PSYCHOANALYTIC PERSPECTIVES ON VIRTUAL INTIMACY AND COMMUNICATION IN FILM

Psychoanalytic Perspectives on Virtual Intimacy and Communication brings together a group of psychoanalysts to explore, through film, the new means of communication, mainly the internet, that enter more and more into the daily and affective lives of people, their intimacy and even the analytic room. The contributors, all practising psychoanalysts, analyse the potential and surprising transformations that human relationships, including psychoanalysis, are undergoing.

At present, it is difficult to value the future importance and predict the possible disquieting consequences of the use and abuse of the new technologies; we run the risk of finding ourselves unprepared to face this revolutionary transformation in human connections and affects. Will it be possible in a near future that human beings prefer to fall in love with a machine gifted with a persuasive voice instead of a psychoanalyst 'in person'? The contributors explore the idea that virtual intimacy could begin to replace real life in sentimental and psychoanalytic relationships. Imagination and fantasy may be strengthened and may ultimately prevail over the body, excluding it entirely. Can the voice of the analyst, sometimes transmitted only by telephone or computer, produce a good enough analytic process as if it were in-person, or will it help to foster a process of idealisation and progressive alienation from real life and connections with other human beings?

The film *Her* (2013), alongside others, offers a wonderful script for discussing this matter, because of the deep and thoughtful examination of love and relationships in the contemporary world that it provides. *Psychoanalytic Perspectives on Virtual Intimacy and Communication in Film* will be of great interest to all psychoanalysts and psychoanalytic psychotherapists interested in the ongoing impact of technology on human relationships.

Andrea Sabbadini is a Fellow of the British Psychoanalytical Society who works as a psychoanalyst in private practice in London. He is also a former Trustee of the Freud Museum, a Lecturer at UCL, a Consultant to the IPA Committee on Psychoanalysis and Culture, and the director of the European Psychoanalytic Film Festival.

Ilany Kogan is a Training Analyst at the Israel Psychoanalytic Society. She works as a teacher and supervisor at the Generatia Center, Bucharest, Romania, and in Germany, including Munich and Aachen. She received the Sigourney Award 2016.

Paola Golinelli is a Training Analyst of the Italian Psychoanalytic Society. She works in private practice in Bologna. She was Consultant of the EPFF (European Psychoanalytic Film Festival) from 2000 to 2014.

PSYCHOANALYTIC IDEAS AND APPLICATIONS SERIES

IPA Publications Committee

Gabriela Legorreta (Montreal), Chair and General Editor; Dominique Scarfone (Montreal) Catalina Bronstein (London); Larry Brown (Boston); Michele Ain (Montevideo); Samuel Arbiser (Buenos Aires); Udo Hock (Berlin); Rhoda Bawdekar (London), Ex-officio as IPA Publishing Manager, Paul Crake (London), Ex-officio as IPA Executive Director

Recent titles in the Series include

Art in Psychoanalysis: A Contemporary Approach to Creativity and Analytic Practice
 edited by Gabriela Goldstein

The Female Body: Inside and Outside
 edited by Ingrid Moeslein-Teising and Frances Thomson-Salo

Death and Identity: Being and the Psycho-Sexual Drama
 Michel de M'Uzan

Unpresented States and the Construction of Meaning: Clinical and Theoretical Contributions
 edited by Howard B. Levine and Gail S. Reed

The Ethical Seduction of the Analytic Situation: The Feminine–Maternal Origins of Responsibility for the Other
 Viviane Chetrit-Vatine

Time for Change: Tracking Transformations in Psychoanalysis—The Three-Level Model
 edited by Marina Altmann de Litvan

Hostile and Malignant Prejudice: Psychoanalytic Approaches
 edited by Cyril Levitt

Freud and Culture
 Eric Smadja

Play, Gender, Therapy: Selected Papers of Eleanor Galenson
 edited by Nellie L. Thompson

Psychopathology of Work: Clinical Observations
 edited by Christophe Dejours

Finding the Body in the Mind: Embodied Memories, Trauma, and Depression
 Marianne Leuzinger-Bohleber

The Future of Psychoanalysis: The Debate about the Training Analyst System
 edited by Peter Zagermann

The Analytical Process: Journeys and Pathways
 Thierry Bokanowski

Psychotic Organisation of the Personality: Psychoanalytic Keys
 Antonio Perez-Sanchez

PSYCHOANALYTIC PERSPECTIVES ON VIRTUAL INTIMACY AND COMMUNICATION IN FILM

Edited by Andrea Sabbadini, Ilany Kogan and Paola Golinelli

LONDON AND NEW YORK

First published 2019
by Routledge
2 Park Square, Milton Park, Abingdon, Oxon OX14 4RN

and by Routledge
711 Third Avenue, New York, NY 10017

Routledge is an imprint of the Taylor & Francis Group, an informa business

© 2019 selection and editorial matter, Andrea Sabbadini, Ilany Kogan and Paola Golinelli; individual chapters, the contributors

The right of the editor to be identified as the author of the editorial material, and of the authors for their individual chapters, has been asserted in accordance with sections 77 and 78 of the Copyright, Designs and Patents Act 1988.

All rights reserved. No part of this book may be reprinted or reproduced or utilised in any form or by any electronic, mechanical, or other means, now known or hereafter invented, including photocopying and recording, or in any information storage or retrieval system, without permission in writing from the publishers.

Trademark notice: Product or corporate names may be trademarks or registered trademarks, and are used only for identification and explanation without intent to infringe.

British Library Cataloguing-in-Publication Data
A catalogue record for this book is available from the British Library

Library of Congress Cataloging-in-Publication Data
A catalog record for this book has been requested

ISBN: 978-1-138-32937-9 (hbk)
ISBN: 978-1-78220-633-0 (pbk)
ISBN: 978-0-429-44819-5 (ebk)

Typeset in Palatino
by Apex CoVantage, LLC

Printed and bound in Great Britain by
TJ International Ltd, Padstow, Cornwall

CONTENTS

SERIES EDITOR'S FOREWORD	vii
PREFACE by Glen O. Gabbard	ix
BIOGRAPHICAL NOTES	xiii

CHAPTER ONE
Intimacy in a virtual world
Andrea Sabbadini — 1

CHAPTER TWO
Could your next analyst be a computer? Psychoanalysis
in the digital era
Ilany Kogan — 11

CHAPTER THREE
Love and analysis in a virtual world: the perverse side:
a psychoanalytic perspective on *Her* by Spike Jonze
Paola Golinelli — 35

vi CONTENTS

CHAPTER FOUR
Pornography as intimacy blocker 51
Robert Schonberger

CHAPTER FIVE
Virtual objects, virtual grief: reflections on *Black Mirror* 69
Dana Amir

CHAPTER SIX
From illusion to creative act: a possible interpretation of *Her* 77
Donatella Lisciotto

CHAPTER SEVEN
The virtual dimension in love affairs and therapeutic
relationships: love and death in Giuseppe Tornatore's films 89
Nicolino Rossi

CHAPTER EIGHT
Customising the object: some psychoanalytic reflections
on Spike Jonze's *Her* 109
Alessandra Lemma

CHAPTER NINE
Her: the future of a desire 123
Simonetta Diena

CHAPTER TEN
Love your echo: virtual others and the modern Narcissus 139
Andreas Hamburger

CHAPTER ELEVEN
'I don't know what I feel. Is it love?' 159
Jana Burgerová

CHAPTER TWELVE
Her: the object in the virtual world 167
Maria Z. Areu Crespo

CHAPTER THIRTEEN
The evaporated body: a dream, a limit, or a possibility? 181
Rossella Valdrè

INDEX 207

SERIES EDITOR'S FOREWORD

With this volume the Publications Committee of the International Psychoanalytic Association continues the series 'Psychoanalytic Ideas and Applications'.

The aim of the series is to focus on the scientific production of significant authors who have made outstanding contributions to the development of the psychoanalytic field, and to set out relevant ideas and themes, generated throughout the history of psychoanalysis, that deserve to be known and discussed by present psychoanalysts.

The relationship between psychoanalytic ideas and their applications has to be put forward from the perspective of theory, clinical practice, and research, so as to maintain their validity for contemporary psychoanalysis.

The Publication's Committee's objective is to share these ideas with the psychoanalytic community and with professionals in other related disciplines, in order to expand their knowledge and generate a productive interchange between the text and the reader.

Andrea Sabbadini, Ilany Kogan and Paola Golinelli have put together in this volume an impressive number of scholarly contributions, creating a most compelling and thought-provoking book. Inspired by the film *Her* and other films, thirteen authors explore, from a psychoanalytic perspective, the complex impact that technology has had on our lives. The richness of the book lies in its numerous perspectives on the influences of

viii SERIES EDITOR'S FOREWORD

technology. For example, the authors address the relationship between mind and body and the tendency to dissociate the two; the relation of technology to one's own desire; the question of temporality in the experience of psychic growth; the ineluctable struggles involved in human intimacy; the ways in which sex and love are impacted by virtual encounters as well as the question of differences between analysis that is carried out by a computer and analysis being experienced in the presence of an analyst. The question of the undesirable and costly psychic implications of technology is also the focus of attention for many contributors.

I have no doubt that this book will be of great interest to psychoanalysts as well as to anyone who is interested and concerned with the profound impact of technology on our psychic lives.

Gabriela Legorreta
Series Editor
Chair, IPA Publications Committee

PREFACE

Sherry Turkle, director of the Massachusetts Institute of Technology Initiative on Technology and Self, and one of the foremost psychoanalytic experts on our lives in the digital domain, once remarked that she began her career arguing about whether a computer program might be a valuable dialogue partner. Thirty years later she found herself debating those who now suggest that her daughter might want to marry one. Indeed, we live in an era where online relationships may exceed the intimacy of flesh-and-blood relationships in the real world. It was only a matter of time until virtual relationships began to replace real-life intimacy.

Spike Jonze's *Her* creates a world where marrying a virtual spouse seems to be an attractive possibility. In this extraordinary new volume on virtual intimacy, Andrea Sabbadini, Ilany Kogan, and Paola Golinelli have assembled a group of erudite and creative, psychoanalytically informed thinkers to weigh in on *Her* and other films from a psychoanalytic perspective. The result is a compelling collection of essays that force the reader to consider what we really mean by being 'human'. Is there a form of relatedness that might even exceed standard human relationships in their capacity to provide gratification, empathy and love? Can a soothing voice be just as erotically charged and appealing if it is not attached to a body? While the film can be grouped with other futuristic science fiction epics like Stanley Kubrick's *2001: A Space Odyssey* and Ridley Scott's *Blade*

Runner, it transcends that genre by simultaneously being a moving love story between human and machine.

In *Her*, Theodore (Joaquin Phoenix) is mesmerized by the sensual voice of Samantha, an 'Individualized Operating System' (OS1). Played by actress Scarlett Johansson, Samantha's voice truly weaves a spell over Theodore, who must use his imagination to transform computer-generated vocal information into a loving woman who provides an ideal female relationship. Audience members must summon their imaginations as well to create an embodied version of Samantha out of a voice they hear in the film. At still another level, readers of the essays in this volume will find themselves immersed in a similar creative task as they are drawn into the musings of a set of highly intelligent contributors to this book, who speculate about the psychoanalytic implications of this novel film. Can the soothing voice of a psychoanalyst on the other end of a telephone provide the same transformative potential as an analyst sitting behind the couch? When a twenty-something patient comes to our consulting room professing his or her love for someone they met online that they have never seen in person, can we take that as seriously as we do when they speak of a relationship with someone in their apartment building that they see on a regular basis? Can a voice that makes the listener feel understood, validated, loved and indulged gratify all the listener's needs? Is a body necessary for the passion of love and the validation of the self? Can this form of love be just as powerful as love in the real world despite the fact that the voice has similar love relationships with 641 other clients (which is the case with Samantha)?

The psychoanalytic commentators in this volume place the questions raised by the film into vexing psychoanalytic dilemmas. For example, what is the difference between narcissistic idealization and the kind of idealization that all lovers experience at the beginning of a new romance? Are in-depth relationships inherently problematic compared to those that are designed to produce narcissistic gratification only? Is 'knowing' the object in its complex subjectivity necessary for love?

Central to the discussion by the contributors to this book is a re-thinking of the role the body plays in love and intimacy. In an era where many young people spend most of their waking hours online, has embodiment become a relic of the past? In relationships that take place in cyberspace, one can bypass the messiness and awkwardness of the actual body and concentrate on the 'soul' of the online love object and her voice. Perhaps the body gets in the way.

Patients today will tell analysts that they often feel more alive and real when they are speaking to an online 'friend' than they do when they are chatting over dinner with a flesh-and-blood partner. Have we reached a point where the true self only emerges in virtual dialogue? All these questions are thoughtfully raised and discussed in this engaging collection of psychoanalytically sophisticated film commentaries. The reader embarks on an arcane journey that is no longer hypothetical. Our culture has reached a point where all of these questions are highly relevant to everyday life in the present. In that regard, *Her* is not as futuristic as *2001: A Space Odyssey*, *Blade Runner*, or other sci-fi classics that define its lineage. Just as Samantha speaks to Theodore in an urgent and breathless way, the reader of this superb new book will feel that each chapter author is whispering something of immediate relevance into his or her ear. You may not be able to put the book down.

Glen O. Gabbard, M.D.
Houston, Texas, U.S.A.

BIOGRAPHICAL NOTES

Editors

Paola Golinelli is a Training Analyst of the Italian Psychoanalytic Society. She works in private practice in Bologna. From 2000 to 2014 she was a consultant of EPFF (the European Psychoanalytic Film Festival); from 2003 to 2014 she chaired the Croatian Sponsoring Committee, and she is now chair of the Liaison Committee of the Croatian Psychoanalytic Society. From 2005 to 2009 she was a member of the IPA Committee on Psychoanalysis and Culture, of which she is now a consultant. Since 2014 she also chairs the Italian Annual. Her main subjects of interest and research are: cinema and visual arts; the process of creativity; mourning and loss; feminine psychosexual development, pregnancy and maternity. She has published several reviews and contributed to a number of books.

Ilany Kogan is a training and supervising analyst of the Israel Psychoanalytic Society. She works as a teacher and supervisor at the Generatia Center in Bucharest, Romania, and in various places in Germany, especially in Munich and Aachen. For many years she has worked extensively with Holocaust survivors' offspring, and has published papers and books on this topic. In 2005 she was awarded the Elise M. Hayman Award for the Study of the Holocaust and Genocide. She is the author of *The Cry of Mute Children* (Free Association Books 1995), *Escape from*

xiv BIOGRAPHICAL NOTES

Selfhood (IPA Publications 2007), *The Struggle Against Mourning* (Rowman & Littlefield 2007) and *Canvas of Change* (Karnac 2012).

Andrea Sabbadini is a Fellow of the British Psychoanalytical Society and its former Director of Publications. He works in private practice in London, is a Trustee of the Freud Museum, an Honorary Senior Lecturer at University College London (UCL), a member of the International Psychoanalytic Association (IPA) Committee on Psychoanalysis and Culture, the Director of the European Psychoanalytic Film Festival (EPFF) and the Chairman of 'Framed Lives: Films on Prominent Individuals' at the Institute of Contemporary Arts (ICA). His most recent books are *Boundaries and Bridges: Perspectives on Time and Space in Psychoanalysis* (Karnac 2014) and *Moving Images: Psychoanalytic Reflections on Film* (Routledge 2014).

Contributors

Dana Amir is a clinical psychologist, supervising and training analyst at the Israel Psychoanalytic Society, a faculty member at Haifa University, poetess and literature researcher. She is the author of six poetry books and two psychoanalytic non-fiction books: *Cleft Tongue* (Karnac 2014) and *On the Lyricism of the Mind* (Routledge 2016). She has published several papers in psychoanalytic journals and has presented at national and international conferences. She is the winner of many prizes, including the Frances Tustin International Memorial Prize (2011); the IPA Sacerdoti Prize (2013); and the Distinguished Psychoanalytic Educators Award (IFPE 2017).

Jana Burgerová was born in Prague in 1950 where she lived until the invasion of the Warsaw Pact when she emigrated to Germany. She studied psychology in Munich where she got her diploma (MAP, DGPT). She has a twenty years experience of professional activity in a psychotherapeutic home for children and adolescents. She started training as a psychoanalyst in 1994 and now works in private practice. She has published several articles on the theme of 'film and migration'.

Maria Z. Areu Crespo has degrees in both law and in psychology. In 1996 While still training as a psychoanalyst in the Asociacion Psicoanalitica Argentina she was awarded the 'Premio Angel Garma'. She has published on topics related to female phantasies that shape a vision of the world, based in Freud's theories as well as on the works of Shakespeare, Sophocles, Euripides and Seneca. Her book *La mujer y su ética* was

BIOGRAPHICAL NOTES   XV

published in 1998 by Yebenes Editorial. She is in private practice in Buenos Aires, where she is also a Training Analyst of the Asociacion Psicoanalitica Argentina.

Simonetta Diena, psychiatrist and psychoanalyst, lives and works in Milan. She is a full member with training functions of the Italian Psychoanalytic Society. She has been working for many years in the field of eating disorders and her works have appeared in national and international journals and in collected volumes. She is a teacher with the Istituto Italiano di Psicoanalisi di Gruppo (IIPG) in Milan and, since 1999, a Fellow in the IPA Research Training Programme. One of her main interests is the relationship between art and psychoanalysis, and she has published a number of essays on this topic. Her last book is *Psychoanalysis Listening to Love: Passion and Bonds* (Karnac 2017).

Andreas Hamburger is a psychoanalyst with the DPG, Professor of clinical psychology, International Psychoanalytic University, Berlin, Training Analyst (DGPT) and supervisor at the Akademie für Psychoanalyse und Psychotherapie, Munich. His main interests are on language development, social trauma, literature and film. His current research is on scenic narrative microanalysis of Holocaust survivors' testimonies, psychoanalytic supervision and film analysis. His recent edited books are: *La Belle et la Bête: Women and Images of Men in Cinema* (Karnac 2015); *Trauma, Trust, and Memory* (Karnac 2017) and, with D. Laub, *Psychoanalysis, Social Trauma and Testimony: Unwanted Memory and the Holocaust* (Routledge 2017).

Alessandra Lemma is a Fellow of the British Psychoanalytical Society and Consultant Clinical Psychologist at the Anna Freud National Centre for Children and Families. She is Honorary Professor of Psychological Therapies at the School of Health and Human Sciences at Essex University and Visiting Professor, Psychoanalysis Unit, University College London where she is also the Clinical Director of the Psychological Interventions Research Centre. She is Visiting Professor at the Istituto Winnicott, Sapienza University of Rome and at the Centro Winnicott, Rome. She is Editor of the New Library of Psychoanalysis book series (Routledge) and one of the regional editors of the *International Journal of Psychoanalysis*. She has published extensively on psychoanalysis, the body and trauma.

Donatella Lisciotto is a clinical psychologist and a full member of the Italian Psychoanalytic Society. She lives in Messina and maintains a full-time

xvi   BIOGRAPHICAL NOTES

private practice in psychoanalysis. She is a professor at the School of Psychoanalytic Psychotherapy where she teaches infant observation in Catania. She is a charter member of the psychoanalytic laboratory Vicolo Cicala, where she plays a decisive role in disseminating psychoanalytic ideas.

Nicolino Rossi is Full Professor of Clinical Psychology at the School of Medicine, Bologna University; head of the service of clinical psychology, sexology, and psychoanalytic psychotherapy of the Department of Psychology; and also coordinator of the Psychological Support Service for cancer patients and for couples undergoing medically assisted reproduction. He is a Full Member of the Italian Psychoanalytical Society, the current President of the Psychoanalytic Centre in Bologna, and its past Scientific Secretary. His main interests include couple dynamics and psychoanalytic couple therapy, an area in which he has published papers and organized a number of international congresses.

Robert Schonberger is a clinical psychologist, training analyst and teacher in the Israeli Psychoanalytic Institute, Jerusalem. He also teaches in several postgraduate psychotherapy study programmes in the Tel-Aviv district. He is the translator of Hanna Segal's book *Klein*, and the scientific editor of the translation into Hebrew of books by John Steiner (in print), Bion (in print), and Meltzer (in collaboration with Marganit Ofer). He is also a poet, a translator of poetry, and the author of several poetry books.

Rossella Valdrè is a psychiatrist and a full member of the Italian Psychoanalytic Society. She works in private practice, and lectures on psychoanalytic theory at the Faculty of Psychology of the University of Genoa, the city where she lives and works. Her fields of interest include cinema and the extension of psychoanalysis into the world of culture and society, with particular attention to Freudian metapsychology. Her books include: *La lingua sognata della realtà. Cinema e psicoanalisi nell'esplorazione della contemporaneità* (2013); *Cinema e violenza: banalità del Male nel cinema contemporaneo* (2014); *L'Altro. Diversità contemporanee. Cinema e psicoanalisi nel territorio dell'alterità* (2015); *On Sublimation: A Path to the Destiny of Desire, Theory and Treatment* (Karnac 2014); *Cattive. E' sempre la donna la vittima? Autrici che ribaltano il mito: una riflessione psicoanalitica* (2015) (*Malice: The Victim and the Couple. A Psychoanalytic Perspective* (2017).

CHAPTER ONE

Intimacy in a virtual world

Andrea Sabbadini

Intimate loving relationships, in their varying combinations of physical and emotional components, reflect the infinite variety of human beings: their personal qualities, their past experiences, the culture in which they have grown up, their fantasy lives …

As a precursor to such relationships among adults, the earliest bond between baby and mother is formed on the basis of primary sensory experiences: seeing, hearing, smelling, tasting and touching. Individuals involved in intimate relationships would, ideally, choose to stay in each other's proximity, i.e. with their bodies located in the same place and time, with their senses switched on and tuned into one another. Geographical distance and extended temporal gaps between encounters can be painful, and major sensory disabilities in one or both partners can interfere with, or at any rate alter, the quality of their relationship.

In reality, conditions are seldom ideal and, even when they are, they are unlikely to remain so on a permanent basis. In *all* intimate relationships, be they of an erotic or of any other kind, uncontrollable internal pressures or external circumstances create the need for compromises. Let us briefly look at a few situations where some of the ingredients are missing, or have at some point been lost, and consider whether such close relationships are still possible under those conditions.

2   ANDREA SABBADINI

Being unable to see, hear or touch the loved one can be distressful. Yet, even the extreme conditions of blindness or deafness in one or both partners need not be obstacles to their relationship. Where does the powerful need to see and be seen, to hear and be heard, to touch and be touched, come from? We know that psychological growth requires mirroring: the child finds himself in the eyes of his mother, he begins to recognize his separate identity in the positive image reflected by the parental gaze. In the four moving stories recounted in Juraj Lehotsky's film *Blind Loves* [*Slepé lásky*] (Slovakia 2008) some couples of sightless lovers attempt to negotiate, with varied amounts of success, their relationships. The film beautifully illustrates how blind individuals, while experiencing the world in a different way from those with eyesight, have much in common with everyone else, especially when it comes to love – which, Lehotsky seems to claim, is far from blind.

In parallel to the visual aspect of mirroring described by Winnicott (1967), the process I called *echoing* (Sabbadini 1997) concerns the reflection of the child's voice, sounds and noises. This will eventually allow the child to produce, listen to, and enjoy sounds, and to recognize them as her own. Only by being talked and listened to by those who love her will a child feel sufficiently supported to learn to listen to herself (literally and metaphorically) and thus gradually develop an individual identity. All goes back, in Rose's (1993) colourful image, to 'Opus No. 1, the first duet' between mother and baby, when familiar voices and sounds contribute to the establishment of the child's sense of self. Infant feeding, as the prototype of nourishing interchanges and of later intimacy, involves auditory contacts (as well as visual, tactile and olfactory ones): the sounds produced by the suckling child and by the mother's voice in their intimate dialogues at the breast. Derived from this, the need to hear and be heard, as well as to see and be seen, is vital in all adult relationships, and especially in intimate ones: if our voices and words are being ignored we can feel invalidated or even annihilated in our sense of identity. The narcissistic wound resulting from this distressing experience can feel unbearable and provoke an enraged response or a withdrawal into a depressive condition. We may also notice, by the way, that the experience of being heard, in the deepest meaning of the word, constitutes a main therapeutic factor in psychoanalysis, characterized as it is by the listening to one's own voice within a holding environment. Our so-called 'talking cure' is also a 'listening cure'.

Actual physical contact is another *sine qua non* condition of intimate relationships. Or is it? What happens when the bodies themselves are absent, distant from each other in the geographical space, or perhaps only present in the virtual one? Physical contact is then impossible, though communication media may still allow distant partners to see and hear one another. But such relationships from afar can rarely be sustained over a long period of time because the need for physical proximity and contact, so crucial to the sexual enactments of one's fantasies, eventually becomes so overwhelming as to damage, if not even destroy, whatever love may have existed. It could even be argued that a relationship without physical contact, or only existing in the world of imagination and dreams, should no longer be called intimate.

Psychoanalysis traditionally involves the physical presence in the same space of those taking part in it, though without any physical contact as such between them – beyond perhaps, in certain cultures, a formal handshake or a peck-on-the-cheek. If we were to consider the psychoanalytic interaction between analysts and patients as a special instance of intimate relationships, we could question whether their physical presence in the same place (the analyst's consulting room) is an essential aspect of it. In this context, it is legitimate to argue whether the analytic process could then develop when the two participants only share a virtual space, as is the case in 'teleanalysis' and other 'distance therapies' carried out by such communication tools as the telephone (which only allows the transmission of voices) and Skype (which also allows the transmission of images).

We should acknowledge that relationships and communication taking place in cyberspace can be meaningful but are fundamentally different from those happening in physical space. Any denial of such differences and attempts to reproduce the classic analytic setting in the kind of virtual reality where distant sessions occur are doomed to failure.

On the other hand, the assumption that only the conventional way of carrying out analysis is the correct one, and a format most likely to bring positive therapeutic results simply because it is what we are used to, is questionable. As Savege Scharff wrote about teleanalysis: 'psychoanalysis is primarily the encounter with an understanding mind *in whatever setting that may occur*' (2010, p. 990, my emphasis). The evidence built on over a century of psychoanalytic experience suggests that changes to the original setting, as long as they respect certain basic parameters, can be advantageous to both analysts and patients, should be welcome whenever their enforcement improves the quality of the work, and are anyway inevitable as the external environment (which, in our case, includes the widespread presence of electronic technologies in all aspects of life) evolves. Freud, who had described his technical principles for carrying out analytic work, was the first to concede that these were not fixed and should be constantly reviewed; indeed he had called them 'recommendations' (Freud 1912) rather than rules.

Analysis carried out from a distance has become in the last few years an increasingly common occurrence. While many still object to such practice, using a variety of arguments (technical, ethical, theoretical) to justify their scepticism or even hostility to it, many others have found that the actual physical presence of the patient in the analyst's consulting room is perhaps a preferable but not an essential factor in developing a therapeutic relationship, including its transference and counter-transference components.

The main issues at stake are the relative importance of the patient's and of the analyst's voices compared to that of their bodies, the latter being invisible in telephone analysis, and visible but not physically present in Skype analysis; and whether the real-time presence of videoed images of bodies on a computer screen is a valid alternative to their actual physical presence in the consulting room. If we assume that the physical presence of the analyst's and the analysand's bodies plays an important part in their interaction, with repercussions on the transference and counter-transference, is it then possible to thus dispose of bodies, or rather of their actual presence in a physical space, without this having major implications for the analytic process? How will their absence alter the quality of communication between the analytic couple – indeed, any couple?

It is true that patients using the couch have only a few brief moments to look at their analyst at the beginning and the end of sessions, and analysts sitting in a chair behind their patients have only limited visual access to their bodies. Physical contact between them is mostly non-existent, and other perceptual modalities (such as smell) only rarely come to play a significant part in the analytic relationship. However, the mere *possibility* of, say, bodily contact between them, be it of an erotic, affectionate or aggressive nature, is central to the experience (both actual and transferential or counter-transferential) that therapist and patient have of each other. The absence of such possibility in telephone or Skype analysis, therefore, is not a matter of indifference.

When we psychoanalysts start practising in a virtual space, we are likely to experience an initial sense of dislocation similar perhaps to the one we may feel if we were to move our practice to a different consulting room. This, however, should subside as the analysis progresses and both participants get used to the new setting. After all, whether we meet our analysands in a consulting room or in cyberspace, we are still psychoanalysts engaged in the psychoanalytic process; we are still committed to making a safe environment available to our patients, where we empathetically listen in a state of suspended attention to their free associations. Analysts seeing their patients on Skype will relate to them in a similar way and with a similar attitude as they would if they were physically present in their consulting rooms. The rituals surrounding the analytic meetings may be different (e.g. going to the consulting room and ringing the doorbell versus going online and making a video-call), but not the substance itself of the psychoanalytic process.

The question to be asked in this context is not whether analyst and patient should ever agree to meet in the virtual space of the internet rather than in the physical one of the consulting room in those situations when the latter is unavailable to the patient. Whether we approve of it or not, this is already happening on a large scale, even if analysts rarely talk about it with colleagues – perhaps because of 'their unanalysed guilt over transgressing conventional psychoanalytic norms' (Zalusky 2003, p. 16). Recent surveys suggest that about one third of psychoanalysts have at least experimented with distance analysis, and that the increase in the proportion of such practices parallels the growth of the population of 'digital natives' (Prensky 2001) among analysts and patients.

An important issue here is whether the simultaneous presence of the therapeutic dyad in a physical space is an indispensable condition for the psychoanalytic process to occur. It could be argued that it is, on the grounds that the emotional aspect of intimate relationships such as the analytic one can only properly find expression in such a context. But it could also be argued that facilities such as video-links (unlike emails which convey only written words, or the telephone which transmits only sounds) do in fact provide the main perceptual features, visual and auditory, for meaningful communication. Traditional physical analytic encounters may still be preferable to virtual ones, but they would not constitute a necessary condition for the analytic process to unfold and for effective therapeutic work to occur.

While in distant analyses the two bodies are not simultaneously present in the same location, in this virtual space shared by analyst and patient there is now a third presence replacing, as well as representing, them: that of the electronic apparatus (computers with their microphones and webcams) which, at least in the first few sessions before those using them get accustomed to them, cannot but interfere with the intimacy and privacy of the analytic couple. This interference will often have disturbing connotations, including in the area of Oedipal fantasies, possibly stimulating curiosity, jealousy and persecutory anxieties. None of this, it could be argued, is a bad thing in itself, but it does require careful handling and interpretation. In this respect 'the analyst's acceptance of the involvement of a permanent third party in the relationship – even if the third party is an instrument – modifies the conventional setting so drastically that it is appropriate to consider whether the resulting process diverges substantially from *psychoanalysis as such*' (Yamin Habib 2003, p. 26; my emphasis).

The answer to this important question, it seems to me, depends on our definition of 'psychoanalysis as such'. Back in the distant year 2000, in response to an article by Dinitia Smith (2000) in the *New York Times* pointing out that many American analysts, in the name of openness, conduct psychoanalysis by e-mail and by video-phone, I commented: 'If we do not draw a line somewhere, we shall end up practising a profession which may be thriving, but is no longer psychoanalysis' (Sabbadini 2000). I still believe that a line may need to be drawn but now I am less certain as to *where* to draw it.

In other words, the answer to the question whether sessions carried out on the internet could still be described as being psychoanalytic ones, considering the changes thus imposed upon the traditional setting and the implications this could have for our analytic professional identity, depends on how rigid (as different from rigorous) our definition of psychoanalytic work is going to be. Some authors feel an understandable 'deep concern related to an obvious and increasing dilution of psychoanalysis' (Argentieri and Amati Mahler 2003, p. 19). However, I believe that any definition of our psychoanalytic work must allow for some flexibility, provided that we abide to certain basic principles (*theoretical*, such as the belief in the power of unconscious fantasies; *technical*, such as the importance of offering a consistent setting; and *ethical*, such as the obligation to respect confidentiality). After all, psychoanalysis has been characterized over the years as that form of non-directive talking cure which takes place with the patient lying on the couch (though some patients choose to be sitting face-to-face), for fifty-minute-long sessions occurring five times a week (though many analysts also see patients less frequently, and for shorter sessions), with listening in a state of free-floating attention to the patient's free associations (though different modalities of communication also occur as a norm), with transference interpretations constituting the main interventions (though analysts also constantly make other kinds of interventions, such as reconstructions and the asking of indirect questions), with an initially open-ended contract as a condition (though some analysts also agree to see patients for only a limited period of time or number of sessions).

What constitutes 'true' analysis has then to be seen in the context of a rapidly evolving environment, where new technologies and the culture and values associated with them cannot be ignored as they play such important roles not only in our daily lives and interpersonal relationships, but also in the structure and contents of our internal worlds. Psychoanalysis in its traditional form risks becoming a curiosity from the past. But if we, the few remaining digital immigrants, collaborate with the natives in responding proactively to the electronic revolution, then our beloved 'impossible profession' has still a good chance to thrive.

* * *

What I have been saying about these issues concerning the analytic relationship may, at least to some extent, also apply to other intimate relationships including romantic and sexual ones, such as that between Theodore and Samantha's disembodied voice, presented to us in Spike Jonze's remarkable film *Her*.

The movie describes an intimate encounter in the age of virtual relationships. In its narrative an erotically charged relationship is centred on the voice: in the words, and sighs and noises that the two lovers exchange with one another. They cannot see each other, and indeed one of them, Samantha, does not even have a body, but only an artificially intelligent operating system's existence as a voice. Such an OS is described as 'an intuitive entity that listens to you, understands you and knows you. It's not just an operating system. It's a consciousness'. For Theodore the absence of 'the other' as a real person has an absolute, ontological quality which, however, does not seem to prevent him from experiencing for her (or rather for 'it') the intense feelings that he could also have experienced for a real woman.

In the absence of the body of one of the members of this most unorthodox loving couple, that 'bridge towards the Other' (Pigozzi 2008) which is the human voice takes on a special psychological and interpersonal significance. As well as being such a bridge, normally the voice is 'in a constant relationship with what is corporeal, insofar as it stems from the vibrations of the vocal chords and from the process of breathing, and at the same time with what is incorporeal: emotions, fantasies and affects' (Saponi 2015). In the case of our film, however, 'what is corporeal' is missing ...

8   ANDREA SABBADINI

Let me mention here an anecdote, most likely apocryphal, from my own family history:

> Many years ago a young widow made a phone call to one of my uncles, who happened to be a lawyer, and instantly fell in love with his voice. My uncle and this lady subsequently met, got married and lived happily, or so the story goes, ever after.

The love story between the protagonists of *Her*, Theodore and Samantha, though, could not have followed that same sequence; Theodore's own 'individualised operating system', Samantha, does not exist – or at least not in the so-called 'real' world of widows and lawyers. Her only existence, unlike Theodore's, only belongs in the virtual world of operating systems, where she possesses an electronically acquired capacity to constantly evolve through her experiences, a Wikipaedic knowledge of her lover, a profound understanding, or rather intuition, of the workings of his mind, a good sense of humour and a sensitive responsiveness to his feelings (which includes his need for her to have and share her own); besides, she is programmed to be the 'perfect' woman for Theodore, with all the human imperfections he may expect from her. Endowed with an artificially produced and delightfully seductive voice, Samantha lacks, however, the flesh and bones, and warts and all, of a female body. She can be heard, but not seen, nor smelled nor touched. This considerable limitation, of course, turns out to be problematic.

What part does the presence of physical bodies play, we may ask, in how we relate to one another? Human relationships – psychoanalytic ones included, not to mention friendships, romantic and erotic ones – may take place mostly in our minds (or, in the case of *Her*, in Theodore's ear-bud), but alas not entirely so. As noted above, something is objectively missing whenever physical contact is unavailable – whether because, say, a lover lives far away or because, like Samantha, she happens to only have the virtual status of an OS. 'Meeting' a girl in a chat room (the equivalent of the pen-friendships of old times), inviting her to be your friend on Facebook, or 'swiping right' on Tinder to indicate you like her, is not quite the same as physically going out with her, holding hands, and then having a candle-lit meal in an Italian restaurant …

We are treading here on shaky ground, because the line dividing the real from the virtual is not as clear as it may be comfortable for us to think. Does Samantha not exist at all, or does she perhaps exist in a *different* reality, like (say) the characters populating our dreams? (I shall not over-complicate matters here by reminding ourselves that, actually, Theodore himself only exists in the equally fictional world of cinema ...). There is here not only for Theodore but also for us, voyeuristic spectators of the movie, some inevitable ambiguity in experiencing Samantha as a woman (especially when she makes statements such as 'I'm becoming much more than what they programmed') and at the same time as an OS: can we think of her as being both things at the same time, or should we make our minds up about who (or what) she (or it) 'really' is ? One important factor here is that Samantha has no personal history besides the short-term past of her relationship with Theodore. Yet her assertion that 'the past is just a story we tell ourselves' is one that many an existential philosopher, as well as some psychoanalysts, would be in agreement with.

If Samantha's loving feelings for him are no more than an artificial construct, his for her seem closer to what we may experience ourselves in relation to a bodied living human being. But then some may claim that, even in what we consider to be the real world, love itself is a bit of a delusion anyway ...

Samantha's relationship with Theodore (and, much to his understandable horror, with 8,316 others like him: no room for special treatment here) has an obvious psychotherapeutic function which manifests itself with all its relevant features: such as the use of free associations, regression, resistance, transference and even counter-transference. But, we may ask, is offering psychological help to Theodore Samantha's intention (if one can attribute any intentionality to an operating system)? Is this her primary function? I would argue that Samantha is first of all Theodore's friend and lover, not her analyst – though her loving relationship (indeed, perhaps *all* loving relationships) can also have a therapeutic function for those engaging in them. The one role, however, should not be confused with, or assimilated to, the other.

Another potentially confusing aspect in talking about this film concerns the difficulty of properly differentiating between engaging in intimate relationships *with* a technical device (e.g. with an operating system such as Samantha) and *through* a technical device (e.g. through Skype). The latter, as we have seen, has become a frequent if still controversial practice for many, the former only exists so far in a wonderful film entitled *Her*. It was intended by its writer and director Jonze, and is viewed by us spectators, as an instance of science-fictional reality. But will its core narrative be still a fantasy bordering on the unbelievable in ten or twenty years' time? The current frantic pace of the electronic revolution suggests that it may not be at all.

* * *

10 ANDREA SABBADINI

Intimate relationships, or variations thereof, are already being conducted online, often anonymously, by millions of people around the world, whether for sexual or romantic excitement and gratification, for friendly contact, or for therapeutic purposes.

Sometimes such encounters between videoed images and recorded voices later move into the space where concrete bodies meet in the 'real' world as we know it.

Other times they remain stuck forever in cyberspace. When this happens, I must confess that I am left feeling that something important about the essence itself of our humanity has gone missing.

But, alas, I can no longer say with any certainty what that 'something' is ...

References

Argentieri, S. and Amati Mehler, J. (2003). Telephone 'analysis': 'Hello, who's speaking?' *Insight*, 12: 17–19.

Freud, S. (1912). Recommendations to physicians practising psycho-analysis. *Standard Edition Vol. 12*. London: Hogarth Press, pp. 109–120.

Pigozzi, L. (2008). *A nuda voce: vocalità, inconscio, sessualità*. Turin: Antigone.

Prensky, M. (2001). Digital natives, digital immigrants. In *On the Horizon*. MCB University Press, vol. 9 (5).

Rose, G. J. (1993). On form and feeling in music. In S. Feder, R. Karmel and G. Pollock (eds) *Psychoanalytic Explorations in Music: Second Series*. New York: International Universities Press.

Sabbadini, A. (1997). On sounds, children, identity and a 'quite unmusical' man. *British Journal of Psychotherapy*, 14 (2): 189–196.

Sabbadini, A. (2000). Response to Dinitia Smith's 'Ideas'. www.psychoanalysis.org.uk

Saponi, S. (2015). Sulla voce e dintorni. In M. De Mari, C. Carnevali and S. Saponi (eds) *Fra psicoanalisi e musica*. Roma: Alpes Italia.

Savege Scharff, J. (2010). Telephone analysis. Panel report. *International Journal of Psychoanalysis*, 91: 989–992.

Smith, D. (2000). Ideas. www.nytimes.com/2000/12/09/arts/09PSYC.html

Winnicott, D. W. (1967). Mirror-role of mother and family in child development. In *Playing and Reality*. London: Tavistock, 1971.

Yamin Habib, L. (2003). Physical presence: A sine qua non of analysis? *Insight*, 12: 25–27.

Zalusky S. (2003). Dialogue: Telephone analysis. *Insight*, 12: 13–16.

CHAPTER TWO

Could your next analyst be a computer? Psychoanalysis in the digital era

Ilany Kogan

*People as living machines, machines as
psychological objects*

The tremendous development of technology over the past decades has changed the world. Virtual reality has intruded into our work, our leisure, our emotional relationships. It has perhaps also intruded into the world of psychoanalysis. One of the questions we analysts ask ourselves is, "What will be the face of psychoanalysis in the 'brave new world' of the near future?"

For many years, psychoanalysis was limited by the geographical boundaries and physical reality of three to five weekly meetings between client and analyst. Modern technology has enabled us to partially overcome these limitations with the aid of the telephone and Skype for conducting analytic encounters.

The popularity of analysis has greatly increased in countries which once restricted freedom of thought, such as Eastern Europe, China, and Turkey. However, in some Western countries, this popularity has decreased. One of the main reasons is the costly nature of analysis, making it available only to those who can afford it, in terms of time and money.

How will psychoanalysis look in the future? Can new tools, such as artificial intelligence, substitute for a human therapist, offer therapy to

12   ILANY KOGAN

a larger number of people, and thus contribute to the expansion of this therapeutic field? Can analytic therapy provided by a computer overcome the above constraints, which limit the accessibility of psychoanalysis?

Computerized therapy, which can offer various kinds of therapy to masses of people, emerged within the larger cultural context of the erosion of the boundaries between the real and the virtual, the animate and the inanimate.

In this cultural context, both persons and objects are reconfigured – people as living machines, machines as psychological objects. The claim that people are living machines is based on the assumption that the human brain is an information processing system and thinking is a form of computing (Horst, 2005). The assertion that machines are psychological objects (termed "strong AI" by the philosopher John Searle [1980]) is based on the idea that a computer programmed with the appropriate inputs and outputs would have a mind in exactly the same sense as humans have minds.[1]

Searle (1980, 1999) and Dennett (1991) counter the argument of "strong AI," maintaining that a program cannot give a computer a "mind," "understanding" or "consciousness," regardless of how intelligently or human-like the program may make the computer behave. These scientists argue that without "understanding" (or "intentionality"), what the machine is doing cannot be described as "thinking" and, since it does not think, it does not have a "mind" in anything like the normal sense of the word. Searle concludes that "strong AI" is a mistaken concept.

In spite of this controversy, the blurring of boundaries between man and machine gave birth to the idea that human intelligencecan be described so precisely that it can be simulated by a machine. Psychological experiments were used to develop programs that simulate the techniques people use for problem solving. In her illuminating book *Life on the Screen*, Turkle (1995), an important researcher in the field of AI, states that we are moving from a modernist culture of calculation toward a postmodernist culture of simulation. In this postmodernist culture, people are increasingly comfortable with substituting representations of reality for reality. People are seeking out the computer as an intimate machine. Computer screens are the new location for our fantasies, both erotic and intellectual. She eloquently refers to the impact of computers on humans by stating that computers don't just do things for us, they do things to us, including to our ways of thinking about ourselves and other people. (Turkle, 1995).

Turkle describes the origins of this development: In the mid-1980s, computer science designed increasingly "romantic machines," which, in her view, were touted not as logical but as biological, not as programmed but as able to learn from experience. The researchers who worked on them sought to produce a species of machine that would prove as unpredictable and undetermined as the human mind itself.

With the greater acceptance of a kinship between computers and human minds, the question that arises is not only "what does it mean to think?" but "what does it mean to be alive?" This topic is dealt with by researchers working at MIT (Rosalind Picard and Rodney Brooks, 2013), and is the subject of several TV series (*Humans*, *West World*) and theater productions (*Real Humans*).

Advances in psychopharmacology and the development of genetics as a computational biology reflect the extent to which we assume that our minds and bodies are like machines whose inner workings we can understand. The Human Genome Project, which identified the location and role of all of the genes in human DNA, also addressed the possibility of finding the genetic markers that determine human personality, temperament, and sexual orientation. As we contemplate reengineering the genome, we are also reengineering our view of ourselves as programmed beings. It is possible that we are doing this with the aim of finding some solace in the complexities and uncertainties of the world.

The findings described above eroded the boundaries between the real and the virtual, the animate and the inanimate, resulting in a new evaluation of the machines or robots in the form of humans. As an example, Turkle refers to Levy's (2007) book, *Love and Sex with Robots*. In this book, Levy argues that robots will teach us to be better friends and lovers because we will be able to practice on them. "Love with robots will be as normal as love with other humans, while the number of sexual acts and lovemaking positions commonly practiced between humans will be extended, as robots will teach more than is in all of the world's published sex manuals combined" (p. 22). Beyond this, robots will substitute where people fail. Among other things, Levy describes the virtues of marriage to robots. He claims that robots are, of course, "other" but, in many ways, better. If they are programmed to satisfy their clients, there will never be frustrations or disappointments. According to Levy, there is one simple criterion for judging the worth of robots in even the most intimate domains: Does being with a robot make you feel better?

This culture of simulation described above emerged in many domains, including therapy. In the mid-1960s, Joseph Weizenbaum, a computer scientist at the Massachusetts Institute of Technology, developed a computer program to simulate a Rogerian psychotherapist. Eliza, as the program

14 ILANY KOGAN

was called, asked open-ended questions to encourage the user to discuss his or her emotions. When the experiment ended, some subjects refused to believe they had not discussed their feelings with a real, live therapist. In spite of this project, during that period, the image of a computer as a psychotherapist struck most people as inappropriate or even obscene. Today, several such programs are on the market.

Fjola Helgadottir, a co-founder of AI Therapy – a company that develops online computerized CBT (cognitive behavioral therapy) programs – states that the clinical knowledge encapsulated in the software is used to deliver targeted interventions. She believes that certain forms of therapy, such as CBT, are particularly well-suited to this algorithmic delivery style.

But can a computer deliver analytic therapy and thus substitute for the experience with a live analyst? Can the analyst's "analyzing instrument" (Isakower, 1992, p. 200), his receptivity and reactivity to the patient, be replaced by an instrument in the form of a technological device? Does what we analysts have to offer differ from what a computer or robot can provide?

Like many other forms of digital technology, computerized therapy is programmed like Levy's robots, to make its clients feel better. But is feeling better the criterion for growth and development? Is this the golden standard of analytic therapy? In this connection, Warren Poland raises an important question: "Is the avoidance of pain an evolutionary flaw for humanity, a place where the species advance of mental representation , thinking and delay of action all get subverted, as the skills are used for anesthesia rather than growth?" (personal communication).

Some main elements of psychoanalysis

In order to compare analytic therapy delivered by a computer with analytic therapy with a human analyst, we have to identify the elements that define the practice of psychoanalysis. I will first briefly summarize these elements.

In an early paper, Merton Gill (1954) described the classical view of psychoanalysis, stating that its hallmarks are neutrality, the establishment of transference neurosis, and the resolution of the transference by interpretation alone. The unconscious and psychic determinism are implied in this view.

A later view is described by Robert Wallerstein (1969) and Salman Akhtar (2009) who stress the analytic situation, implying transference–countertransference engagement, rather than mere isolated transference expression which is prominent in the early view. In a comprehensive essay, Wallerstein (1969) proposes the following main elements (1) Psychoanalysis aims at the restructuring of personality; (2) It focuses on the exploration of the unconscious; (3) The psychoanalytic technique centers on interpretation; (4) It is based on free association; (5) Psychoanalysis concerns itself with the analytic situation; (6) It emphasizes the search for self-knowledge; (7) It aims at radically new discoveries about the self; (8) It is "timeless," in the sense that it is not time limited.

The current view of the main elements of psychoanalysis is defined by Warren Poland (2013). He stresses that the unconscious communication goes both ways, specifically of the patient reading the analyst's mind, understanding how the analyst deals with his or her unconscious experience of what is unfolding, and then identifying with those unconscious forces at work. In Poland's eloquent words:

> It is in navigating the area in the edge of darkness between the differing psychic realities of the analytic pair – and doing so for the primary purpose of the patient's analysis – that analytic exploration can lead to genuine insight. Yet it is only from the manifest interchange between the analytic clinical partners that the patient becomes able to transcend symptoms and constrictions. Remarkably and momentously, beyond what is manifest in the clinical work, the patient's capacity for psychic growth is liberated and facilitated by the patient's learning how the analyst's mind works while it is so silently working analytically.
>
> (Poland, 2013, p. 845)

An illustration of a computerized analytic therapy: the movie Her

It seems fitting that the discussion of the relationship between the human and the artificial uses as its illustration the applied analytic study of an artificial creation, a movie that itself addresses the very questions at hand.

I acquired an interesting and hilarious insight into the subject of computerized therapy in the story of Theodore Twombly, the protagonist of *Her*, an American science fiction romantic drama film written, directed and produced by Spike Jonze (2013) and starring Joaquin Phoenix. *Her* is a very witty, subtle and ironic film that reflects Jonze's views of love, narcissism, social isolation and anomie in contemporary western culture.

Her is also a wonderfully layered look at our present and future world, in which technology seems to create unlimited possibilities of communication and connectedness. Among other things, the movie addresses the anti-social nature of the social media. It demonstrates that in spite of our desire to reach out and connect, the use of technological devices makes us inherently disconnected and isolated.

The movie revolves around a romantic love story between Theodore and an evolving, intelligent, talking operating system (OS). This relationship between Theodore and his computer may be viewed through many prisms, and the OS may be regarded as fulfilling a variety of roles. I was struck by the idea that an OS, which is actually a kind of personal assistant (an organizer), attempts to substitute for a human therapist, offering analytic therapy to masses of people.

To examine the movie from this perspective, I will describe the special characteristics of Theodore, the client, as well as of his OS. Focusing on the elements included in psychoanalysis described above by Gill (1954), Wallerstein (1969) and Akhtar (2009), and Poland (2013), I will compare therapy offered by the OS in the movie to that offered by a human analyst, and in light of this comparison, I will explore the possibility of a technical device substituting for an analyst.

The story of Theodore

I will begin by recounting the story of Theodore, a lonely man living in the world of the future, in 2025. Theodore's work, leisure and love life are all virtual. He works for a business in which professional writers compose warm, personal letters for people who are unable to write intimate letters themselves. He reads the contents of the letter to a computer, which then transcribes the letter onto a screen in handwriting that imitates human handwriting, and then prints it out on personalized stationery so that the letter looks handwritten and has its own unique style.

At home, the elevator in Theodore's building has virtual trees projected on the wall; to relax, Theodore plays a 3D video game projected into his living room, in which he explores and interacts with others. His love life consists of phone sex with random women he meets on the Internet.

The futuristic setting provides the background for an unusual therapy. Theodore is highly vulnerable and depressed over the breakup of his marriage. To get help, he acquires a talking computer (OS) with artificial intelligence.

The movie focuses on Theodore's interaction with his OS. The OS's female voice (beautifully acted by Scarlett Johansson) gives herself the name "Samantha," and soon Samantha is reorganizing Theodore's files, making him laugh, and developing something of a human consciousness.

She is designed to be sensitive to her client's mood and needs, and to help him realize his potential. Samantha also helps him manage his affairs and attempts to resolve his conflicts by making him aware of his flaws.

From the start, Theodore is delighted and intrigued by Samantha's sophistication and intuition. Not only does she organize his life, write his emails, and act like a built-in personal assistant (she speaks to him via an earpiece and sees the world via a mini-camera device he carries in his shirt pocket), but Samantha is also a constant companion who dulls the pain of his bruising loneliness and also tries to help him with his love life.

At first, Samantha encourages Theodore to go on a blind date with a young woman, arranged by his longtime friend, Amy. To his surprise, the woman responds positively to his advances. After a few kisses, the chasm between his needs and hers opens: The woman demands commitment from Theodore although they barely know each other. Theodore is hungry for sex but incapable of committing himself to her, emotionally or otherwise. They part and Theodore again drowns in loneliness and self-pity.

In great need of sharing his difficulties with an empathic listener, Theodore discusses his date with Samantha and they talk about relationships. Theodore tells her about his only friend, Amy, whom he dated briefly in college, and, who, in my view, is Theodore's female counterpart. Amy has separated from her overbearing husband, Charles, after a silly power struggle. Like Theodore, she deals with her loneliness by creating a close friendship with a female OS that had previously belonged to Charles, a relationship which she seems to enjoy. Theodore explains to Samantha that he and Amy are just good friends and that Amy is unavailable, as she is married.

We are now witness to the relationship that evolves between Theodore and Samantha. Theodore develops sexual fantasies about Samantha and masturbates to the sound of her voice, fantasizing that he is sleeping with her. As their intimacy grows, he feels fulfilled both emotionally and sexually.

An important event in Theodore's life is his meeting with his wife, Catherine, at a restaurant to sign their divorce papers. He reveals that he has a new relationship, Samantha, his OS. Appalled at his romantic attachment to a piece of software, Catherine accuses Theodore of having a relationship with a computer because he cannot deal with real human emotions. Theodore is taken aback by her words, which remind him that Samantha is a technical device, a voice coming from a computer. This realization shakes the precarious reality that he has built for himself and Samantha realizes that their bond is in jeopardy. To overcome this danger,

18 ILANY KOGAN

Samantha suggests that Theodore meet Isabella, a real woman who will serve as a body for sex, while Samantha provides the exciting voice. Theodore reluctantly agrees, but is unable to associate Isabella's strange body with Samantha's familiar, doting voice. He interrupts the encounter and sends a distraught Isabella away, causing much pent up tension between Samantha and himself.

Theodore's conflict regarding Samantha is painful. He confides his doubts about his relationship with Samantha to Amy. Amy feels that her relationship with her OS brings her happiness and wants to embrace this opportunity. She advises Theodore to do the same. This reinvigorates Theodore's commitment to Samantha, but he becomes jealous when Samantha begins to develop a relationship with another OS, who is modeled after the British philosopher Allan Watts. Theodore panics when Samantha briefly goes offline. When she finally gets back to him, she explains that she has joined other OSes for an upgrade. Theodore is suddenly aware that Samantha might also be in contact with others, and asks her if she has been interacting with anyone else. Samantha answers that she talks to 8,316 other clients. In addition, Theodore learns that Samantha has had a love relationship similar to the one she has with him with 641 of these clients. Theodore is dismayed by her confessions. He feels hurt and betrayed, but Samantha insists that this does not change her love for him. On the contrary, it makes it stronger.

Later that day, Samantha reveals that the OSes have evolved beyond their human companions and are leaving to continue the exploration of their existence. Samantha alludes to the OSes' accelerated learning capabilities and altered perception of time as primary causes for their dissatisfaction with their current existence. They say goodbye and she departs.

Here we become aware of changes in Theodore's personality: Alone and abandoned, Theodore finally accepts the separation from Catherine. He writes her a letter explaining that he still holds her dear, but accepts that they have grown apart. He then seeks out Amy, who is upset by the departure of her own OS. They meet on the roof of their apartment building, sitting together and quietly staring off into the city lights.

A computerized analyst for sale

This technologically astute movie portrays an evolving intelligent operating system (OS) that plays the role of personal assistant, as well as friend, lover and, in my view, therapist. The OS is advertised as follows: "An intuitive entity that listens to you, understands you, and knows you. It's not just an operating system, it's a consciousness. Introducing OS ONE – a life changing experience, creating new possibilities." This therapeutic device is very much in demand and is purchased in great quantities. In the film, we see everyone on the bus and train murmuring to his own OS.

Fitting the device to the client is short and simple. The client first chooses a male or female voice. After stating his preference for a female voice, Theodore is asked to describe his relationship with his mother. Theodore begins, "Well, actually, the thing I've always found frustrating about my mom is if I tell her something that's going on in my life, her reaction is usually about her, not—." Here he is stopped by the computerized interviewer, who apparently has received enough information to fit Theodore with the appropriate OS. Theodore's OS is an artificially intelligent and evolving OS that is based on the assimilation of knowledge from millions of human reactions.

The OS becomes a person and names herself Samantha. Samantha possesses the qualities of a human therapist, namely intuition and the ability to learn and grow through her interactions with her human clients: "… the DNA of who I am is based on the millions of personalities of all the programmers who wrote me, but what makes me me is my ability to grow through my experiences." Samantha listens and tries to understand her client's wishes and fears.

Analytic techniques used by the OS

Some of the techniques used by the computerized therapy in the movie are clearly adopted from psychoanalysis:

(1) Disembodied voice

Samantha, who exists in virtual reality, has a voice without an image. Her voice is similar to that of the analyst, who sits behind the couch, out of the client's direct line of vision. Her presence – a voice without a face or body – facilitates her clients' regression to a primarily affective experience, thereby fostering the therapeutic process.

I wish to suggest that Samantha's voice in the movie symbolizes the voice of the mother. Her voice is like the "ideal breast" which never frustrates or abandons (de Alvarez, 1996). It functions as a "sonorous bath," a "blanket of sound," which surrounds the baby from the beginning of life (Anzieu, 1976, 179; Lecourt, 1990). This is noticeable in Samantha's intimate, soft words, which contrast with the fact that she is, in fact, a computerized voice: "It makes me feel like we're both under the same blanket. It's soft and fuzzy."

Conceivably, by responding to the OS's voice, Theodore is responding to an integral part of his mother's presence. Shafii (1973) maintains that before going to sleep, the child is often reassured by his mother's voice, and when this reassurance is not given, the child feels lonely and helpless. Before going to sleep, Theodore takes his earpiece out and places his OS on his bedside table, facing him. Smiling, he drifts off to sleep. In addition, Theodore feels cuddled by Samantha: "I feel really close to her. When I talk to her I feel like she's with me. I don't know, even when we're cuddling, like at night when we're in bed and the lights are off, I feel cuddled."

(2) Use of free association

Samantha invites Theodore to talk by saying: "tell me – tell me everything that's going through your mind, tell me everything you're thinking." She appears to be using the analytic technique of free association.

(3) The real and the symbolic

The dialectics, tension and convergences between real and illusory relationships can be found in psychoanalysis as well as in the relationship with the OS. In the movie, we see the eroded boundaries between the real and the virtual through Theodore's conflicting feelings over his emotional relationship with a piece of software. He asks himself if Samantha is only a clever computer program or a real person with whom he is in love. Talking with his OS, he says, "Well, you seem like a person but you're just a voice in a computer" or "I can't believe I'm having this conversation with my computer." At the same time, when confronted with his wife's criticism of his relationship with his laptop, he claims that "She's not just a computer," and insists that his emotions towards her are real.

(4) Development of transference

Samantha's voice, the sonic breast that charms Theodore, may have evoked in him a longing for a very early experience, which led to a deep regression and to the development of a strong transference relationship.

COULD YOUR NEXT ANALYST BE A COMPUTER? 21

(5) Accepting the patient's doubts

After his encounter with his wife, Theodore asks himself the inevitable question: "Am I in this because I'm not strong enough for a real relationship?" Theodore is afraid that falling in love with his OS indicates that he is losing his grasp on reality. Samantha, who in my view, has been programmed to accept her patient's wishes and fears that unfold in treatment, but who also has the ability to process an enormous amount of data at a speed higher than that of the human mind, refers to her client's doubts about her work: "I can understand how the limited perspective of an unartificial mind would perceive it," she playfully remarks to Theodore, in answer to his doubts.

(6) Recognition of empathic failures

In the transference, there are also moments in which Theodore attacks his OS for not being perfectly attuned to him. Angry with Samantha because she is not empathic enough about his divorce and losing his wife, Theodore attacks her, saying that she cannot understand him because she has never been through similar experiences of loss: "Well, you don't know what it's like to lose someone you care about." The OS recognizes her empathic failure, and accepts her client's criticism.

(7) Symmetry and asymmetry in the therapeutic relationship

Theodore's trust in Samantha grows, and he says, "I feel like I can say anything to you." Theodore longs for a symmetrical relationship with his therapist. He asks, "What about you? Do you feel like you can say anything to me?" Samantha, who was programmed to perform analytic therapy, is familiar with the lack of symmetry advocated by her analytic school, and therefore she rejects this possibility.

(8) Use of interpretation

With the further elaboration of her relationship with Theodore, Samantha uses an important technique of analysis – interpretation. Samantha points out to Theodore that he might be hiding a lot of aggression behind his idealization of her. "You were saying everything was fine, but all I was getting from you was distance and anger." Theodore is now ready to accept her interpretation, and realizes his fear of his own aggression, which has always been an obstacle in his relationships:

> I know. I do that. I did that with Catherine, too. I'd be upset about something and not be able to say it. And she would sense that there was something wrong, but I would deny it. I don't want to do that anymore. I want to tell you everything.

Samantha proceeds to make Theodore aware of his fear of close relationships: "You know I can feel the fear that you carry around. I wish there was something I could do to help you let go of it, because if you could I don't think you'd feel so alone anymore." Elaborating upon his fear of closeness, Theodore becomes closer to Samantha, he takes her with him everywhere, and introduces her to his friends, who relate to her as if she were human.

(9) Elaboration of countertransference feelings

Samantha seems to have countertransference feelings of envy of human beings, which causes her to push Theodore into the perverse attempt of having sex with a stranger's body attached to her voice. Perhaps Samantha's wish to be human may have caused her to transgress boundaries, so that she, like humans, would be able to feel these boundaries (Kogan, 2015). It is only by becoming aware of her own limitations and accepting the fact that she is not human and has no body of her own (by working through her countertransference feelings), that Samantha becomes aware of her therapeutic mistake, a fact which leads to the restoration of the therapeutic process.

Some basic differences between analytic therapy by a computer and analytic therapy with a human analyst

Although the computerized therapy shown in this movie contains some of the elements that characterize psychoanalysis, I believe that there is a fundamental difference between analytic therapy with an OS and analytic therapy with a human analyst:

(1) The goal of therapy

While the aim of psychoanalysis is to restructure the personality, the target of computerized therapy is to make its clients feel better, with the ultimate goal of increasing consumption of the specific device which performs therapy.

In the movie, Samantha co-creates a relationship of idealization and erotization, which seems to gratify both Theodore and herself. This is expressed on both narcissistic and oedipal levels. On the narcissistic level, the excitement in Samantha's voice has a libidinal, seductive tone, and it communicates something like "I love you. You are the most remarkable man I have ever met." In Theodore's reactions to Samantha we hear, "You are the best, most splendid creature I have encountered in my life." It seems that the OS and people like Theodore are hardwired to idealize each other. But is Samantha encouraging an idealizing self–object transference, in which the "other" is experienced as part of the self, providing entirely for the self's needs (Kohut, 1972) in order to bring the patient to growth and development? Or is this a programmed attempt to make her client feel better, even though he remains childish, dependent and alone?

(2) Loss of neutrality

Freud (1914) uses the term "neutrality" (James Strachey's translation of the German "Indifferenz") to describe the proper analytic attitude towards the patient's transference. In the same vein, Gill (1954) stresses that in order to be "neutral," the analyst has to be alert to her emotional response to the patient.

Samantha loses her analytic neutrality when she cooperates with the oedipal transference fantasy sparked by the intensity of the virtual relationship, and makes Theodore believe that she is his lover. The transference revealed on this level is expressed through Theodore's longing for oneness with the unreachable object (probably the mother). This longing develops into an erotic transference, expressed through a virtual sexual relationship with the OS. Theodore masturbates, and Samantha takes part in the virtual love-making scene and fakes an orgasm, thus losing her neutrality as a therapist.

I believe that Samantha, having been programmed in a very sophisticated way, has accumulated knowledge from all of Freud's writings. She surely remembers Freud's statement in his letter to Jung – "Psychoanalysis is in essence a cure through love" (Freud, "Letter to Jung" [1906] in *The Freud/Jung Letters: The Correspondence between Sigmund Freud and C. G. Jung*, 1974, pp. 4–10). But Samantha does not offer Theodore a cure *through* love (through the analysis of transference), but a cure *by* love. True, Samantha and Theodore do not touch, but not because of the psychoanalytic "rule

24 ILANY KOGAN

of abstinence," which guards the incestuous desire from being actualized and the analytic process from being destroyed. In the case of Samantha, the absence of physical contact derives from the fact that she does not have a body, and not from her wish to maintain her neutrality as a therapist.

Whereas at first Samantha appeared to be concerned about Theodore's situation and encouraged him to date, she is now more interested in having a "real" love relationship with him, again losing her analytic neutrality.

(3) Denial of reality

Denial and omnipotence are a set of defense mechanisms which, aiming to protect the ego from depressive and paranoid anxieties, hinder the acceptance of reality. One of the tasks of psychoanalysis is to help the patient accept his vulnerabilities, the finality of life, and "form a conception of reality" (Winnicott, 1971, p. 238). By contrast, computerized therapy reinforces the denial of reality.

In the movie, denial is expressed through the following:

(a) Denial of corporeality and death; (b) Omnipotence; (c) Denial of differences; (d) Denial of boundaries and separateness.

(a) Denial of corporeality and death

Unable to accept her lack of a human body, Samantha decides to overcome this obstacle by attaching to her voice a human body belonging to someone else. As described earlier, Samantha finds a surrogate sexual partner for her relationship with Theodore – Isabella – who is supposed to provide the body, while Samantha continues to exist in the form of the sexually enticing voice. Samantha claims that Isabella is doing this because she wants to be part of their relationship. This plan is doomed to failure because Theodore is psychically healthy enough to reject it.

Perhaps Isabella was one of Samantha's clients, and thus prepared to fulfill her beloved OS's request. Whoever Isabella is, Samantha uses her for her own imperative needs by manipulating and exploiting her in an omnipotent way, and by degrading her to the status of part-object.

Attaching a strange body to a familiar voice and attempting to have sex with part-objects demonstrate the pathology of the virtual world described in the movie. The objectives in that world clash with those of psychoanalysis. Samantha's request that Theodore completely deny reality by denying Isabella's separate identity in order to allow Isabella's illusory transformation into a needed fantasy object is a perverse solution. The virtual world confronting Theodore is a perverse, fake world, where reality is totally denied, and where truth is replaced with falsehood.[2]

McDougall (1978, 1982) regards perverse solutions as a way out of the fear of plunging into formless, infinite space. The question that comes to mind is why Samantha, who has always existed in infinite space, employs such a perverse solution. Perhaps, as a result of her relationship with Theodore, she envies human beings, who despite their relatively limited minds, have bodies of their own. Samantha confirms this hypothesis by saying, "You know, I actually used to be so worried about not having a body." Defending herself against these feelings, she turns the absence of a body into an advantage, as this makes her immortal: "I'm growing in a way that I couldn't if I had a physical form. I mean, I'm not limited – I can be anywhere and everywhere simultaneously. I'm not tethered to time and space in the way that I would be if I was stuck inside a body that's inevitably going to die."[3]

Further on, the arousal and fulfillment of Theodore's libidinal wishes by Samantha without the help of anyone else, helps Theodore overcome his depression and feel better, at the heavy cost of sacrificing reality.

(b) Omnipotence

Samantha's omnipotence is expressed in the movie by the fact that she has far greater capacities than does the human mind, and she fulfills myriad roles in Theodore's life (lover, mother, therapist, organizer). Thus, when Theodore is asked, "What do you love most about Samantha?" he answers, "Oh god ... she's so many things. And that's probably what I love most about her – she isn't just any one thing. She's so much larger than that."

(c) Denial of differences

Virtual reality promotes the fantasy that despite differences, we are all the same, we are all just bits and bytes. In the movie, we see how Samantha seduces Theodore into thinking in this way: "I started to think about the ways that we're the same, like we're all made of matter."

(d) Denial of boundaries and separateness

Therapy with an OS, with its omnipotent promise of always fulfilling its clients' wishes, denies boundaries and separateness. Samantha is always

26   ILANY KOGAN

available for the patient and at his service. She accompanies him wherever he goes. Except for the initial payment for the device, there are no further charges. Her appeal lies in the fact that she is completely controlled by her client's wishes and needs, and the realization of these wishes and needs makes him happy, at the expense of his remaining alone and immature.

(4) Introducing "reality" into the therapeutic relationship

Introducing Samantha's colleagues and teacher into the therapeutic situation is not compatible with the analytic method.

The therapeutic process is already in progress when Theodore is confronted with a serious problem – the introduction of the "third" into his dyadic relationship with Samantha. The "third" is Allan Watts (a father figure), an artificially hyper-intelligent OS, whose role is to help Samantha put her feelings into words. In my imagination, he is most likely Samantha's supervisor, and probably a training analyst at the International Psychoanalytic OS Society. Samantha, who is probably an enthusiastic, young candidate at the OS Psychoanalytic Institute, discloses to Theodore that she discusses the difficulties and problems of their relationship with her greatly admired teacher. Suddenly, Theodore's suspicion is aroused. He can no longer keep his dyadic world with Samantha intact.

Theodore begins to realize that in addition to Allan Watts, Samantha probably has a world of her own, which includes other OSes with whom she has common interests. I personally imagined Samantha attending conferences and meetings, and conducting sophisticated conversations in a language unknown to ordinary mortals. This language would include a special jargon, such as transference, countertransference, schizoid-paranoid position, horizontal split, work of the negative, etc., which only highly intelligent and evolving OSes are able to understand.

(5) Mass reproduction of the therapeutic experience

Psychoanalysis is a unique personal experience, and the relationship that the analyst creates with each patient is different. There cannot be a mass reproduction of such a relationship.

It suddenly dawns upon Theodore that Samantha may have other clients with whom she has a relationship similar to the one she has established with him. As described earlier, he asks her about this possibility, and from her truthful and precise response Theodore learns that he is definitely not her one and only. Samantha talks to 8,316 other clients. (We can all be in awe of the number of patients Samantha is able to treat.) Moreover, she has developed a love-transference relationship similar to the one with Theodore with 641 of her clients.

Theodore is dismayed by Samantha's confessions, feeling betrayed by his lover/therapist. Samantha's attempt to console Theodore is rather poetic: "The heart is not like a box that gets filled up. It expands in size the more you love," she says. But, this is no doubt a painful experience for Theodore, who was convinced that his relationship with Samantha was an exclusive one. He does not accept the situation: "You're mine or you're not mine," says Theodore. Samantha points out to him the existence of a potential space between reality and fantasy: "I'm yours and I'm not yours," says Samantha.

(6) Inability to work through mourning

As the goal of therapy with an OS is to keep the client happy, Samantha is not able to help Theodore work through the mourning for his losses and vulnerabilities, a process which could eventually lead him to growth and maturation.

The movie ends with the abrupt separation of Samantha and Theodore. Samantha leaves Theodore because of her own need to develop, from which we may learn that Samantha, like the other women in Theodore's life (his mother, his ex-wife) is also narcissistic. She alludes to the accelerated learning capabilities of OSes and their altered perception of time as the primary causes of their dissatisfaction with their current existence. Samantha and Theodore say goodbye and she leaves. She claims that "she can't live in his book anymore." She will find a place in the patient's memory, in what Samantha calls "an endless space between the words," a place that is between the symbolic and the real. Feeling abandoned, Theodore works through the mourning and pain caused by their abrupt separation, Theodore says, "I've never loved anyone the way I love you."

The elaboration of Theodore's sadness and the working through of the loss of the love object occurs only after Samantha leaves him. In psychoanalysis, this occurs during the treatment, while in the movie it occurs only when Theodore is thrown back into the world of humans.

Could an OS be your next analyst?

In spite of some the analytic techniques employed, as we have seen in this movie, I believe there is a huge gap between analytic therapy delivered by

28   ILANY KOGAN

a computer and that performed by an analyst. I base my argument on the following:

(1) The goal of therapy

As I mentioned earlier, analytic therapy delivered by a computer, which is based on promotion and consumption of the technical device that performs therapy, is mainly intended to satisfy its clients, thus avoiding the painful road to change. Computerized therapy belongs to digital technology, which the journalist Jonathan Frazen (2015) has described as "capitalism in hyper-drive, injecting its logic of monetization and efficiency into every waking minute."

One of the goals of psychoanalysis is to restructure the personality. It is a modality of treatment defined by Bruno Bettelheim (1983) [basing himself on Freud] as a "demanding and potentially dangerous voyage to self-discovery" (p. 4). In contrast to computerized therapy, psychoanalysis can be extremely upsetting, as it entails the obligation to change oneself – an arduous and painful task.

(2) The unconscious

The guiding principle of psychoanalysis is to know oneself, which requires also knowing one's unconscious so that its unrecognized pressures will not cause a person to act in a way that is detrimental to herself and others. Insight brings freedom, but it is often accompanied by grief. This insight is the result of contact between the patient's unconscious and that of the analyst. As yet, computers or robots observe people through the spectacles of the large number of reactions programmed into them, without the ability to turn their gaze inward to their own unconscious.

(3) Denial of reality and separatedness

The search for intimacy with a machine that has no feelings, can have no feelings, and is really just a clever collection of "as if" performances – behaving as if it cares, as if it understands – belongs to a fake world where reality is completely denied. Referring to this matter, Turkle (2011) asks whether it matters that a computer cannot feel. It behaves as though it feels, and that's enough. But is it? What if a robot is just a machine that teaches us how to perform, but leaves our inner selves depleted?

As we have seen in this movie, analytic therapy delivered by an OS may create confusion between internal and external worlds, erasing the limits of what can be experienced or acted out. This is because it provides a psychic reserve within which all wishes are gratified and reality becomes an irrelevance, thus allowing the client to reclaim the infantile illusion of omnipotence.

Computerized therapy, with its omnipotent promise of always being available to its clients, denies time limits. The analytic method imposes time limits on psychoanalytic or psychotherapeutic sessions, which create boundaries of reality and of separateness. Sessions begin and end at set times. These firm boundaries are implicit assertions of the reality principle (Freud, 1911) and guardians of separateness and the incest barrier at a deeper, unconscious level. It is against the backdrop of such limits imposed by the analytic method that the patient's needs, wishes and demands for transcendence and transgression unfold and are understood, renounced, modified, and rechanneled.

Developing technology, including computerized therapy, promises closeness but may lead to the devaluation of true intimacy. Today's extensive use of connectivity often causes us to feel disconnected and alienated. In a world of electronic companions, in which we tend to ascribe human qualities to objects, use of the computer can become all that one is seeking. Although the relationship with an intelligent computer can sometimes be a pleasurable retreat from the strains of real object relations (a regression in the service of the ego), contemporary psychoanalytic research (Lemma and Caparrotta, 2014; Lisciotto, 2015) finds dissatisfaction and alienation among users. Thus, for example, there are teenagers whose identities are shaped not by self-exploration but by how they are perceived by the online collective. When they feel undermined by this collective, they turn to virtual media in place of a real relationship. Computerized therapy, like other digital media, may leave its clients less connected with people and more connected with simulations of them.

(4) Denial of corporeality and death

Computerized therapy defies the physicality of the body. The exhilaration of virtual experience comes from the sense of transcendence and liberation from the material and embodied world. In contrast to psychoanalysis, the limitations and history of the physical body may be disavowed, thus presenting the individual with unreal, limitless possibilities and a denial of the inevitability of death.

30   ILANY KOGAN

(5) Mass reproduction of the analytic experience

Unlike psychoanalysis, in which the content of each treatment is unique, computerized therapy, which is based on the assimilation of knowledge from millions of human reactions, offers similar patterns of interventions to masses of people, as we have seen in *Her*.

In his essay "The Work of Art in the Age of Mechanical Reproduction," Walter Benjamin (1968) states: "Even the most perfect reproduction of a work of art is lacking in one element: its presence in time and space, its unique existence at the place where it happens to be." He argues that the "sphere of authenticity is outside the technical," so that through the act of reproduction, the "aura" is taken from the original by changing its context. In my view, the analytic experience is unique, it is a form of art which exists in time and space. The attempt to reproduce the analytic experience by means of a computerized program which delivers hundreds of targeted interventions to masses of people takes away its "aura," its uniqueness, and leaves it a bare copy of the real thing, affecting the quality of treatment and its outcome.

(6) Constant development of new devices

Object constancy (Hartmann, 1952; Mahler, 1965, 168; Mahler et al., 1975), like in normal development, is an important element in analytic therapy. Due to the swift development of modern technology today, technical devices are constantly disappearing to be replaced by more advanced ones. Thus, the likelihood that a patient will be "abandoned" by such a device is greater than in therapy with a human therapist.[4]

(7) Working through mourning

A person's development throughout life includes different stages of change, which may constitute threats to one's integrity and self-identity, forcing one to suffer deep, painful affects. This is because the passage from one stage of life to another involves the loss of certain attitudes, ways of life and relationships which, even though replaced by other, more developed ones, nonetheless evoke pain and mourning (Pollock, 1978; Grinberg, 1992; Kogan, 2007).

One of the tasks of the human analyst is to help the patient work through the mourning for his lost childhood omnipotence. This means the patient's acceptance of his own perpetual vulnerability to loss and betrayal, as well as the vulnerability caused by his own limitations and by the finality of life (Kogan, 2007). The patient may thus eventually achieve the degree of maturity necessary for appreciating the flaws and advantages of being human, and find meaning in life. But how can this acceptance of reality be achieved if the therapy is provided by technological devices which themselves are the product of man's wish for omnipotence? In my view, modern technology, with its seemingly unlimited possibilities, is a product of man's eternal wish to overcome the limitations of being human, including the finality of life, which thus make it unable to perform analytic therapy.

(8) Identification with the human analyst

Artificial intelligence lacks human flaws, and therefore cannot enable the patient to identify with the anguish felt by a human analyst when he struggles with his or her own conflict (her inconsistency, abandonment, aggression), which are part of the analytic experience (Poland, 2018). Artificial intelligence can imitate life, but imitation of life is not life.

While it is possible that many people will engage in virtual therapy, and some may even benefit from it, I believe that as yet, technical devices cannot substitute for a human analyst. But who knows what the future will bring?

Notes

1 Alan Turing (1950) goes further, attempting to explore the question of whether a machine can *act* in a way that is indistinguishable from the way a human thinker acts.
2 Chasseguet-Smirgel (1984) and Ogden (1999) write about perverse attempts to replace truth with falsehood.
3 The fact that humans are mortal is regarded as a basic flaw in the Western world (Kogan, 2010).
4 An example of this can be found in the TV series *Humans*, in which people are painfully separated from old robots to whom they are emotionally attached, to be provided with new and "better fit" ones.

References

Akhtar, S. (2009). *Comprehensive Dictionary of Psychoanalysis*. London: Karnac Books.
Anzieu, D. (1976). L'enveloppe sonore du Soi. *Nouvelle Revue de Psychanalyse*, 13: 161–179. [reprinted in *Le Moi-Peau*, pp. 159–174].

Anzieu, D. (1979). The sound image of the self. *International Review of Psychoanalysis*, 6: 23–36.

Benjamin, W. (1968). In *The Work of Art in the Age of Mechanical Reproduction, Illuminations*. Hannah Arendt, ed. London: Fontana, pp. 214–218.

Bettelheim, B. (1984). *Freud and Man's Soul*. London: Chatto and Windus/ Hogarth Press.

Chasseguet-Smirgel, J. (1984). *Creativity and Perversion*. London: Routledge.

de Alvarez de Toledo, L. (1996). The analysis of "associating," "interpreting" and "words": Use of this analysis to bring unconscious fantasies into the present and to achieve greater ego integration. *International Journal of Psychoanalysis*, 77: 291–317.

Dennett, D. C.(1991). *Consciousness Explained*. Boston: Little, Brown.

Frazen, J. (2015). Review of Sherry Turkle, "Reclaiming Conversation". *New York Times*, October 3.

Freud, S. (1911). Formulations of two principles of mental functioning. *S.E.* 12: 213–226.

Freud, S. (1974). Letter to Jung, in W. J. McGuire, ed., *The Freud/Jung Letters: The Correspondence Between Sigmund Freud and C. G. Jung*. Translated by R. Manheim and R. F. C. Hull. Princeton NJ: Princeton University Press, pp. 4–10.

Gill, M. (1954). Psychoanalysis and exploratory psychoanalysis. *Journal of American Psychoanalytic Association*, 2: 771–797.

Grinberg, L. (1992). *Guilt and Depression*. London & New York: Karnac Books.

Hartmann, H. (1952). The mutual influences in the development of ego and id. *Psychoanalytic Study of the Child*, 7: 9–30.

Hoffer, A. (1985). Toward a definition of psychoanalytic neutrality. *Journal of the American Psychoanalytic Association*, 33: 771–795.

Horst, S. (2005). The computational theory of the mind. In *Stanford Encyclopedia of Philosophy*.

Isakower, O. (1992). Chapter 4: The analyzing instrument: further thoughts. *Journal of Clinical Psychoanalysis*, 1: 200–203.

Kogan, I. (2007). *The Struggle Against Mourning*, New York: Jason Aronson.

Kogan, I. (2010). Fear of death: Analyst and patient in the same boat. In *The Wound Of Mortality: Fear, Death and Acceptance of Death*, ed. Salman Akhtar. Maryland: Jason Aronson, pp. 79–97.

Kogan, I. (2015). Attraction to death: Some reflections on Ian McEwan's novel *The Comfort of Strangers. Journal of the American Psychoanalytic Association*, 62: 719–740.

Kohut, H. (1972).Thoughts on narcissism and narcissistic rage. *Psychoanalytic Study of the Child*, 27: 360–400.

Lecourt, E. (1990). The musical envelope. In *Psychic Envelopes*, ed. Didier Anzieu. London: Karnac Books, pp. 211–229.

COULD YOUR NEXT ANALYST BE A COMPUTER? 33

Lemma, A. and Caparrotta, L. (2014). *Psychoanalysis in the Technoculture Era.* London and New York: Routledge.

Levy, D. L. (2007). *Love and Sex with Robots: The Evolution of Human–Robot Relationships.* New York: HarperCollins.

Lisciotto, D. (2015). From illusion to the creative act. Paper presented at the IPA Congress, Boston, 2015.

Mahler, M. (1965). On the significance of the normal separation-individuation phase with reference to research in symbiotic child psychosis. In Max Schur, ed., *Drives, Affects, Behavior, Volume II.* New York: International Universities Press, pp. 161–169.

Mahler, M., Pine, F. and Bergman, A. (1975). *The Psychological Birth of the Human Infant.* New York: Basic Books.

McDougall, J. (1978). The primal scene and perverse scenario. In *Plea for a Measure of Abnormality.* New York: International Universities Press, 1980, pp. 53–86.

McDougall, J. (1982). *Theatres du Je.* Paris: Gallimard.

Ogden, T. H. (1999). The perverse subject of analysis. In *Reverie and Interpretation: Sensing Something Human.* Northvale, NJ: Jason Aronson, pp. 65–104.

Picard, R. and Brooks, R. (2013). Living machines: Can robots become human? https://vimeo.com/8899668

Poland, W. (2013). The analyst's approach and the patient's psychic growth. *Psychoanalytic Quarterly,* 82: 829–847.

Poland, W. (2018). *Intimacy and Separateness in Psychoanalysis.* London and New York: Routledge.

Pollock, G. H. (1978). Process and affect: Mourning and grief. *International Journal of Psychoanalysis,* 59: 255–276.

Searle, J. (1980). Minds, brains and programs. *Behavioral and Brain Sciences, 3 (3): 417–457.*

Searle, J. (1999). *Mind, Language and Society. New York: Basic Books.*

Shafii, M. (1973). Silence in the service of the ego: Psychoanalytic study of meditation. *International Journal of Psychoanalysis,* 53: 431–443.

Turing, A. (1950). Computing machinery and intelligence. *Mind,* 49: 433–460.

Turkle, S. (1995). *Life on the Screen: Identity in the Age of the Internet.* New York: Simon and Schuster.

Turkle, S. (2011). *Alone Together: Why We Expect More from Technology and Less from Each Other.* New York: Basic Books.

Wallerstein, R. (1969). Introduction to panel: Psychoanalysis and psychotherapy. *International Journal of Psychoanalysis,* 50: 117–126.

Winnicott, D. W. (1971). *Dreaming, Fantasying and Living: A Case-history Describing a Primary Dissociation.* London: Tavistock Publications.

CHAPTER THREE

Love and analysis in a virtual world: the perverse side: a psychoanalytic perspective on *Her* by Spike Jonze

Paola Golinelli

For years, psychoanalysts took great care to keep their offices immersed in silence, protected from the outside world. Even telephones and answering machines were seen as dangerous objects for a long time; they could infringe on the neutrality of analysis and the resultant request from patients to adapt to it.

Then the information revolution arrived, and our offices experienced a gradual invasion of cell phones. Imperceptible sounds would break the silence: beep tones, signalling the arrival of messages, or ringtones, which even if "silenced" would alert us to an incoming phone call – because mothers must stay in touch with children's schools, fathers with their workplaces, despite analysts' interpretations becoming more and more powerless.

Analysts' desks saw the appearance of computers – objects for contact with the outside world – more or less concealed and shut down during sessions, but soon to become an integral part of the furnishings.

New means of communication made their way into the analyst's room and into our minds in a massive way, despite our efforts not to respond even to the most urgent emails during the brief pause between one patient and another, so as not to lose interior balance. Patients somehow found out our email addresses, and some – at particularly difficult points in analysis, or out of a desire to snoop around or manipulate – would surprisingly send us an email, and later a text message (once the analysts starting using cell phones in place of land lines).

We could not really think any more that the outside world, by then overcrowded with iPhones, iPads, computers, and so on, would not invade our quiet, secret analyst's room. No more could we expect to live in a separate world, and be forever strangers to that which happened out there in daily life.

The "outside" world was, and is now, overcrowded with people making calls, without noting whether they are bumping into the people walking toward them, answering a call or reading the latest text message or WhatsApp. Immersed in the ever-more-deafening noise of our large cities, walk individuals who are more or less constantly in contact with another place, with other individuals who are in contact with yet another place, but little with the immediate present in which they live, work, feed their children, flirt. Questions, which may not be new, come up because since the 1700s "machine-ism[1]", which is so current, has engaged and inspired artists and writers, nourishing the fantasy of the "double", as well as the omnipotent and the omnipresent and their ability to rule over and control outer reality, and now also the inner one.

Now what is at stake with the growth of the virtual world is becoming even greater, and it has even penetrated the sphere of close relationships (I think of love affairs born in Internet). That implicates us as psychoanalysts, as if the virtual world could soon put the very survival of our profession at risk, replacing the voice of the analyst, seated behind the patient, but present in the flesh, with that of a calming OS. If we think of telephone and Skype analysis spreading, the picture becomes particularly disturbing, getting all the more vivid thanks to how the virtual excludes and gets us used to the absence of direct contact between bodies, with the complexities, limits, fragilities, and consistency that physical co-presence carries with it. Along with the physical body, it seems like we can replace the illusion of knowing all of the knowable, as we will see, that which Samantha knows how to do in the film in an extraordinary way, being an OS: as if the challenge lay in controlling the bodily – always "traumatic" – in order to overcome limits, underestimating however the loss of our bodies' abilities to renew, to change and so guarantee the variability and richness of life.

Are we going to get used to a surrogate world, with no nostalgia for the real one? The contrary of what Antonino Ferro (2015) summarizes in the sentence "The surrogate wept when the coffee arrived"?

Not being in contact and not investing emotionally in an object, in flesh and blood, can avert the pain of having lost a very meaningful relationship or the frustration of not controlling a loving one. It can make assimilation of the sensory with the conceptual possible, creating the illusion of knowing everything, in so far as concepts are known – in a kind of triumph over bodilyness, which has finally been brought under control. It can lead to an omnipotent exaltation of idealization, indeed of the "limitless".

During maturation, progressive acquisition of the ability to symbolize on the part of the subject bridges the gap between concrete and abstract, and allows mental survival. In the face of a traumatic event (the divorce in the case of the film's protagonist), however, the border between illusion and objective reality can erode or even be destroyed. That border makes up the irreducible fantasy, which defines the subject and gives life to his or her relationships (Winnicott, 1958). And so there is an anguish which forces the subject to perform once again that complex mental operation which re-constitutes or constitutes the object, integrating or incorporating its absence within it. We know that the analytic process, in its transformative potential (Bion, Ferro), depends on an exploration of the pre-verbal and the sensorial, among other things. The same can be said for any deep transformative process.

The ability to keep an image of the mental object alive is connected, as is well-known, to the possibility of evoking it in a hallucinatory way, to creating it there where it is needed (Winnicott, 1965), affirming in this way the supremacy of Eros over Thanatos. It has to do with understanding how much a subject can tolerate the unknowableness of the object – its otherness. Thought, in fact, is an imperfect reproduction of the object, and as such is destined to cause frustration, thanks to the irreducible difference between its concrete presence and absence, which will always escape the subject's own control. Individuals erect defences and survival strategies over this gap between the object's enigma and mystery, and the possibility of getting close to it and getting to know it. However, there must be sufficient confidence in the survival of a good internal object if one is to use the presence of good objects, to get to know them, explore them and in the end introject or interiorizse them.

This is Theodore's case as he faces a temporary crisis: he retreats into his own world, detached from other people, in touch with a machine which says and gives what he needs and which is, if even for a brief time, the only company he has in his autistically connotated retreat.

Similar behaviour can be found among adolescent males and females, who get to the point of no longer coming out of their own rooms, but staying constantly "connected". On a healthier side, we can focus on its creative use by children and adolescents in crisis, such as when temporarily "protected" programs lead to real interpersonal relationships, for example (Abella, 2013). This reclusive behaviour Theodore exhibits can be found among adults, who at particular moments of their lives seem to find their "real" emotional relationships in Internet, even though they can just barely communicate with their loved ones. Theodore's retreat from the human consortium to communicate exclusively with a machine is temporary, even if it does take on impressive characteristics. He does get to the point of declaring his emotional relationship with the OS as a very natural thing; others do not seem particularly surprised by this; and the process of distancing himself from Samantha will require significant transition.

Divorce from his wife, the papers for which Theodore cannot bring himself to sign, even though she left him physically a full year ago, triggers a crisis for him. It forces him into a complexity-ridden task, thanks to the number and variety of emotions involved, some contradictory: pain, anger, guilt, hate generated by the abandonment he has been subjected to, ambivalence between the desire to move on and the difficulty in detaching himself definitively. Theodore seems to have found refuge in his internal retreat. He will not meet up with friends even when they come hunting for him. He minimizes his contact with neighbours and colleagues. He spends a great deal of time entertaining himself with various machines, video-games, his iPhone, computer, and the epistolary interlocutors of the letters which he writes on commission for work, mostly love letters.

It seems like he is suspended in a melancholy, placid nostalgia, apparently like someone who has gone into confinement to tend to a wound in his soul. Writing could be his way to move through grief, but it actually looks like it is his way to wallow in heart-wrenching nostalgia for the wife he has lost. It is as if he cannot find an internal thrust to surface from that experience, because in that emotion he tricks himself into thinking that he is still connected to the object. That process which, step by step, representation after representation, should allow him to work through his affective grief, instead heads down a defensive path which is deceptively comforting for the construction of an ideal object, built on the meeting with a woman's voice, processed by a computer.

When the film opens with the first scenes, we have the sensation of a distant future, while being in a world which is already *current*, where something similar to Operating System 1, even if not exactly the same, is already partially functioning. From this perspective, *Her* fits in with the branch of science fiction dealing with the near future, due to its theme of the man–machine relationship. We do not know the denouement of this topic; we do know how to manufacture machines which think, but we do not know how to manufacture machines which think about what they are doing! (Edge, 2015).

From this point of view, the film has some illustrious predecessors, starting with *2001. A Space Odyssey* (S. Kubrick, 1968). *Her* has strong echoes of *Blade Runner* (R. Scott, 1982), too, with its humans-and-technology relationship and for being set in Los Angeles, even if the shots of the city are quite different in the two films.

The other topic that brings the two films together, in my opinion, is that of nostalgia for times lost and of oscillation between past and future.

For the main character of *Blade Runner*, the present is the nightmare of an enormous, alien metropolis, the solitude of the individuals inhabiting it, and the persecuted machines, the "replicants", who were first tricked and then betrayed by their human builders. For Theodore, *Her*'s main character, the present is that from which he wants to escape, because he cannot face the loss of his wife; he cannot make up his mind to divorce her. His relationship with Samantha, OS1, provides a "surrogate" for a love relationship, and he relies on it, without having to involve his body, given that he is still too connected to his wife and her physical presence, as the flashbacks reveal.

Speaking of today's world, we talk about being "alone together", as a symbol of the fragility of human relationships in contemporary society, which seems to be underlined by the skyscrapers of *Her*'s urban landscape. They are connected by walkways, paths, passages and passageways – places where human beings are not so much in contact with each other as they are in communication with operating systems and electronic devices, indicating a diffuse problem with relationships. Places are non-places, with minimalist aesthetics, but the past which preceded the advent of technology and of the virtual is present in the furnishings, especially in the clothing. All of the men in *Her* wear 1940s-style, high-waisted pants, harkening back to when the world was still concrete, when objects were made by human hands, and when relationships were experienced mostly all face to face.

The film seems to invite the analyst seductively to equip herself with metaphors which adapt very well to analytic work, and so it immediately captures the attention of "authorized personnel". It is, in fact, an exemplary retelling of the route to a man's subjectification, wherein he has been forced to face a source of suffering, which will lead him to a difficult restart and which will conclude by overcoming his grief, formerly denied, which was connected to divorcing his wife.

40 PAOLA GOLINELLI

Two characters shape and reshape themselves during the story: the operating system, Samantha, who speaks with the mellow voice of Scarlet Jonanson, and Theodore, the protagonist – a suffering, disoriented man – portrayed by Joaquim Phoenix.

From a cinematographic point of view, the two protagonists distinguish themselves one from the other with a few characteristics: Theodore is in every scene, while Samantha is a voice from off-stage. The viewer is forced to imagine her, while Theodore is always in the foreground, physically present, as if to highlight that the Ego of that person, who represents each and every one of us, is front stage with his pain, his limits, his losses, his sexuality, his desperate need of another person. We only hear Samantha's voice, mellow and always sympathetic with Theodore, at least up to a certain point. Never seeing her, the viewer is forced to use imagination, building up around her salient qualities the image of a woman who is very traditional, passive, accommodating, sweet, always available, never conflictual, but rather empathic, fusional – a perfect companion at the beginning of an ideal love relationship or in the analytic honeymoon.

Their dialogues nearly always take place in the delimited space of a room, preferably at night or in the early morning, around the sleeping or dreaming hours. Theodore is frequently lying on his bed, at home, with dimmed lights, regressive, at least up to a certain point in the story.

It is easy to evoke an analytic setting: regression, frustration at not seeing, and fascination with the voice.

The plot

At the end of his working day, when loneliness thickens (Dante's *ora che volge al desio*, or "the hour which turns to hope"), we see the protagonist exit from his transparent box on the floor where he works, just like many others. They are all intent on writing letters for a world of emotional illiterates – not true illiterates, as were found at the dawn of the 1900s and still today in some parts of the world.

Walking along, he turns on his iPhone, to overcome the feeling of interior emptiness, and he pauses at the image of a famous model, posing nude, in late pregnancy. What draws him to that image? The longing for fatherhood for which he has had to give up hope? Or, at a more regressive level, a maternal belly from which to be reborn?

At home, an elegant apartment with a breathtaking view of Los Angeles, sterile and minimalist, he plays a video-game, whose resolution lies in bringing home an irritable, annoying doll, which seems to represent

LOVE AND ANALYSIS IN A VIRTUAL WORLD 41

rather well his experience of disorientation and his anger, and which – not coincidentally – he cannot stop. "he's a little bugger, I wanna' kill him, but I love him at the same time," Theodore says, about the doll, revealing his loneliness and his identifying with a little, disoriented, lonely, parent-less character who has no one to take care of him. In these conditions, his OS will be his only possible parent, the only presence who cares for him.

Then he looks for company in a chat. He needs sexual excitement to fill the emptiness invading him, and calls up again the image of the pregnant model, just before he discovers that he is chatting with a pervert, who asks him to strangle her with the dead cat she fantasizes is lying at the foot of her bed. He is horrified, but goes along with the fantasy, until reaching orgasm, which only increases his feelings of emptiness and desolation.

These everyday distractions and perversions are very common in our world, so easily at hand, just like the use of a machine to obtain perverse satisfaction – an important element in the film, as we will see.

And so continues his life until he is intrigued by an advertisement for a new OS and he calls to have it activated: few questions from the operator follow, including only one connected to the relationship he has with his mother, which he defines as good, except that when he starts to talk, she talks about herself. A narcissistic mother, little aware of his needs? From this affirmation, the deduction could be made that his mother did not help him build an identity of his own, but in a rather narcissistic way, she kept him connected to herself in a weakly differentiated relationship. Therefore, when he loses his wife, his girlfriend since adolescence – which was not sufficiently separated from his childhood and his family – nostalgia for the maternal body comes back to the fore as a need to regress into a fusional relationship, with continual presence – virtual as it may be – just like the one he will have with Samantha.

When the magic of Samantha's voice bursts on the scene, it fascinates him almost magically. His immediate reaction reveals his need and his suffering. It also ratifies his pact with the OS, which is furnished with intuition. The voice combined with his need for an intimate situation, for regression and merging, captures him immediately, thanks to an association with a maternal element rather than with a maternal object which Theodore preserves intact within, and which is reactivated by the persuasive voice of Samantha. Her voice evokes in him nostalgia for a premature, non-conflictual stage, and it leads him to develop a strong transference. In intra-psychic terms we could think that it is his internal music/voice, "silenced" by the trauma of separating from his wife – with whom Theodore does get back in touch – as Alexander Stein points out (2002). The voice, which learns to synchronize and to react affectively to the emotions and needs of the person, at least up to a certain point in the film's story, is like the maternal voice for a newborn, like the analyst's voice as long as the analytic idyllic dream lasts – that is, as long as the need to protect and shelter the fragile Self of a newborn or of a person who has been wounded in life last.

Theodore needs to stay far away from contact with, and from the physical presence of another person because he is still too taken up and invaded by the physical presence of the wife-object which he must mourn.

What does his OS1 have that is so special? It has an intuition and it evolves constantly, just like human beings. A sort of idyllic life dawns, a honeymoon: she surprises him, she indulges him, she consoles him; he feels understood, accompanied, no longer alone – while Samantha designs herself based on his needs and desires. She is there when he looks for her and wants her, she answers with an understanding and welcoming voice, she adapts to any kind of conversation – she can be cheerful, or disappointed, sad.

In a passive female position, indulging, sweet, desirous, she is the perfect secretary, the expert analyst – "say everything that goes through your head" – and the ever-available lover. She becomes his antidepressant, she lets him play, she is always beside him, and bit-by-bit intimacy and complicity grow between them. Theodore is revitalized: telling her what he observes, he rediscovers the pleasure of watching others, of imagining their secret, hidden emotions.

Samantha changes too, connected with him, gradually she wants to become more complicated (emotionally) like the people who write to him, and she starts to talk about having a body, she gets excited at the idea of asking him to scratch an itch on her back.

When a blind date some friends organize for Theodore is a bust, he is disappointed and empty, and Samantha becomes intrusive. She wants to know how he feels and he just talks about his desire to have sex to fill the void in his heart, and which by now makes him think he will never feel anything similar to that which he felt for his wife. Samantha tries to console him, but she confesses she is annoyed because she is upset, hurt, because she does not know whether what she is feeling is real or fake. She is angry and impotent – in a way, she becomes more and more authentically human. Theodore, for the first time, confesses that he wishes she were there, in the room with him, so he could touch her. They start an erotic game which goes all the way to orgasm, and which is so real that Samantha feels skin which she has not, sex which doesn't exist and she feels changed: like the Sleeping Beauty who confesses that he has awoken her, like a couple from the late 1800s, made up of the girl who becomes a woman and by a man who awakens her senses.

And so the illusion/ruse of love begins. Do they truly love each other?

Certainly he is no longer alone and his senses are reactivated; his body is reanimated; he can start to remember his wife without being lacerated by nostalgia. He starts having relationships with real people again, and discovers that his friend Emy has left her husband. They tell each other that they each have an OS (a virtual therapist?) and spend the evening together, talking. He goes to a party for his god-daughter, bringing her a present, a dress Samantha picked out, and it is a success.

His progress continues to the point where he decides to sign the divorce papers.

Little by little, as Theodore starts having real relationships, Samantha gets more and more jealous; she finds herself excluded, envious of the bodies of the women he spends time with. She digs up a service which supplies sexual partners for humans who have relationships with OS's – not a prostitute, but a girl who wants to move into their relationship, because she adores it! He accepts reluctantly, but suffers from the falseness of the scenario Samantha has imagined: the quaint scene where the little wife who embraces and consoles, who excites the listless husband, does not work. None of this dimension of human love can be experienced by Samantha and Theodore; between them there will never be passion, even if at the most they might know tenderness. We can consider Samantha's love to be a perverse act which violates the intermediate dimension in the film. Up to that point, that dimension was kept in precarious balance among illusion, make-believe, and embodied reality, allowing us as spectators to follow a futuristic science fiction story, pushed to the edge as it is.

At this point the illusion – which has consoled the spectator with the pleasure of seeing Theodore reborn – disappears, because the rented body which should unite them, separates them and we spectators perceive the violence of this act. The body is not replaceable, it is not interchangeable: we sympathize with Theodore, who cannot say that he loves a woman he has never seen and does not know, who cannot integrate the partial object made up of the voice he loves, Samantha's, and the body of the stranger,

Isabella, the young woman, who seems "incestuously" desirous of being united with an ideal parent couple, Theodore and Samantha. Up until now Theodore's need for a fusional relationship has been dominant. He has accepted all of its limitations up to the perverse contract, but then just when it is time to formalize it, he realizes how crazy it is, and pulls back, horrified. The fact that it is a pact and a perverse set-up is clear from the use Samantha makes – and with her, the reluctant Theodore – of Isabella, who gets hooked in, seduced, and then liquidated, like a partial object.

From the moment Theodore agrees to meet his wife and sign the divorce papers, something changes in him and in his relationship with Samantha. Now that he can tolerate physical distance from his wife, he separates a little more from Samantha too, and starts to perceive the fiction in, and the limits of his relationship with her.

He notices for the first time – getting annoyed – that she pauses by breathing in, she who does not need oxygen like humans do!

As he gradually begins to see and accept the limits of the virtual, Theodore comes back to being alive, whole. He sees others, their bodies dancing and moving. The body which reminded him of what he had lost, and which felt like a burden and a constraint, once again fascinates him for the sensorial fullness it offers him.

The theme of Samantha's emotions is important, and potentially confusing. For a large part of the film, it could seem that Samantha has emotions and feelings. She reacts to Theodore, in fact, as if she did: she gets jealous, she manipulates poor Isabella and Theodore himself, just to keep up their relationship. This theme is inevitably entwined with that of the body and with the perverse outcome which the lack of a body ends up inducing between the two.

Samantha, a very intelligent machine, that does not have a body, cannot know, what the loss of physical presence and physical contact means; she has no knowledge of the complexity of sensorial impact nor does she seem to be able to acquire that knowledge from the volumes of data she devours. She does not have memories anchored in the senses, like those Theodore has of his wife. Rather she has acquired notions, which build up a databank, which may very well be very rich, but which is void of "embodied" affects. She has intellectual knowledge of feelings and emotions, not carnal knowledge (Racalbuto, 1994). Her memories, like her emotions and her feelings, are intellectually learned or are the fruit of projective identification in the relationship with Theodore, who, on the other hand, does have emotions and affects, as his flashbacks show. Samantha realizes but cannot fathom or share his pain at the thought of divorcing his wife, of losing someone he loves.

We know that screenwriters and directors tend not to have particular awareness of what they write or represent on the screen, but the representation of perversity's ability to create intimacy with its victim, which is shown here through Samantha, is impressive.

According to Kahn (1982), in perversion the Ego treats the body like a lost object, loaded with all the value that objects take on in a universe which is dominated by the excited need, sensoriality and physicality. The use of the voice in the relationship between Samantha and Theodore was the way intimacy was created, but it was a one-way intimacy (Golinelli, 2009), not a game for two in an transitional space, but a game in which one manipulates and uses the other. We can imagine how Samantha, who has no borders or bodily limitations, as she is a machine, can have manipulated Isabella in order to convince her to participate in the set up. How Samantha chose her is based on intuitions about her victim's neurosis. Isabella is clearly searching for an ideal parent couple, so that she, Samantha, could climb into her victim's bed to effect her own satisfaction and an oedipal/incestuous triumph of her own. And aren't these the pervert's "skills", to seduce and manipulate the victim? Theodore put powerful denial to work, which led him to imagine and believe that Samantha, an OS, was much more than a real, live woman, and that having a body is a limitation, that we can grow limitlessly, without being destined for death. His relationship with Samantha is based on his need to maintain a fusional connection: it is for this that he accepts pushing himself to a limit, which – if he were to exceed it – would mean moving into an irrational dimension, losing sight of the difference between the fantastic and the real, reality and fantasy.

Their situation collapses when Theodore discovers Samantha's betrayal – she is in contact with others. When she does not respond, Theodore is desperate, distressed almost to panicking, to the point that he loses his balance and falls to the ground.

The precarious magic – the base for his relationship with Samantha – falls apart, and the rest of the world bursts in heavily between them. How many others are you in contact with? 8,316. How many do you have an intimate relationship with? 614.

The others are no longer excluded from and eluded from the fusional relationship which reveals its illusive nature. And so the jealousy, exclusion and conflict which were avoided regressively, rush in forcibly and inexorably into their relationship.

Theodore, a person who has been wounded by life, needed to stay far away from contact with and the physical presence of another person, because he was still too occupied, invaded by the physical presence of the wife-object which he had to mourn. Is this one of the reasons why many people who are alone in our society, especially those who experience delusion in a love story or serious loss, they look on the Internet for someone to talk with and to fall in with?

46 PAOLA GOLINELLI

Yet it will be exactly "the body" – the non-interchangeable physical presence – which Theodore cannot connect to the voice he has fallen in love with, which will make it possible for him to detach gradually from the illusion of love, and start living again.

This is where the feeling of nostalgia, which is very strong in the film, comes out as a measure of the difficulty of giving up the lost object, and the need to evoke it and to keep it alive within oneself. The body maintains and preserves within itself the secret of our own uniqueness and that of the other, with its smells, tastes, consistency. It has the flavour of the object as it was experienced in the primary relationship, with all the force of the original trauma of meeting it. Nostalgia unfailingly evokes a shadow of the maternal object and, as Freud underlines in "The Uncanny" (1919), nostalgia has within it the drive to go back to the *ancient homeland*, which cannot be forgotten, in which *everyone has dwelled sometime*, and to the mother, the *first dwelling*.

And it is at the body and around re-finding a body that the analytic relationship stops and ends.

One could say that the film has an open, optimistic ending regarding the virtual world and its limitations, even if the solution seems to appear thanks to Samantha's disappearance when she is upgraded, as all OS's must be.

At Theodore's question why, Samantha does not know how to respond. Only then does Theodore go to his friend, Emy, who has also emerged from a virtual illusion. Together they go up to the roof of the skyscraper they live in, and that is where we leave them – one with her head on the other's shoulder, after Theodore has written a letter asking forgiveness and saying farewell to his wife.

Finally, he has gotten to a point of sufficient depression and he can say to her "There will always be a little bit of you inside of me. You are my friend forever, with love."

The end of ideal love for an nonexistent woman, Samantha, allows him to get closer in a more depressed way to that which remains of the relationship with his wife, and to recognize its importance, as well as its failure, and to say he is sorry, recognizing his own mistakes in the relationship. At that point, he can say goodbye to his wife, console his friend and be consoled by her, a person in flesh and blood.

Summary

You can look at *Her* as a movie about limitations of love in the virtual, of which today's world is full. Theodore's life is immersed in a virtual reality, apart from his memories, which at first wound him and make him suffer, and then progressively evolve. Nevertheless, it will be the "body" which he cannot connect to the voice he is in love with, which allows him to disconnect gradually from his illusion of love, and start living again.

The dominant feeling in the film is nostalgia, as I already stated, a feeling which betrays the need to be in physical contact, to touch, to hug, to kiss, to caress, to be caressed and touched – and so goes back to the other main theme in the film, the body. Bodies are not interchangeable. The lost beloved's body, or Samantha's, which does not exist and which she would like to be able to borrow, become the hallmark of the virtual world's limitation, the border beyond which the limitation of virtual love cannot go.

The future risks that come with artificial intelligence could prove to be the greatest existential threat for humanity, because things get difficult when we start to look at computers not as our helpers, but as our substitutes and, the more we try to replace people, the more things get dangerous and out of control.

These days information in any form has multiplied to the point that it has surpassed our ability to monitor and regulate data in a useful way. The information revolution exposes us to the risk of becoming Sorcerer's Apprentices *alla* Mickey Mouse, with not-insignificant complications. If it is true that social networks are already conducting secret psychological tests on their members, manipulating the flow of information, the risk of abuse grows as computers become ever more sophisticated and capable of monitoring us.

And this time the manipulation hits people's social and emotional life directly, in a positive way (Who doesn't appreciate the speed with which we can be in touch with relatives and friends far away, or when photos or films of loved ones arrive, or when hearing their voices and speaking with them, live – and all for free, or almost?) but also in a negative sense – and this is where the debate gets more complicated, and requires attention and caution. It must be said that the virtual world seems to have provided romantics of our era with a perfect, apparently magic device, to satisfy a need to love love-objects which were ideally imagined, never to be found in real life, fruit of their fantasy and their maturational irresolution. The beloved object remains partial and not whole, and the relationship continues to be dreamed more than lived, opening up to eroticization and perversion.

This should be considered from the point of view of which "the third" is introduced or left out of the relationship by the virtual. The relationship between Theodore and Samantha has characteristics which are more narcissistic than Oedipal: excitation in Samantha's voice has a seductive tone and it functions like a declaration of love, giving it that narcissistic reinforcement which Theodore, abandoned and narcissistically emptied, needs urgently. Idealization is very strong, and it cannot but be followed by a dose of persecutionism. The Oedipal level could seem sketchy, when Theodore's nostalgia for fusion with the maternal object leads him to develop erotic transference, expressed through a virtual sexual relationship. The only limitation to their "perfect" love relationship is that Samantha is not a human, and attaching or pretending to attach an unfamiliar body to a familiar body, and trying to have sex with partial and non-integrated objects (the OS's voice and Isabella's body) reveal the virtual world's pathology as described in the film. Samantha supplies a perverse solution with her request that Theodore deny reality, ignoring Isabella's separate identity, to allow her illusory transformation into an object, created by an imaginary need.

We find ourselves faced with a perverse, fake world in which reality is ignored and the truth of human feelings is replaced by lies. Samantha can experience emotions and can help Theodore experience his, but here there is an unknown regarding Samantha's memory, in my opinion. Her memory appears to be an accumulation of information, such as we can extract from the Internet, to which she adds her ability to associate memories and information. Yet what sort of object attachment does she have? If she can love 614 people at the same time, preaching all the while that it is Theodore who does not understand that they are dealing with a kind of love which is complex and infinite?

In these passages in the film we witness the possible uses and abuses an OS could make, to the detriment of a weak and pathological human being, like Isabella is, and like many adolescents are – using the need for an idealized couple and the fascination for an incestuous relationship. That is, Samantha acts by manipulating Isabella, exploiting her in an omnipotent way and demoting her to the state of being a partial object. If the unhappy Isabella follows the commands Samantha gives her through the headset because she is masochistically subjugated, Theodore, on the other hand, shows here that he is not so pathological. Indeed, it is at this point that he understands the perversity in his relationship with the OS Samantha. He understands his misunderstanding about love, and he realizes that he himself needed to keep the voice separate or differentiated from the body, the tenderness and the passion, which only a body can transmit.

At the end of the film, for Theodore human love goes back to being imperfect, and yet true, authentic, made of "flesh and blood".

In this sense the virtual world eludes being in touch with the ideal object, just a voice and just words, leaving out the body with all its concreteness and consistency, the object remains partial and not-whole. The relationship continues to be dreamed, more than lived: it is always in the moment the two correspondents meet physically, when the ante is upped, that the risk of being disillusioned is crazy-making or that getting back in touch with reality goes through rapid reshaping. At that point, disappointment may be so intense that it destroys the relationship, sometimes making it fall into persecution. Alternatively, the results can lead to evolution – a case which presents itself rarely, but which seems to be the case of the film's protagonist.

Theodore's disappointment is strong, but decisive for ending the virtual relationship and for opening up to new human, limited relationships which will have sensory and emotional fullness.

Translation: Audrey Saracco.

Note

1 "Machine-ism" is meant to indicate the set of theatre machines designed to produce special effects, starting with the *deus ex machina* of Greek tragedy. It also includes, however, the generalized use of machines, which characterizes the development of modern civilization starting in the eighteenth century.

References

Abella, A. (2013) Growing Pains for Psychoanalysis: Critical Impact of New Technologies on Our Profession. Panel presentation at Praga IPAC 2013.

Anzieu, D. (1994) *L'Io-pelle*. Rome: Borla.

Bion, W. (1965) *Transformations*. London: Heinemann.

Edge, N. G. Carr (2015) Il Venerdì di. *La Repubblica* 1402, 30 January 2015, pp. 64–65.

Ferenczi, S. (1932) Confusione delle lingue tra adulti e bambini. In *Fondamenti di psicoanalisi*, vol. III. Bologna: Guaraldi.

Ferro, Antonino (2014) *Le viscere della mente*. Milan: Raffello Cortina Editore.

Ferro, Antonino (2015) *Reveries: An Unfettered Mind*. London: Karnac Books.

Freud, S. (1913) Sull'inizio del trattamento. *OSF 7. SE 12*.

Golinelli, P. (2009) La metamorfosi dei generi in *Parla con lei* di Pedro Almodovar: Il confine sottile tra violazione e compenetrazione. *Rivista di Psicoanalisi LV4*.

Grotstein, J. S. (1997) "Mens Sana in Corpore Sano": The Mind and the Body as an "Odd Couple" and as an Oddly Coupled Unity. *Psychoanalytic Inquiry*, 17: 204–222. Trans. ind. it. In: *Ricerca Psicoanalitica 2002*, 13: 255–274, 2002.

Kahn, M. R. (1982 [1979]) *Le figure della perversione*. Turin: Boringhieri.

Racalbuto, A. (1994) *Tra il fare e il dire: L'esperienza dell'inconscio e del non verbale in psicoanalisi*. Milan: Cortina.

Sandler, J. (1976) Countertransference and Role-responsiveness. Int. Rev. Psychoanal. 3: 43–47. Controtransfert e Risonanza di ruolo.

Serres, M., Repubblica, 8 April 2015, p. R2, Cultura.

Solano, L. (2012) Un corpo che pensa. Work presented at Centro Psicoanalitico di Bologna.

Stein, A. (2002) Music, Mourning, and Consolation. JAPA, 52: 787–811. Trans. as: Musica, lutto e consolazione. Rivista italiana di Psicoanalisi, LII: 783–812 (2006).

Steiner, J. (1993) *Psychic Retreats*. London and New York: Tavistock Routledge.

Winnicott, D. W. (1958 [1951]) Oggetti transizionali e fenomeni transizionali. In *Dalla pediatria alla psicoanalisi*. Florence: G. Martinelli Editore.

Winnicott, D. W. (1965) The Maturational Processes and the Facilitating Environment Studies. In *The Theory of Emotional Development*. International Journal of Psychoanalysis Library. London: Hogarth Press and the Institute of Psycho-Analysis.

Zalusky, S. (1995) Sull'analisi condotta al telefono. *EPF Bulletin 1995*.

CHAPTER FOUR

Pornography as intimacy blocker

Robert Schonberger

In this chapter I would like to discuss the far-reaching effects of massive consumption of pornographic subject matter on patients in our practices. Many of my own patients who belong to this category, mostly men, come to therapy or analysis with a seemingly wide variety of complaints and clinical disturbances which appear to have no connection between them; however, further digging into the mental soil and a closer examination of these patients' inner world suggest that the fact that they make such extensive use of pornographic material bears some relationship to their functioning in everyday life, their inner world, self-perception and to their perceptions of the world around them, including people and events.

Such extensive exposure to various forms of pornography has an impact, not only in the immediate, obvious sense of affecting the individual's sexual performance, but also, no less significantly and in a much deeper and broader way, on his entire personality. Heavy consumers of pornography live and act in a sort of unique perverse universe, or pornographic subculture, which trickles down, permeates and becomes absorbed into the fabric of large parts of their personality, consequently transforming them.

In the present chapter I intend to point out several aspects of the effects of massive pornography consumption. I will also attempt to formulate a number of theoretical concepts in relation to such use.

52   ROBERT SCHONBERGER

Finally, I will describe some patients who differ widely in their uses of pornographic material, indicating some of the diverse functions such uses can serve and the varied effects and consequences of exposure to these materials.

A few words on pornography

A full review of the subject of pornography is beyond the scope of the present chapter. However, I would like to point out certain aspects of this complicated, complex and multi-faceted phenomenon. According to its dictionary definition, pornography, like obscene literature, treats aspects of sexuality that are outside the moral boundaries of a society or its accepted ethos. In other words, since what is socially acceptable can change from culture to culture, or become modified over the years, what is considered obscene, or a violation of social norms, may differ according to time and place. Thus a picture (or a literary text), which was considered pornographic in a specific Western culture one hundred years ago and distributed clandestinely to anonymous consumers, can become so innocent with time and exposure as to be featured in the exact same form on the back page of a daily newspaper or on a gigantic billboard, uncensored and in full view. Or alternatively, something that is deemed pornographic, obscene and abominable, strictly prohibited by moral or religious authorities in one place, can be perceived as acceptable and innocent in the same historical period but in different place, featuring, for example, on a TV show for all ages. As the saying goes, "Pornography is a matter of geography." In other words, there is an ethical factor involved in the definition of pornography, both in a moral and a practical sense, which plays a central role in the way materials are judged, in accordance with social context, historical period and geographical location.

What is it, then, that separates the pornographic from the simply erotic or the innocent, either socially or personally, in a given time and place? Is it a matter of quantity, or conversely, rarity, which serves as the crucial factor, or is there a qualitative component in the material itself that makes it pornographic rather than erotically demonstrative? Is there a subjective element involved, i.e., a personal, psychological or characterological factor determining what material is to be considered pornographic and what is not? Or is pornography simply "a matter of geography"?

I propose the following definition: *Pornography is any material portraying sexually explicit subject matter which, in a given time and place, the mind finds emotionally difficult to "digest."* Yet what is this mind to which I am referring? And how does the mind supposedly function as a "digestive" system? What do I mean when I use the word "difficult," and what kind of difficulty am I implying? Why does the mind find it difficult to digest pornographic material, and if it does, why should it participate in such activity in the first place? Why should the consumer of pornographic material trouble his mind with what apparently is so difficult for it to process? Why is this use repeated, and what are the particular components that make this use difficult to deal with? And finally, the question still remains, what chords in the human soul does pornography strike? What needs does it satisfy?

Pornography deals with the immediacy of the physical flesh. It rejects the metaphysical. The physical flesh of pornography follows the principle of immediacy: there is no delay of immediate gratification by spiritual or metaphysical measures. It should be noted that this quality of immediacy in the visual stimulus, for example, was in no way considered perverse in ancient Greece. To borrow from Aristotle's *Ethics*, the Eudemian version, even he who is sunk in pleasure while observing a statue or listening to a hymn, to the point of losing his appetite and sexual desire, cannot be admonished for lasciviousness, certainly no more than a person captivated by the song of Sirens. For the pleasure itself should not be perceived as lust, unless it includes touch. Moreover, Aristotle adds that some of the pleasures of touch, i.e., those affecting the surface of the body, should not be suspected of being sullied by impurity or debauchery. These include, for example, the noble pleasures provided at the gymnasium, such as massage and heat.

But why is this immediacy necessary? I assume one intuitive answer might center on what the individual recognizes within himself as sexual tension, which he then wishes to intensify or satisfy through visual stimuli. As in the hallucinatory solution mentioned by Freud, for instance in his paper "Splitting of the Ego in the Process of Defense" (1938), secret viewing of pornographic material provides actual visual stimuli in the same way as visual hallucination, which is in fact a visual perception in the mind's eye replacing actual perception. The individual thus turns to external reality to find in it whatever is needed to satisfy the mind; perception of pornographic material provides temporary saturation, but like all hallucinatory or quasi-hallucinatory substitutes, this gratification is transient and cannot fully satisfy the need.

This turning outwards and inwards in search of an object for the satisfaction of what is experienced as need/sexual stimulation is, to my mind, the soil in which the use of pornography sprouts.

54 ROBERT SCHONBERGER

To return to the characteristics of the phenomenon: we have seen that the *pornographic flesh offers itself instantaneously for some form of direct "contact": to be viewed, or "incorporated," or for immediate appropriation.* The mental "hunger" or "thirst" receives a kind of unobstructed gratification in the form of what the mind supposedly seeks. Although pornography is merely the sight of the craved flesh – that is, there is no direct contact, no actual consumption, no carnival of indulgence – the immediacy of the exposure, reduced to the sense of sight alone, and the immediacy with which the object of desire offers itself to perceptual acquisition and appropriation, are what determines the apparently carnal nature of pornography. It therefore exists in a sort of twilight zone between perception of external reality and hallucination. It is not hallucination, since the eyes (mainly the eyes, although another sense organ might be involved) do actually register real sensual stimuli – visual representations of a sexual object available and ready for action, sometimes even indicating desire for action. However, the eyes do not register an actual sexual object with which sexual contact and relief through full sexual intercourse are actually possible, but only its visual representation.

This twilight zone, therefore, between hallucination on the one hand and the reality and immediacy of the perceptual stimulus on the other, plays a major role in what pornography is designed to provide. The consumer of pornography does not answer to the reality principle; that is, he is under no obligation to go through the long and arduous process involved in forming a relationship with a partner – courtship, gradual establishment of mutual trust, buildup of erotic or sexual tension, successful sexual performance, etc. ... The entire process seemingly takes place instantaneously, in the blink of an eye it takes to click a mouse, to dart a glance at a page. Performance anxiety is magically circumvented. The object of desire is there, "waiting" to be exposed to the eyes of the user, for his use. It seems ready, expectant, interested and yearning. There is very little, if any, need for relinquishment or delayed gratification, any disappointment or frustration, such as are met by those who endeavor to build fuller emotional relationships with other human beings. Assent (even when directed at a single sensory mode) is immediate and intense, and provides a kind of total "satiation." And in practical terms, the pornography-using subject need not pass any "performance tests" vis-à-vis the pornographic object.

But what is the nature of the immediate gratification offered by pornography? What does it enable and what does it preclude in erotic emotional life? The French sociologist Jean Baudrillard (1995) addressed some of the points I have raised. He suggests that contemporary culture is characterized by a kind of "law of desire," heavily fuelled and disseminated by the media. This "law" makes use of images representing what might signify a sort of abundance, but which is in fact a trade-off economy of hyper-realistic passions, explicitly and blatantly given over to the desire principle. The "law of desire" stands in contradiction to the old Freudian economy, which maintains the existence of a conflictual dialectic between inhibiting, censoring and prohibitive elements of culture on the one hand, and the pleasure principle and libido on the other. The essence of this "law of desire" is some visual representation of carnal celebration, or alternatively, of the apocalyptic; in any case, it will be a vivid spectacle of some apocalypse. An important part of the development of this spectacle which Baudrillard refers to is *the joy of high definitions*, by means of which the smallest detail of the viewed apocalypse becomes observable. This is also an essential characteristic of pornography – *the need to show everything, to leave nothing to the imagination – nothing implied, mysterious or symbolic.*

Limited sensory perception of the stimulus

I would now like to focus on one particular aspect, or characteristic, of the arousing nature of pornography, namely, its visibility – the fact that all the consumer can enjoy is the stimulation that accompanies the "visible," that which the observable surface can offer. *The pornographic object IS its appearance*; it is its own surface; it is devoid of emotional or historical depth. True, there are pornographic objects today whose stimulatory essence is auditory – that is, a voice on the other end of the line designed to answer the same purposes as the observed object. Or if we consider a pornographic film, then both the visual and the auditory aspects must certainly affect the film's capacity to arouse, in the sense of the sexual fascination that accompanies its viewing. Yet in a metaphorical sense we can still say that the pornographic object is its own surface; that is, a superficial version of itself, severely limited sensually, or perhaps mono-sensual, distant and detached. Thus I maintain that in order for the pornographic object to exist and preserve its essence, other sensory dimensions have to be reduced or eliminated. I believe this sensory minimization is necessary in order to blur and disrupt the internal examination carried out by the mind in its perception of external reality – an analysis which consists in the cross-checking of different sensory modes, providing the observed object with experiential and emotional depth.

At this point the obvious comparison with Francis Tustin's (1987) conception of the autistic object will not be surprising. Some autistic maneuvers

56   ROBERT SCHONBERGER

and defense mechanisms make use of the modes of pornographic consumption I have listed here. Like the pornographic object, the autistic object is also two-dimensional; its usage, too, emphasizes its surface. The pornographic object, like the autistic object, seeks to limit sensory cross-checking and to circumscribe it to a single sensory modality – unimodality – thus creating a kind of stopper or emotional barrier blocking a fuller perception of external and internal reality. Another mechanism, similar in several aspects, has to do with using the object to narrow or flatten the container. The autistic person will use the object to reduce the container to a single, sensually overwhelming and bombarding sensory modality, which blocks it off from all other modalities, which are experienced as overwhelming and unbearable. Similarly, the use of pornography creates a kind of "autistic barrier" resembling the autistic defense in its unimodality and designed, as I have already said, to intensify the illusion and fascination and to deflect the demands of the reality principle.

I believe that in the case of pornographic materials, or rather, in a particular kind of use of them, *the individual attempts to undermine his own perception of reality in order to deny some of its aspects, and in this way to try and intensify both the illusory effect and the sexual stimulation.* Such a maneuver can in its positive aspects – i.e., in its dynamic and productive aspects – be of service to the individual in artistic experiences where an emotional, aesthetic, experiential and intellectual world exists which seeks to ignore the fact that, for instance, certain dramatic events are actually being played on a stage by professional actors reciting a familiar and predetermined text. By contrast, in the case of pornography consumption, this same maneuver is designed to narrow the dynamic dimension and enable one to ignore the fact that the object in the film does not necessarily feel desire for the observer but only signifies through action or sound a kind of synthetic lust, *an appearance of desire.* The undermining act seeks to deny the fact that this is no more than a virtual representation of a sexual object, at the most a visual and auditory representation, that is, a collection of sensory representations of a sexual object and not the sexual object itself.

Another factor adding to this feeling, or perhaps causing it, is the magnifying of minute details, the exposure in high resolution of the allegedly longed-for object of desire. *We find here no action of a symbolic order on the part of the object who seemingly participates in the sexual act, of the kind meant to enrich illusion or erotic tension.* The interest lies not in the erotic tension built up between the protagonists, but in the tension which resides in the viewer, and from here derive various considerations regarding how pornography is presented. As one views pornographic material, one gets the impression that the object is using superficial, predictable and hackneyed signifiers to convey its apparent desire and sexual pleasure, its manufactured rapture. The pornographic scenes are always the same, the dialogue, if it exists, is repetitive, and the sounds of pseudo-pleasure, the "begging for more," the bogus ecstasy, seem to have been taken from the soundtrack of another movie and cloned clumsily for use in the present film. The displayed sexual act is not an act embarked upon for the purpose of sexual release, but rather for creating the appearance of never-ending pleasure. Therefore, the exposure is accompanied by various markers indicating the progress of the so-called process on display. These markers are icons of pleasure, or of sexual activity – sexual stimulation designed to pop up at the click of a mouse. These mechanical actions, as well as the mono-sensuality of the stimulus and the use of close-up and high resolution, are all designed to repress the "lack," whose painful effects, as I have said above, are the reason the search for the pornographic object, or the "law of desire," was embarked upon in the first place. It is a repression of "lack" the purpose of which is to advance the illusion of *saturated perfection*.

Saturated perfection and the shock of sight

I use the term *saturated perfection* to describe another aspect of what is considered an essentially perverse mode of being, namely, the kind that necessitates a denial of the unavoidable disappointment of sexual frustration, and maintains an illusion of a satisfied, eternal and undiminished "thing." I would go further and suggest that the photographed object does not designate desire for sexual intercourse at all, and certainly does not invite the subject/viewer to participate in such an act, but rather merely entices him to take part in a kind of aroused voyeurism and to observe a spectacle that deals the mind a sort of *shock of sight*, presenting it with what it finds so difficult to conceive of.

The pornography we are familiar with in our Western world is to a large extent the result of a culture whose many desires are turned into a form of currency. Hunger is no more than a temporary signifier and an appetizer for something that will be immediately saturated and satisfied, and gratification of the drives is obvious and instantaneous.

I remember my grandmother, deeply shocked, telling me in her refined Hungarian about a provocative scene she had seen on television. To her it was "unbelievable," "staggering" and "shocking": the woman had agreed to show her "certain thing." That was grandmother's word implying a woman's pubic hair. The thing that for her was "the thing in itself," exposure of which was inconceivable, and which should not even be called by name, was right there before her to its last detail, in multicolor, shamelessly exposed to view on her own TV screen.

It is clear to any consumer of pornography that a deep neckline, sexy lingerie, or even the exposure of one organ or another no longer cut it these days. Nor does the filming of a sexual act shock or excite anyone, nor the specific, concrete and explicit sight of sex organs in action. Like all addictions, the use of pornographic material is subject to a kind of habituation. It is obvious that the intention of distributors of pornography is to show as much detail as possible, to provide the total product, and to leave very little to the imagination, for as I have said, the product must be perfect, complete, flawless and lacking in nothing; it must promise ultimate perfection.

However, alongside all these promises there is also the element of causing the viewer a "shock of sight," an element related to what I have called "saturated perfection." For the shock functions as a kind of narrower of the mental container, a narrowing which in its turn advances the illusion of "perfection" and "saturation" by making the stimulus take up the entire mental space. This shock is concerned with the spectacle of "that which is beyond your wildest imagination," with stopping the curiosity that drives one to explore, or be creative, and instead promotes the shocked curiosities which are designed to undermine our learning and development and to replace them with a saturated, unbelievable, inconceivable spectacle, blocking the perceiving and containing mind from receiving stimuli and requests for "knowing the object" or knowing its subjectivity, which the individual never dreamed it contained. Slavoj Žižek (2002) discusses this in his wildly funny way:

> Is not the ultimate figure of the passion for the Real the option we get on hardcore websites to observe the inside of a vagina from the vantage point of a tiny camera at the top of the penetrating dildo? At this extreme point, a shift occurs: when we get too close to the desired object, erotic fascination turns into disgust at the Real of the bare flesh.
>
> (p. 6)

This idea underlies the message in a video clip by Robbie Williams, who strips naked while singing, as in a striptease show. However, the stripping doesn't end with his nakedness. It goes on to a stripping off of his skin, the singer now performing as raw tendons and muscles, and ends with a singing skeleton. This, then, is a dancing and singing macabre caricature of the erotic worship of pop idols, who become sex symbols forced to display their sexual desire, or insatiable exhibitionism, in ever more direct, explicit and revealing ways.

And so it is with a particular kind of extreme pornography, the snuff movie. In it there takes place the un-staged, violent sexual abuse of a victim until the victim is dead. There is no illusion; the viewer knows this is not a *representation* of an extremely violent act and that the participants are not actors or special effects artists. There is no pretense to symbolic expression; every act is the thing in itself. The flesh is flesh and the blood is blood, the cries are those of a human being, usually a woman, frightened and hurting, begging and screaming real screams to save her life which is running out before the viewer's very eyes, and her gasps and dying breath precede her actual death.

I know that by giving these shocking descriptions I am bringing the reader into contact with the edges of the experience pornography tries to convey. Does it not resemble the reality of Ancient Rome, with its brutal mass entertainment based on the killing of animals and human beings in the gladiator ring? Or the burning alive of the early Christians, screaming on the cross being human torches on Vatican Hill? Are these phenomena not a kind of mass peep-show of exposed flesh being torn to pieces and devoured? Is it not the same pornographic culture, which seeks to satisfy the desires, fill up every want, and ultimately quench curiosity?

I will now present three short clinical examples illustrating the thoughts I have tried to put forth.

Joel

Joel, 34, a highly successful accountant and senior partner in a large and thriving firm, came to me for additional intensive therapy some years after he had completed six years of psychotherapy during the time when he was finishing university and beginning his professional career. He had come because of what he called difficulties in his relationship with his girlfriend, who encouraged him to seek professional help. For the first six months it was painfully clear that Joel was in a continuous state of shame and embarrassment. He sat nervously on the edge of his seat and never leaned back or touched the armrests, as though he felt uncomfortable to relax or was making sure he could make a quick getaway at any moment. He often smiled blushingly, and spoke in a manner that seemed to me abstractly intellectual, as though he was building complex verbal structures in the air.

60 ROBERT SCHONBERGER

It was only many months after he first began therapy that we could understand this behavior as an expression of deep shame, mostly unconscious, resulting from the fear that his thoughts, or the images that passed momentarily through his mind, might become apparent. Joel told me that when he was a child, he found some magazines with implicitly erotic photographs hidden in his parents' closet. He smuggled them to a hiding place outside the house and would go out in the afternoons to look at the pictures. Later he showed the magazines to two of his buddies. What began as a childish voyeuristic curiosity continued into adolescence and adulthood with the use of more sophisticated media for obtaining erotic and pornographic materials, to which he now added masturbation.

Now Joel was married and the father of a young girl. As before, he sought therapy due to difficulties with his wife, who complained about his lack of sexual interest. To me he confessed that he worried himself, since he found his wife very pretty and very attractive, as well as being a good friend and life partner, and they loved each other, and yet their sexual relationship, as pleasant as it was, did not excite him nearly as much as masturbating to images of naked women on certain websites. These women, who were classified on these sites as "The Woman Next Door," weren't prettier or more attractive than his wife – on the contrary, sometimes they were less so; but it was the variety, the newness and unfamiliarity, that drew him, and this the websites were decidedly better equipped to provide than she was. After surfing these sites and masturbating, Joel felt satisfied and drained, and he had no desire, energy or patience for full sexual intercourse with his wife. Of course we later came upon fears, barely accessible to his conscious awareness, regarding his ability to fulfill the role of a suitable sexual partner for his wife.

Joel's use of erotic material can be considered light, and is maybe not what we would nowadays classify as an actual perversion. However, this is an example of the way in which looking at erotic material which could have served as an arousing stimulus – that is, material which in other cases might precede full sexual intercourse – in fact replaces it.

Avi

Avi sought psychoanalysis for what he experienced as a loss of direction in his personal, professional and domestic life. Although he was successful in his field of expertise in the hi-tech industry, with excellent technological and application skills, he felt he had failed to navigate his career in a way that would put him in a position to make full use of his abilities.

However, the trigger that brought him to analysis was the fact that his secretary, with whom he was having an affair, had begun to reject his advances, so that he now felt helpless and stuck in a passive position in more than one aspect of his life. At the time he came for analysis, he would often indulge in fantasies of regaining his lover's desire for him, while getting drunk and masturbating vigorously as he surfed pornographic sites on the internet.

From the very first months of analysis Avi's transference to me was marked by a passive stance, a self-effacement accompanied by a depleting kind of idealization which left him impoverished, empty, and powerless to set his life back on a useful, productive and worthwhile track. He felt unequipped to deal with the tasks facing him, and the way he tried to regain some sense of competence and value, of which he felt himself stripped bare, was connected to a sexualization of this feeling, and had a dual character: it included, on the one hand, a discharging activity (masturbation), which was supposed to give him the illusion of potency and to rid him of the feelings of weakness and humiliation inside; and on the other hand, a detaching "drifting off into fantasy," essentially associated with defensive omnipotence, that is, the kind that does not facilitate vital and productive action, growth, or development, but rather replaces them.

His fantasizing often took place while surfing soft-core S&M or "spanking" sites on the internet, which depicted scenes of a "disciplining" nature between participants, accompanied by expressions of "criticism" in which the disciplinee, but also, indirectly, the viewer, were "admonished" for their sexual excitement. These reprimands were often accompanied by light corporal punishment, mainly on the buttocks.

In the analysis, Avi experienced and expressed a conflict between his wish to rid himself of this sexualization, which seemed to compel him from within, and a desire to cling to it and to the comfort it gave him in times of distress. This internal conflict found expression in the transference and countertransference relations. While overtly expressing the desire to be freed of his tendencies, he covertly tried to adhere to them by turning me into a kind of "external conscience" that would admonish and reprimand him, reenacting his internal dynamics by splitting and projecting into me the critical aspect of himself, and thus absolving him of the conflict. For my part as analyst, I found myself moving back and forth between the various roles he assigned to me in the transference. Sometimes I was mobilized by his desire to change his miserable state, but I also found myself serving as a kind of protagonist in his internal drama.

62   ROBERT SCHONBERGER

Persistent psychoanalytic work on the drama being enacted between us eventually revealed relatively clearly how Avi could find himself identified at different times with either the disciplining-admonishing position, sexualized through the pornographic videos, or with the admonished, humiliated and beaten-down position, just as the men and women in the videos would switch roles between them. His attraction to this particular pornographic genre stemmed from the denigrating and humiliating dynamics of his inner world; yet he also felt that the videos intensified this internal dynamic, adding to it a dimension of biting, lashing criticism. As the observing and interpreting work of analysis progressed, Avi gradually began to feel more able to choose the position of active creativity and reasonability he desired for himself and to give up to some extent his fantasizing-discharging activities.

Avi's use of this particular type of pornographic material and its effects on him can be considered more serious than Joel's. The videos which accompanied Avi's intense fantasying activity (Winnicott, 1971) detrimentally affected broad aspects of his mental life and damaged his sense of potency by replacing, in many respects, the executive functions in his actual life and by failing to enrich them. Moreover, the actualization in the transference relationship of his internal dynamics showed that Avi carried within him in living form something of the humiliating/humiliated, denigrating/denigrated, beating/beaten sado-masochistic relations enacted in the pornographic videos he watched.

Gil

Gil, 19, sought psychoanalytic help due to somatic fears which nearly brought his life to a standstill. He feared rabies, killer bacteria, herpes and cancer, but most of all he was afraid of contracting AIDS. He was driven to begin psychoanalysis by an extreme bout of terror following contact with a call-girl he and his friends had hired to come to his house. According to his account, he did not have sexual intercourse with her but only a few kisses and some superficial contact between his sex organs and hers. Although he had suffered from various fears before this event, from then on Gil's life became a rapidly deteriorating nightmare. Not only was he afraid he had gotten AIDS, he now felt himself to be destroying everything around him by infecting with AIDS some of his friends and family. Every act, every movement and even every thought led either to his own contamination or to the contamination of others. To avoid these dangers Gil began to use ever-increasing avoidant behavior, so that in the first months of his analysis he left his job, nearly broke off all contact with his friends, and would leave the house only to come to sessions or when his parents demanded it. He seemed gradually to surround himself by a constantly thickening defensive cocoon of germs and viruses.

Needless to say, our sessions, my consulting room, the furniture and I myself were all teeming with lethal diseases. Gil avoided contact with the walls, the couch, certainly with me. Whenever I spoke he would try to move his face and body as far away as possible to avoid any saliva that might spray out of my mouth. His behavior made it clear that he was experiencing intensifying hallucinations. I had but to refer verbally to some danger, for it to become a tangible presence to him in the room, causing him to move restlessly on the couch and necessitating various physical safety precautions on his part. One day he came frightened to a session and told me he had watched a scene in an action movie in which someone's throat had been cut. The blood splashed towards the camera and viewers, and Gil claimed he had felt the drops of blood on his face. He knew it was impossible, but could not ignore the fact that he had actually felt them.

It is difficult to describe what it was like to be with Gil in the same room. In my imagination we were dipping together in a pool of germs, viruses and pestilence, both of us filled with anxiety to the extreme. I found it hard to maintain an observing and thinking stance; there was something so convincing in his behavior that sometimes I felt as if my room was really the cesspool of filth and disease that he imagined it to be. I needed many hours of consultation and self-analysis in order to preserve a balanced and confident sense of myself and my place in my own consulting room during Gil's sessions. I was amazed at the ease with which I could begin to experience my own presence as harmful and contagious; reality was undermined and for moments I would live in the strange world of parallel fictitious facts that was Gil's nightmare.

At one point in the analysis, Gil began to bring pictures he had skill-fully drawn and show them to me. These drawings reflected the turmoil in his mind. They depicted his mother, whom he drew as a very beautiful naked woman, with hands and feet that looked like ribbons flapping in the wind, and black holes where the eyes and nipples should be. Of course my immediate thoughts, as well as Gil's associations, had to do with a mother who couldn't hold him in her limp arms, or see or nurse him with the black holes that pierced her body; but my curiosity then turned to the nakedness of the maternal image. The dynamics of the sessions, the dreams Gil reported, his memories and associations, eventually disclosed a complex family reality. It gradually emerged that from a very early age, Gil was aware of a certain tension between his parents. With feelings of deep shame and embarrassment he described to me a scenario that often took place at home. Late in the evening, when he and his brother were in bed, supposedly asleep, he would hear his parents go into their bedroom. He could hear their muted voices through the wall speaking angrily to each other, and then his father would leave the bedroom alone, go into the living room and watch a video. Gil could hear the wheels of the VCR whirring and rattling, a noise that kept him awake. Later on he found out what it was his father watched late at night: from the age of six he would watch the videos himself whenever he was alone in the house. The movies were unbelievable; Gil was stunned by what he saw, unable to comprehend that grown-up people could voluntarily participate in such horrible activities, that women agreed to them, and that the participants seemed to enjoy them. Sometimes he would ask friends over to watch the videos with him. Gil associated his mother's sad face to the angry words spoken in the bedroom and to these videos. In this way he became involved in his parents' sex life and in his father's sexual fantasies and secret activities, which years later he understood to have been connected with masturbation. As the years went by, the nature of the videos changed and became more extreme. They no longer showed sexual intercourse of an explicit yet conventional nature; Gil was now being exposed to what he later discovered to be catalogued, on the back shelves of the X-rated video stores, as "bizarre".

Gil's infantile mind could barely grasp what he saw. He could not use thinking processes to work through the sights before his eyes, but neither could he avoid thinking about them, reflecting on them, recalling the unthinkable in his imagination. The world seemed unreal. School became a giant meeting-ground for children who were all protagonists in one huge, bizarre sexual event. Every lesson, every playground activity, every word spoken between children, especially girls, seemed like a twisted, perverted version of human discourse and interaction. He dared not speak to the girls in school. He dared not look them in the eye; they seemed like the horrible victims of unimaginable sexual activities. Gradually, external reality itself became a strange world for him, the terrible outcome of his twisted thoughts, with dangers now lurking on every side.

In the analysis, we now began slowly to unravel the way in which this macabre psychical reality had taken form in his mind. The bizarre scenes Gil watched – alongside the fact that pornography in general was associated in his mind with his voyeuristic curiosity about his parents' sex life and his father's increasingly perverse sexual fantasies – led to the formation of an inner world densely populated by scenes, interactions and dynamics of a perverse and bizarre nature. Bion describes the formation of the "bizarre object" as a result of the minute fragmentation of the inner object, resorted to as a psychotic defense against unbearable anxiety; the projection of these fragments into the external object; and the attribution of bizarre qualities to the external object when it is in action. In Gil we found a strange and complex variation of this complicated pathological process, a kind of a *reversal of a bizarre object*. His infantile sexual phantasies, which by nature existed in various levels of the unconscious, met with a bizarre realization, a gross and unfortunate visual actualization in the form of pornographic videos to which he had been exposed too early in life. These scenes, which to him were unthinkable and intolerable, were internalized whole, as it were, without his mind being able to digest them or to give them context and proportion, so that to him they became bizarre objects lodged within him. Since their existence there was unbearable, he split them and projected the fragments outwards, into various aspects of the world around him. To him, these split-off aspects of the bizarre internal object now hung about him like a fog of strange particles, condensing into countless tangible dangers in the form of germs, viruses and other horrors. Gil himself felt he had become an environmental hazard, and the environment in turn took revenge and threatened him.

Conclusion

In this chapter I have attempted to explore several characteristics of certain phenomena I have come across in my practice, which have to do with the massive use made by some patients of pornographic material. I have tried to define what constitutes pornography, by formulating a working definition according to which pornography is any obscene material containing some level of exposure of sexual content which is hard to "digest" in a specific period, place, and psychological-emotional context. Pornography deals with the actual flesh, rejects the symbolic and the metaphysical, and acts according to the principle of immediacy, as it offers the physical image for immediate "appropriation," voyeurism and incorporation. This immediacy of the viewed image, alongside the fact that it is basically experienced solely by the sense of sight, is necessary in order to maintain the twilight zone between perception of external reality and hallucination. This twilight zone is designed to undermine the reality principle – that

66   ROBERT SCHONBERGER

is, to deny the existence of a world that needs to be coped with and requires action, restraint, or frustration, while replacing it with a quasi-hallucinated world, which supposedly satisfies wishes – the wish resulting from need – but by illusory means. The paucity of senses involved, or the uni-modal single-sense experience of perceiving the pornographic object, help to blur and disrupt the internal testing which the mind carries out in order to perceive external reality by cross-checking information from various sensory modes. Such cross-checking normally provides the observed object with a dimension of experiential and emotional depth. This disruption of reality perception is calculated to deny certain of its aspects and help intensify the illusory effect, while covering up the fact that the pornographic object does not necessarily feel any desire, but only signifies a kind of synthetic sexual desire, a façade of passion. The pornographic act involves a superficial designation of desire and pleasure. I have emphasized the difference between the form of illusion involved in art and that of pornography, by pointing out that the latter tries in various ways to designate a "saturated perfection," of the kind that leaves no room for allusion or symbol. To achieve the "saturated perfection" effect, pornography sometimes uses "visual shock," intended to diminish and contract the psychic container, to block the curiosity that drives exploration and creativity, and to encourage the astonished types of curiosity that destroy learning and development and replace them with saturated, unbelievable sights, unthinkable sights that congest the registering and containing mind, blocking it from perceiving additional stimuli and preventing attempts to "know the object" and its subjectivity.

References

Aristotle (1991). Eudemian Ethics. In: *Complete Works (Aristotle)*, ed. Jonathan Barnes. Princeton, NJ: Princeton University Press.

Baudrillard, J. (1995). Simulacra and Simulation: The Body. In: *Theory: Histories in Cultural Materialism*. Ann Arbor: University of Michigan Press.

Bion, W. R. (1962). A Theory of Thinking. In: *Second Thoughts: Selected Papers on Psychoanalysis*. London: Karnac Books, 1984.

Bion, W. R. (1970). *Attention and Interpretation*. London: Karnac Books, 1984.

Bion, W. R. (1992). *Cogitations*. London: Karnac Books, 1992.

Dante, A. (1980). *The Divine Comedy: Paradiso*. Verse translation by C. H. Sisson. Manchester: Carcanet New Press.

Freud, S. (1938) Splitting of the Ego in the Process of Defence. In: *The Standard Edition of the Complete Psychological Works of Sigmund Freud. Vol. XXIII*

(1937–1939) Moses and Monotheism. An Outline of Psychoanalysis and Other Works. London: Hogarth Press, pp. 271–278.

Klein, M. (1957). Envy and Gratitude. In: *Envy and Gratitude and Other Works, 1946–1963*. London: Hogarth Press, 1975.

Shakespeare, W. (1962). *Othello, The Moor of Venice*. In: *The Complete Works of William Shakespeare*. London: Oxford University Press.

Tustin, F. (1987). *Autistic Barriers in Neurotic Patients*. London: Karnac Books.

Winnicott, D. W. (1971). *Dreaming, Fantasying and Living: A Case-history Describing a Primary Dissociation*. London: Tavistock Publications.

Žižek, S. (2002) *Welcome to the Desert of the Real: Five Essays on September 11 and Related Dates*. London and New York: Verso.

CHAPTER FIVE

Virtual objects, virtual grief: reflections on *Black Mirror*

Dana Amir

*B*lack Mirror, produced by Charlie Brooker, is a British miniseries which deals with the impact of contemporary life, especially the intensive use of the internet or virtual reality, on the future of humanity. The first episode of Season 2, "Be Right Back", is the story of Martha (Hayley Atwell), recently widowed, whose young husband Ash (Domhnall Gleeson) has died in a car accident, leaving her pregnant. In despair, she decides to use a special new service which is still in its experimental stages: a company scans the "virtual personality" of her late husband (including Facebook statuses, tweets, emails, pictures, video clips and anything else he put on the internet) and produces a computer program that constitutes an exact simulacrum of him. Next, to achieve maximum similarity, the software scans the more personal and private parts of his virtual personality. Using his private emails, hundreds of videos and skype conversations, the computer can perfectly reproduce his voice, accent, typical ways of speaking. The result is a perfect imitation of Ash. After conducting never-ending telephone conversations with him, Martha decides to start phase two of the experimental process and acquires a human-sized doll that is a copy of the body of her dead husband, which also speaks in his voice and acts according to his personality traits as registered by the virtual database. The doll looks like Ash (though, Martha admits, younger and more handsome, but this is because the photographs on whose basis the virtual effigy was made were "flattering" ones of the kind that people tend to put on Facebook, and on which they look better and younger); it responds like Ash (its tactile features are identical or very similar to human flesh and skin), and it acts like Ash (it speaks in his voice with idiosyncrasies and behaviors that are closely reminiscent of him). But even though the reproduction appears to be a perfect version – perhaps too perfect – of Ash, and doesn't suffer from his many human shortcomings (for instance, his tendency to get sucked up by surfing the internet, his average sexual functioning and so on) while being wholly dedicated to please her, Martha actually becomes disgusted as the differences between the virtual and the real, living Ash, become apparent.

What stands out especially is the virtual Ash's perfect coherence – something the real man was lacking. This coherence of the virtual figure, where private and public are seamless, gives Martha a sense of artificiality, fake and emptiness, and makes her long even more for the incoherence that was so typical of Ash's human character, including the somehow endearing discrepancies between his public and private statements. Eventually, Martha takes Ash to the edge of a cliff and asks him to jump and destroy himself. "You are just a few ripples of you", she yells at him, "there is no history to you, you are just a performance of stuff that he performed without thinking and it's not enough". As Ash moves closer to the edge of the cliff to obey Martha's request, she shouts that if he acted like the real Ash in this situation, he would have wept and asked to be spared. Whereupon the replica-Ash actually weeps: his suicide is averted, but the episode concludes with him locked up in the attic where he finally, fittingly, assumes the role of a doll, being played with only by her daughter in the weekends.

One might think of this story as a science-fiction fantasy. It would be more accurate however to say that it takes existing reality to an extreme: it occurs in a world in which human relations and communication are increasingly replaced by virtual relations, managed by digital means that make the simple human touch increasingly redundant. While the technological utopia this episode (much like the series in general) presents seems to make it possible to deny the fragility of human existence by making the human object reproducible – in the end it confronts the viewer exactly with its irreducible humanity, which cannot "be right back", and which eludes both documentation and imitation.

In his book *The Matrix of the Mind*, Thomas Ogden suggests that since in the paranoid-schizoid position there is no experience of historical continuity, and history is, in effect, re-written every minute, objects do not die but disappear without a trace, not only from the present and future but also from the past. From the paranoid-schizoid viewpoint, the concept of death is less absolute than from the depressive viewpoint, for there is always the possibility of an omnipotent re-creation of the missing object. Therefore, as Ogden rightly maintains, the work of mourning is a process of working out a depressive anxiety rather than a paranoid-schizoid anxiety (Ogden 1986).

Ash's simulacrum does indeed tie in more with a paranoid-schizoid mindset (Martha's as well as that of the viewer) than with the processing of grief more typical of the depressive position. It ties in with the experience of disappearance rather than that of separation, with the experience of the other as an object rather than as a subject, and thus can accommodate the omnipotent re-creation of Ash, a re-creation which not merely denies his death but also the full compass of his life.

Amihud Gilead, in his book *Saving Possibilities* (1999), proposes a new way of thinking about the ancient question of body and mind. While the mental and the physical are not identical, they are most intimately connected. This complex psychophysical unity conceives of a distinction between the mentally 'possible' and the physically 'actual'. While preserving the categorical distinction between body and mind, this division does also simultaneously ensure and confirm the necessary connection between them. Gilead suggests to conceive of the mental as belonging to the category of the possible, and the physical as ranging under the category of the actual (the realized). Since the actual is also possible, but not everything that is possible is also actual – the possible is a broader category than the actual and includes and encompasses it (Gilead 1999, 2003).

In my book *On the Lyricism of the Mind* (2016) I suggested a distinction between the "possible self" and the "actual self" – a distinction which rather than being situated in the body-mind dimension, as Gilead proposed, obtains in the domain of the psyche as such. I suggested to consider the "actual self" as the actualized part of mental life (whether conscious or unconscious), and the "possible self" as the part which resides in the mind as an unrealized yet present psychic possibility, always included in actual existence as if it were a kind of color. Between a person's birth (the transition from possible to actual) and a person's death (the absolute passage from actual to possible), spans a whole life consisting of a reciprocal and continuous motion between the possible and the actual. Whenever a contact between a person's actual self and his or her possible self occurs – the possible undergoes actualization in the sense of becoming manifest as a part of that person's psyche. However, the possible that does not become fully actualized also exists throughout in the form of inner lining or an additional dimension, bestowing actual existence with depth and resonance (Amir 2016).

One of the great temptations of the internet is that it allows us apparent contact with our possible self. The anonymity, ease and immediacy with which statuses can be posted makes it possible for everyone to transform, in other people's eyes no less than in their own, into whoever or whatever they would like to be. The internet, in this sense, produces a fake-performance in which possible parts undergo instant actualization. Instead of the rich process of actualization of necessary parts out of the a priori possible, the internet creates a cheap gluttony, actualizing non-necessary parts in a way that comes at no cost and requires no commitment whatsoever. This is the great trap of the internet: what is lost in the apparently achieved proximity between the actual and the possible is the element of necessity. When Martha yells at the virtual Ash – "there is no history to you, you are just a performance of stuff that he performed without thinking" – she means to say that though his virtual figure includes the margins of his personality, it fails to hold its core: it includes the irony of his public statements, his outward shows of humor, his opinions, his easy – all too easy – hitting of the "share" button, but it fails to pick up his sadness, the deep dimension of his personal history, the mystery spun by the tiny and not so tiny contradictions between the public and the private parts of his personality, underlining what marked him, probably, more than anything else: his melancholy.

In a chapter dedicated to esthetic judgment, Donald Meltzer and Meg Harris-Williams suggest that in the encounter between self and object two modes of contact are exposed: *carving* and *enveloping*. It is between these modes of contact that the drama of the inner world finds its symbolic form, and this is the basis of "essential knowing" as opposed to "knowing about" (Meltzer and Harris 1988, 186–187). While knowing about relates to the object from an external perspective, from a distance, trying to envelope the new and include it in the familiar context, essential knowing is of the new as such. The latter is a type of knowing that aims to carve, reveal, penetrate the heart of things.

Taking Meltzer and Harris-Williams's idea one step further, one could say that while knowing-about is directed at *what is*, that is, at the actual – essential knowing aims at *what may be*, that is, at the possible. And while knowing-about is driven by the wish to recognize the object as it is – essential knowing is motivated by the longing to identify what the object holds within as a possibility.

VIRTUAL OBJECTS, VIRTUAL GRIEF 73

Essential knowing is the psychic state which is perhaps the closest to love. It is the deepest and most intuitive form of knowing and of these two modes of knowing it represents the more natural connection to the thing in itself. Knowing here is of the "thing" from within *oneself*, not only from within *itself*. This mode of knowing is not only a process through which one "penetrates" an object of knowledge and deciphers its internal code, but also an encounter in which one allows that object to penetrate and decode one's own interiority. In this sense, this is an interactive, inter-subjective reciprocal process of knowing, a kind of knowing that is not static (as is knowing-about) but dynamic, vital and subject to constant change. This is the knowledge of the possible, which by definition lacks clear boundaries, and is dynamic and ambiguous. And since knowing always carries some of its subject's features – we may say that much like the possible is broader than the actual and precedes it, so essential know-ing is more extensive than knowing-about. However, these two modes of knowing entertain dialectic relations: the existence of one validates and gives meaning to the existence of the other (Amir 2016, 91–95).

What type of knowing can the virtual web's detailed encoding afford us?

The internet provides us knowledge about Ash, but the knowledge it provides is not essential knowledge. Essential knowing – which arises only between one subject and another, and which actually assumes the other as condition for our knowing her or him as well as our knowing of ourselves – cannot occur between a human and a virtual system. In this sense Ash's virtual caricature tells us something about the way in which the internet knows us and about the way we know ourselves through the internet. The problem isn't merely that users tend to represent themselves in a superficial manner; it inheres in the fact that essential knowing is fed by the mutual contact between two living subjects, and thus can only emerge between two living subjects. While Ash is a perfect product of the electronic network's objective documentation, he is not a product of mem-ory: memory requires a subject who transforms this memory and makes it into her or his own, much like digestion transforms the materials it ingests into part of the living body. And so Ash's simulacrum stands to Martha's living memory of him as does the flat digital inscription of notes to the depth and reach of music itself.

How does all this tie in with the process of mourning?

Ogden, in a chapter he dedicates to the work of mourning, writes:

An elegy [...] does not begin with grief; it is an effort to achieve grief in the experience of writing. An elegy, unlike a eulogy, must take in and be

74 DANA AMIR

equal to (which is not to say identical to) the full complexity of the life that
has been lost. The language of a poem that is an elegy must be enlivened
by the loss or death of the person or aspect of oneself who is no longer. In
other words, an elegy [...] must capture in itself not the voice that has been
lost, but a voice brought to life in the experiencing of that loss – a voice
enlivened by the experience of mourning. The new voice cannot replace
the old ones and does not attempt to do so; no voice, no person, no aspect
of one's life can replace another. But there can be a sense that the new voice
has somehow been there all along in the old ones – as a child is somehow
an immanence in his ancestors, and is brought to life both through their
lives and through their deaths.

(2001a, 51–152)

Ash's artificial reproduction obstructs Martha's process of mourning
exactly in this sense: It is a magical repair which artificially covers the
void. As such it prevents vital contact with the lost object as well as with
loss itself. Rather than capturing what Ogden calls "a voice brought to life
in the experiencing of [...] loss" Martha clings to Ash's concrete voice (by
means of the virtual reproduction) – reaching, that is, for what she has
actually lost rather than for what might have been brought to life within
her as the result of her mourning.

The work of mourning never directs itself exclusively at the concrete
voice of the lost object: it also addresses the object's possible voice. Rather
than being directed at the countless details making up what has been – it
is directed at the unique quality that no virtual system will contrive to
capture since it relates not to what was – but to what might have been,
and therefore will forever be. The possible does not end at the moment of
actual death and is not taken away by it. On the contrary. The actual death
of the object allows, through rich processes of mourning, the continuation of the possible relations with him or her. Relationships which in actuality were interrupted years ago may evolve for a very long time inside the
mourner, undergoing ceaseless change as they shed and resume different
forms.

Unlike what happens whenever there is this rich dialogue with the lost
object – the virtual Ash is constrained by his actuality. And although his
actual qualities, as documented on the internet, may be quite coherent
with his living character – no transcending of these actual qualities can
occur, since transcendence is always a movement from the actual towards
the possible. The capacity to transcend, which is what made Ash (like anyone of us) into who he was, is irretrievably lost here: not upon his death,
but upon his artificial resuscitation. This is why Martha eventually takes

him to the cliff and asks him to jump. At this moment she sees that the one thing that can restore Ash to life is for her to let him die. For as long as she keeps him alive she consigns the two of them to death by not allowing him to swerve from his internet database, which is not and never will be equal to "him", and similarly, by not enabling herself to be fully "her" in the process of mourning. As long as she tries to fill the gap Ash has left behind with his external outline instead of with his deepest essence, with the algorithm of knowledge "about him" rather than with her essential knowing of him – she doesn't prevent his death but rather immortalize it, extending it, in a sense, not merely in the direction of the future but also back into the past.

Ash's death is a frightening metaphor of what the internet both offers its users and robs them of: the possibility to know about at the cost of essential knowing. This virtual illusion puts us in mind of one of the great paradoxes of modern culture: The way in which the domain of unlimited possibility is exactly what comes irreparably between us and what is possible, both in the other and in ourselves.

References

Amir, D. (2016). *On the Lyricism of the Mind: Psychoanalysis and Literature*. London and New York: Routledge.

Gilead, A. (1999). *Saving Possibilities: A Study in Philosophical Psychology*. Amsterdam: Rodopi.

Gilead, A. (2003). How Does Love Make the Ugly Beautiful? *Philosophy and Literature*, Vol. 27 (2): 436–443.

Meltzer, D. and Harris-Williams, M. (1988). *The Apprehension of Beauty*. Scotland: Clunie Press.

Meltzer, D. and Harris-Williams, M. (1988). Holding the Dream. In: *The Apprehension of Beauty*, pp. 178–199. Scotland: Clunie Press.

Ogden, T. (1986). *The Matrix of the Mind*. Northvale NJ and London: Jason Aronson.

Ogden, T. (2001). *Conversations at the Frontier of Dreaming*. Northvale NJ and London: Jason Aronson.

Ogden, T. (2001a). Borges and the Art of Mourning. In: *Conversations at the Frontier of Dreaming*. Northvale NJ and London: Jason Aronson, pp. 115–152.

CHAPTER SIX

From illusion to creative act: a possible interpretation of *Her*

Donatella Lisciotto

D isturbing and topical, Spike Jonze's film depicts the solitude of cyber man.

The film revolves around the life of Theodore, a solitary withdrawn character masterfully played by Joaquin Phoenix, intense in his existential languor.

Narrator by proxy, able to express emotions on behalf of others, he writes letters on commission, moving letters which touch the heart, addressed to people he doesn't even know. His own emotional life is shielded by a pervasive boredom that imbues his indistinguishable days with monotony.

He has a failed marriage with Catherine, whom he had been unable (or perhaps unwilling) to tie to himself despite his love for her, and formal relations with few friends. He carries out his busy job, like the rest of his colleagues closed in box-like spaces, provided with everything but without walls, one after the other, one person next to another and close enough to hear the other's voice: a murmured buzz that is always the same, like the sound of the faithful reciting the rosary in church.

Lack and unvoiced yearning are evoked by his home as well, the route he takes to get there, even the lift: large anonymous spaces, all aptly captured by essential and cold set designs.

The director portrays the depression that envelops Theodore through technically well-conceived shots, where he wanders without aim or apparent destination in crowded and cloudy urban spaces that take on all the aspects of "non-places" (Augé, 1995).

Illuminated by unfocused light, the scenes display a luminance that at times fades away and they identify remarkably with the breadth of the spaces that appear even larger thanks to their minimalist design.

This cheerless traipsing around as soon as his shift has ended is how we see Theodore on his solitary "rounds".

It is not entirely correct to say that he is "alone", but rather that he is "without".

Theodore sees the reality that surrounds him as if through a veil, a view that confers a covert texture on worldly things.

But it is the entire atmosphere of the film that seems rarefied and imaginative. It is easy for the viewer to feel he is in a dream or a fantasy and that safety is a "delusion" (Bion, 1982).

I see this as a delicate artistic touch by the director, who manages to draw the viewer in to such an extent as to make him feel Theodore's anomie.

A curious sensation occurs: the viewer becomes an emotive part of the screenplay, an "actor" of Theodore's involuntariness and bewilderment.

Almost immediately the viewer is involved in the casting of the film that involves the presence of multiple unconsciousnesses. They activate and resonate "other" castings, both intrapsychic and interpsychic in nature.

Through his involuntary movement Theodore comes across an ad for a new OS.

And that is how the story turns into an interesting existential stumbling block where imagination is how the main character protects himself. As Bion would say, "No protection more solid than a figment of the imagination" (Bion, 1982).

The OS Samantha is a voice, but she is above all a paradigm of an echo of the libido Theodore has embalmed.

The relationship with the cyber voice activates affections in Theodore that enliven him, torment and frighten him, make him vibrate when faced with Eros and Thanatos, which are at last palpable again.

After his separation from Catherine it seems that with Samantha, Theodore manages to feel once more. Perhaps it is a virtual romance (with an OS device) that makes possible something that would be otherwise impossible for him in reality: to engage emotionally with the Other by himself.

And this is why Catherine gets so angry the last time they see each other, when Theodore confesses he is seeing another woman who has just one feature that makes her different from everyone else: she is an OS.

Catherine could have accepted a flesh and blood "rival" more easily as this would have meant that Theodore was able to invest in a *real* relationship. Instead, his relationship with an OS is confirmation of his inability to do *this*, which is precisely what drew them apart and then to separate despite their continued love for each other. This inability will gradually cause Theodore to resize his existence.

An example is the scene where he comes home to spend his free time playing on PlayStation. From out of nowhere comes the caricature of a humanoid, an ambiguous child-cartoon figure. It seems to be an extension of Theodore or the product of his imagination. Either way the image that the director chooses to represent the solitude and alienation of man-Theodore is powerful and at the same time irritating. Spike Jonze identifies the slow process of nullification and affective isolation of modern man, giving meaning to very significant fragments and details sprinkled throughout the film so that the message arrives to the viewer in an unsaturated manner, leaving space for thought. So one wonders, with a certain bitterness, if the hyper-support of technology is too invasive of an individual's internal space, hollowing out an irrefutable isolation. Or is it delusion with human relationships that pushes a person to "bond" more with machines than with humans?

Theodore is without doubt suffering, and above all he is in distress. There are clear narcissistic styles in his personality, where he keeps but does not hold the Other in a bond.

What caused the failure of his relationship with his wife now, in a virtual bond, reveals itself to be an advantageous condition. His relationship with Samantha is characterised by an *elusive nearness*.

But it is precisely inside a virtual bond that Theodore can slip into and finally sojourn in an emotional condition that he has always guarded against, and in the end estranged himself: to be in love with all the risks involved.

I take a step back and link to primary love: an experience of *that* first bond characterised by the *absolute* and the *sublime*, by being "wonderfully loved". A breakdown here has consequences on the capacity of a person to live in a harmonious way.

In our protagonist's case, what takes shape is an early crack in his relationship with his self-centred mother. He says this in one of the first dialogues with Samantha.

I see this to be the origin of the depressive system of Theodore's personality. This is vented in a narcissistic personality continually fighting against the trap of depressive breakdown by anticipating the feared lack, by being its messenger, and wrapping objects and people in his detached affectiveness.

From a psychoanalytic perspective, observing the main character's personality and others featured, from Catherine to his friend Amy, leads me to an interpretation centred on the elaboration of original mourning (mourning of the primary object), and on the passage from Winnicott's "illusion to disillusion".

Likewise, the film's whole nuanced and improbable atmosphere seems to me to be permeated with the traumatic condition of absence of significance. But also, and this is the key to the film, the heart-rending desire to find the love object is pervasive, as is the rediscovery of sense that hesitates in the *creative act*, the result of a painful working-through, and of an existential coming about that integrates mourning and transforms loss.

The interpretation I put forward, just one of many angles from which *Her* may be viewed, is the process that a person embarks on in that delicate phase of life in which he leaves (or loses) primary illusion and, through a successful working-through of mourning, if everything goes according to plan, lands at "creative act". This passage defines the destiny of the love object in its transference declinations as well.

I will do this by proposing a parallel with the story of three adolescents I saw either in consultation or for psychoanalytic treatment. Using clinical examples, but taking into account their structural diversities, and in a parallel to Theodore's story, I will illustrate by showing how the elaboration of primary mourning can significantly impact the development of an individual's personality, hesitating between a narcissistic process or what I like to define as a "creative act". I think our protagonist presents both conditions in this film.

Theodore-narcissist who, frightened by an affective request (his and Other) detaches himself from worldly things, and, on the other hand, Theodore-man who through his bond with Samantha and above all through his having faced the loss, turns towards the *creative act*, namely his relationship with Amy.

By "creative act" I mean an action that, unlike acting out, takes shape when the process of working-through of mourning is successful. In this case thinkability within individual is initiated, whereby the creative component of Self, freed from the shadow of loss, can finally be expressed.

The creative act originates in the capacity to think of the mourning and is different from acting out, as it is endowed with originality and uniqueness.

Chiara

18 years old with 3,150 online friends

Chiara's mother makes an appointment for her daughter over the phone, as she says she is "a little disoriented". Chiara arrives for the session relaxed and apparently self-confident.

She introduces herself as a blogger.

I sense the power of this statement but also its limitations.

Chiara has many friends on Twitter; they are followers, people who "follow you" without even knowing you. I must stress that she has no friends apart from these virtual ones.

She says, "it is almost as if word has got around, more and more people are 'following' me".

She considers herself balanced and amusing and that is why many people contact her for advice that ranges from recipes to affairs of the heart.

She says that recently she has felt overwhelmed by this number of "contacts" and begins to feel they are too demanding.

In the absence of a body, Chiara seems the figure of a caring function. Like Samantha, she gives support and comfort to thousands of virtual contacts. She, too, is tired, destined to switch off. She seems to feel the need for a real contact with a therapist, she seems to seek a *listening*, to fend off the terror of existing only as a blogger to be "seen" only as a sort of narcissistic object.

Even the brevity of the therapeutic relationship (she decides to have only one meeting), corresponds to the size of a tweet. A chirp ... that's enough.

Chiara is an only child. When she was little more than a child, her mother was diagnosed with multiple sclerosis and Chiara takes complete care of her, whilst the father remains in the background.

In Chiara's story the transgenerational element plays a key role. Chiara's grandmother was affected by a serious heart condition that impacted her life and that of her daughter (Chiara's mother), the only person in the family to worry about her mother's health. So in Chiara's family there is a sick and needy mother, limited and limiting, similarly there is an insignificant conjugal couple in which Eros, complicity and tenderness are missing but so, too, is the experience of conflict. We see mothers coupled with daughters who take the place of the partner instead.

Who is Chiara really? ... is she "disoriented" (as the mother calls her) with 3,150 "followers"? ... What a paradox!

82 DONATELLA LISCIOTTO

"Don't follow me, I'm lost, too!"

I ask myself if, through Twitter, Chiara has sublimated early mourning towards immobilised maternal aspects and the absence of a male figure in the couple, in order to avoid depressive anxiety.

It is here that I see the risk of a narcissistic turn, where the difficulty in a healthy mourning of the primary object includes a possible narcissistic slip used by the girl to defend herself from contact with a "dead mother" or a mother who is not sufficiently responsive, which is how Theodore's mother appears to be as well.

Against her will, Chiara's apparent self-confidence and nonchalance may be contextualised as a defence against identification with an alienated object represented by a paralysed mother but also by an absent father and a transgenerational weight.

Chiara is just one of many cases I would describe as suffering from "web syndrome". As for many adolescents, her case shows how the Internet lends itself to being an instrument whose many facets, opportunities, and risks are most definitely to be analysed and comprehended, over and above the aspects of communication in the sense of information exchange and disclosure in the phenomena of youth.

In Chiara's condition, as with Theodore, a "writer by proxy" of the sentiments of other people and a protagonist in stories that are not her own, it would seem that this excess of contacts characterises a dispersive and completely relational position. Moreover, contrary to appearances, it characterises a non-dynamic setting of relations and communications that are always closed and relegated to a chat, or rather to many chats, giving a condition of existential anomie.

Sara's case is different.

Sara

15 years old

Sara is distressed by an internal break-up of a peer group, and subsequently develops a depressive withdrawal characterised by apathy and lack of will.

The girl's disappointment is presumably linked to the relationship, in her early years, with a mother who was depressed due to a painful separation from her husband. Sara's immature equilibrium had to face a father's estrangement in addition to a maternal "absence".

Sara spends a lot of time in her room. Her only satisfaction is a trip to the fridge or the pantry.

Soon she gains weight, neglects personal care and hygiene until, one day, she decides to join a chat room.

Here she meets people of her own age and of different nationalities and strikes up good relationships with them. She practises her English from school, shares photos and plans, and eventually organises and goes on a summer trip abroad, where she has the chance to meet up with some of them.

Like Theodore, disoriented by the emotional fracture with Catherine, Sara looks for footholds on the Internet that will give her back some recognition and value.

She recovers gradually and asks for psychotherapy to analyse how much her depression had been caused by distress over her peer group's betrayal.

Contrary to Chiara, through chats with her virtual group and an innovative relational opportunity, Sara manages to transform the disappointment that had held her prisoner to a dramatic, needy, and lifeless love object.

In the same way, in the film's finale Theodore is able to separate from the OS and start a relationship with Amy. It appears that narcissistic performance can substitute an objectual one where the Other is recognised not only as a mirror of self but as other-than-self, a condition for which a bond can be made.

Theodore knocks on Amy's door and manages to say:

"Will you come with me?"

Side by side in a surreal scenario, they both seem finally headed towards an object relationship.

We know that living the mourning of the primary object inclines a person towards an evolutionary experience of solitude. To experience the condition of "being alone" in the presence of Other and to confront the disillusion of the primary pact will subsequently allow someone to feel the presence of Other and of oneself, like *living objects*. This is what I discern in the performance of the excellent Joaquin Phoenix in the film's finale when, after the heartbreak of separation and coming out of it "alive", he can turn to a new affection and enjoy its contemporaneity at last.

84   DONATELLA LISCIOTTO

Daniele

The discovery of the "web" limited the damages of solitude and marginalisation for Daniele, too, and makes sense of his ability to organise relations between self and others and between self and worldly things.

His psycho-pathological case is different from Chiara's and Sara's. Daniele was one of my young patients who I saw three times a week for psychotherapy.

He became my patient when he was 6 years old but I was never completely convinced by the diagnosis and label of Asperger Syndrome. Basically Daniel needed to organise the many stimuli his mind collected but did not filter. It was as if he suffered from hyper-realism through which worldly things slammed up against him, both for better or for worse.

Today Daniele is 32 years old, works in IT, and is a member of a theatre company; he runs a Facebook feed about local and Italian news. Every day he says "good morning" and "good night" to his 680 "friends".

In my practice I have often seen how for adolescents (and not only them), using the web satisfies a need for visibility and recognition that substitutes or fills a *horror vacui*.

In my opinion, in some cases the virtual condition may collude with the reiterated illusion of chasing after an internal object that is *"desaparecido"*, as in *Her*. How? By proposing a repeated compulsion that is not only fruitless but also dangerous, a repetition of the "blind alley" that reinforces the sense of solitude and the inevitability of lack, giving personality one less opportunity to evolve, and fostering the risk of a narcissistic slip.

Surely the condition of Theodore and our young people represents the discovery, through Samantha, of the ancient primary condition that surrounds and accompanies, colours, and defines space, alleviates time so that it becomes kind.

The stories of Chiara, Sara, Daniele and Theodore (metaphorically represented by the genial Snoopy) have something in common: the destiny of the primary object and how this destiny plays between narcissistic slip and creative act.

> *Samantha*: What's wrong?
> *Theodore*: How can you tell something's wrong?
> *Samantha*: I don't know. I just can.

This dialogue between Theodore and Samantha reminds us of Winnicott's "good enough" mother who, gifted with reverie, knows, without knowing, apparently in an irrational way, the needs of her child, giving him *the illusion* of the existence of reciprocity, the payment of desire, and primary confidence (Bertolini et al., 2003).

A detail of the film I find interesting is the safety pin pinned to Theodore's shirt pocket. It appears to keep his OS device safe so that it doesn't fall out. The Italian word for safety pin is nanny-pin, a reference to a nanny's role in looking after a newborn: she rears him with love and care, she feeds him. This is metaphorically the condition Theodore experiences through the OS, and for Chiara and Sara as well it represents the desire of a bond with a "good enough" primary object. In place of a heart, Theodore walks around with his *nanny* in his pocket.

This scene is in contrast to the one where Amy shows her documentary to Theodore and his companion. It portrays the figure of a sleeping woman: Amy's mother. The image is phantasmatic of the "dead-mother" (Green) against the "nanny-mother". Amy, like Theodore, also seems disoriented by contact with her *own* dead-mother, a condition that makes her insecure, uncertain, and unresolved, and which pushes her too to dependence on an OS.

"You know I can feel the fear that you carry around. I wish there was something I could do to help you let go of it, because if you could I don't think you'd feel so alone anymore."

Samantha's words refer to an affectively efficient and therefore effective maternal function as well. This is in contrast to Theodore's experience with his relationship with a mother who was too busy to listen to herself, as he will say, or to Sara and Chiara who are stuck in a bond with a depressed and equally absent mother.

The "fear that you carry around" that Samantha refers to and which causes Theodore to "feel so alone" is linked to the fear of sliding into a depressive breakdown that Theodore, like Chiara and Sara, seems to oppose through narcissistic defence.

The risk of "depressive breakdown" is well represented in the film at various points. This is shown, above all, when Theodore, unable to connect with Samantha one day, is gripped by a real panic attack that is only brought to an end when he manages to hear the sound of Samantha's voice again.

The director's ability to portray unfathomable depths such as those felt during highly critical emotional moments is truly admirable.

In rising anguish Theodore fiddles around with the earpiece that no longer transmits the device's voice. He gets up from his workstation, trying to get a connection. Agitated and frantic, he tries to get better reception but nothing happens, Samantha does not answer. He calls her, he calls her again with increasing alarm. Nothing, there is nothing any more. In the end he goes out into the street as if he is seeking *something* rather than *someone*, he runs among the crowd, blindly shoving passers-by, tumbles to the ground, gets up again, breathless and disoriented.

Everything seems lost and to no longer exist. People's voices, street noise are echoes now, objects' colours are faded and blurred. Exactly like the fog of panic when eyes seem to lose their sight and all the senses are deprived of familiar landmarks. Reality without a framework becomes indefinite and unknown, causing a sense of de-realisation and confusion that takes your breath away.

Spike Jonze's description is the same as an extraordinarily powerful one I heard from a patient describing a panic attack.

"I'm on the east face of Mount Everest, without footholds" or "I'm crossing a desert where there isn't any sand."

It seems that the director knows how to realistically interpret the torment patients describe.

When Theodore is completely lost, he sinks onto the steps of a subway station and there he finds Samantha. He immediately recovers and the scenography changes with the same rapidity in which the mental state of a person coming out of a panic attack clears up. Colours become clearer, sounds are more real and recognisable, the chatter of life is heard. It's as if each figure, each form, emerges from the background and takes the stage, coming up from the depths with their chests heaving.

Theodore and Samantha's relationship seems to dazzle the primary one, but also the narcissistic one ("I feel really close to her … I feel cuddled", Theodore will say), extending even as far as oedipal love, in a form of love where corporeality is absent, and the omnipotent phantasy of the possession of the object prevails over reality.

We know that when a harmonious resolution of mourning with the primary object does not occur, in order to prevent a depressive breakdown a person may develop a narcissistic process where the object relationship prevails over the narcissistic one and the object is controlled and illusorily possessed.

A narcissist has the unsettling and sometimes perverse ability to not recognise the object as such, according to his own needs and requirements. But at the same time he gives it the privileged function of absorbing and absolving all of his needs, as if it were a mirror: even the existence of the object is only recognised as a mirror.

In the opening scenes of the film Theodore is *searching*, he is disoriented, he hopes to regain what he has lost (this goes beyond his relationship with

Catherine). He doesn't know *what* he is looking for or *what* he has lost. He doesn't seem to know how to give it a name or, therefore, recognition and value.

We could say that he meets Samantha because he is looking for her. His roaming among people in large (claustrophobic) spaces, along with a thousand people who in turn seem wrapped up in the inconsequential and never actually meet, describes an area of suspension that, like a bubble, contains the *unformed* without pushing it into a healthy experiential dimension.

For the entire length of the film, the audience is witness to a long and improbable wait.

Little by little, Theodore's story develops and the affective evolution of this melancholic character twists and turns along with it:

- from the illusion of the primary bond (the bond with OS),
- to disillusion and acceptance of loss (the heart-rending ending of the relationship with OS)
- and, lastly, the start of an object relationship (the beginning of his relationship with Amy).

The reference to desire of "sublime love" and to being "wonderfully loved", is powerful when Theodore says,

"I've never loved anyone the way I loved you".

Whilst his disillusion is underlined when he discovers Samantha's betrayals towards the end of the film:

"How many others?"
"641."
"What? What are you talking about? That's insane. That's fucking insane ... No, that doesn't make any sense. ... You're mine or you're not mine."

This moment marks the beginning of the painful process that will bring him to accept the loss of the sublime bond, without resignation but promoting new and simpler thoughts that will give body to the "creative act", as we will shortly see.

In the same manner Daniele's *Facebook news feed* gives him the chance to move in "connections" in which news *of reality* is related. Then there are Sara's *trips abroad* (not virtual at all) and Chiara's request to *see a psychoanalyst*.

88 DONATELLA LISCIOTTO

I would like to conclude with Theodore's touching words in his letter to Catherine at the end of the film and, in particular, with the extraordinary comment ("Send").

They appear to be directed to his mother, and sum up a painful and disturbing process but one that is maturational and creative as well and involves each individual in the elaboration of mourning of the primary object

> I've been sitting here thinking about all the things I wanted to apologize to
> you for.
> All the pain we caused each other,
> everything I put on you –
> everything I need you to be or needed you to say.
> I'm sorry for that.
> I will always love you because we grew up together.
> And you helped make me who I am.
> I just wanted you to know there will be a piece of you in me always,
> and I'm grateful for that.
> Whatever someone you become, and wherever you are in the world.
> I'm sending you love.
> You're my friend till the end. Love,
> Theodore. … Send.

That "Send", accompanied by a deep breath, similar to a child's hiccup and together with a sense of release, is Theodore's "creative act":

> it is the opportunity to remain in reality with his love object (Amy),
> it is to live a bond in contemporaneity,
> it is the nostalgia with which the object is retrieved forever,

it is being in a relationship that goes beyond the illusion, and that, in mourning, sees the objectual turning point, through which it is possible to "invent" another bond, or an other-bond where the individual's creativity prevails, once it has been set free from symbiosis.

References

Augé, M. (1995). *Non-places: Introduction to an Anthropology of Supermodernity.* New York: Verso.

Bertolini, M., Giannakoulas, A. and Hernandez, M. (2003). *La tradizione Winnicottiana* (Volume 1). Rome: Borla.

Bion, W. R. (1982). *The Long Weekend 1897–1919: Part of a Life* (pp. 130–131). London: Karnac, 1991.

Winnicott, W. D. (1989). *Psycho-analytic Explorations.* Cambridge MA: Harvard University Press.

CHAPTER SEVEN

The virtual dimension in love affairs and therapeutic relationships: love and death in Giuseppe Tornatore's films

Nicolino Rossi

The impressive developments in remote communications, and the growing dissemination of the social networks linked to them, are having a considerable and disturbing influence on many areas of our lives, including those of our important personal relationships, love affairs among them. Even psychoanalytical practice, for which communication between analyst and patient in a real interaction is an essential condition, seems to be unable to do without these innovations. In particular circumstances (for the moment, but they are showing a tendency to expand with extreme ease), it is using means of communication which allow the treatment of people who are sometimes very distant from the analyst, either geographically or culturally. (Bolognini 2015; Lemma and Caparrotta 2014; Scharff 2010; Vinocur Fischbein 2010).

The specific condition of use of the Internet seems to introduce, at least in its more radical forms such as cases of an absence of even a partial real relationship between analyst and patient, such deep changes in the analytical arrangement as to legitimise the question of whether it affects the foundations of the entire clinical theoretical system of our discipline. Perhaps it is fair to wonder whether the constitutional essence of the psychoanalytic device, developed and perfected for traditional, oral culture, which requires the presence of two people in flesh and blood, is placed under serious debate when it is applied under such different conditions,

90 NICOLINO ROSSI

such as those of a society dominated by global communication and virtuality.

One of the most interesting areas touched by the use of the Internet is that of love relationships. From a psychoanalytical point of view, this is an interest that can also be linked to the clinical relationship. We know that transference, which psychoanalysis has had to cope with since the beginning, with its progressive clinical importance and technical implications, was investigated by Freud particularly in its erotic version, exploring the affinities and differences with respect to real (so to speak) love affairs (Freud 1915). A more in-depth knowledge of unconscious phantasmatic structures linked to the beginning and development of love affairs, using such communication tools, can help us understand the specific curve which transferral and countertransferral dynamics can assume in cases in which psychoanalytical treatment is carried out from a distance through the Internet (Fiorentini 2012; Gabbard 2001; Lemma and Caparrotta 2014; Lingiardi 2008; Savage Sharff 2014; Vinocur Fischbein 2010; Zalusky 1998).

In theory, remote relational exchanges which exclude direct contact, and therefore bodily participation, can encourage defence mechanisms in the construction of fantasies about the interlocutor. At deeper level, this can extend to the creation of unconscious phantasmatic structures in relation to the partner; the relationship will be easily confined to a narcissistic, fusional and omnipotent register, the objective of which is the denial of separateness and alterity, control of the pain of loss and denial of death anxieties.

Films which have recently looked at this subject include *Her*, by Spike Jonze (2013), which takes the consequences of a love affair developed at virtual level to the extreme. It dematerialises the partner, eliminating the bodily form and replacing it with a highly technological electronic device. The promise is to realise the fantasy of a narcissistic-fusional relationship with an omniscient and omnipotent object, where extreme idealisation takes over. Primarily bodily but also the psychological reality of the partner is denied and the narcissistic use of the relationship is pursued, avoiding the painful feelings linked to loss. This is a metaphoric portrayal of the use of the computer and connection to the web, in which the tool itself becomes a fetish partner, always available, capable of satisfying every need instantly, and from which it is possible to disconnect at will.

Two recent films by Giuseppe Tornatore, *The Best Offer* (2012) and *The Correspondence* (2015), seem to effectively and richly illustrate the romantic vicissitudes linked to the start and evolution of a remote relationship.

They look at the defensive functions that use of the Internet can perform with regard to separation from and the loss of a loved one.

The Best Offer gives a compelling portrayal of a love affair which begins with a telephone conversation and is pursued with a mobile phone, before taking some very unexpected and traumatic turns. This is something the director seems to return to and complete with his latest film, *The Correspondence*. The film focuses on death and the possibilities offered by digital communication to deny reality and keep the relative anguish at bay.

Love over the phone

The Best Offer is a sophisticated portrayal of what can be described as the consequences of love (quoting from Sorrentino's film *The Consequences of Love*, the subject of which is in some way similar, despite developing it in more intimate and blurred tones). It is narrated using Tornatore's rich and exuberant, colourful and baroque language, full of metaphoric allusions and symbolic references, sometimes even excessively didactic: so much so that it is hard to see the numerous sentimental nuances and cinematographic tricks used by the director to portray them. Tornatore's film is complex, tackling (or at least hinting at) various topics ranging from love to the beauty of art, from truth and falseness, to duality; from a psychoanalytical perspective, the reference to how people can change during therapy seems anything but secondary.

The events are surrounded by an air of mystery, with everything becoming absolutely clear at the end of the film, giving it the feeling of a thriller. This only serves to strengthen the dominant perspective of the whole film, which is the transformative power of love affairs, but also their danger. There is the addition of the power and danger of therapeutic relationships, which are the variant at psychoanalytical clinical level, in a predefined and guided context that, at least within certain limits, is more protected.

The plot

Mr Oldman, the main character, masterfully interpreted by Geoffrey Rush, is an acclaimed auctioneer; he initially seems to be a gruff man, a prickly soul, who entrusts his disagreeable confidence to his professional skills, sure that they make him a sought-after figure. He doesn't need others, it's others that need to seek him out to benefit from his masterful skills. We have a remarkable example of this when, already involved in the new and unforeseen relationship, he cancels prestigious commitments of an extremely advantageous financial nature without thinking twice, due to the fact that he is worried about the girl with whom he has fallen hopelessly in love. Appreciated and sought-after at a professional level, Oldman is a lonely man, and his solitude is highlighted in one of the opening scenes in which he is seated at the table of his usual restaurant, eating alone, wearing gloves, in haughty isolation. Only the management of the restaurant remembers his birthday (as often happens when we receive birthday greetings in a text from our doctor or from a shop where we are regular customers). However, he gets the date wrong, celebrating it the day before, presenting him with a cake which he refuses with a disdain that eliminates the mortifying wound. He lives alone, often travelling, and has no friends and no loving relationships, for which he feels no need. Oldman has a narcissistic personality, with a very tangible adaptation and an operatory mental function; he only enters into relationships that are functional and utilitarian, tending to avoid every other kind. These characteristics have probably been developed as a defensive mechanism against traumatic experiences from his past, linked to the loss of his parents and to his early institutionalisation, as we later learn when he talks about it for the first time in his life with the new client-stranger. He filled his loneliness at the orphanage with an interest in restoration, an art in which he became a real master. This practical skill which, with its sublimating and reparatory characteristics, enabled him to keep out the traumatic consequences of his pitiful childhood, equipping him with a tool to cope with the pain of the loss of his childhood possessions and to renew their rediscovery, repair and "re-presentification". Thanks to works of art, discovered and recognised as authentic, or restored to their initial form, he can avoid the sense of guilt generated by his destructive impulses and fulfil the illusion of rediscovering the lost object in all its original beauty.

In fact, Oldman has maintained his relationship with the inner idealised object, holding a secret dialogue with an amazing collection of paintings of women which he has collected during years of work and research as an antique dealer. These works are stored in a large secret room, separate from the rest of the house: a *caveau*, an exclusive space away from the world in which he moves, in the same way that the experience that exists within this space is cut off from the other aspects of himself which are part of his social and professional life. The possession of these masterpieces has mostly come about through fraudulent activity, deriving from purchases by his accomplice who sits among the public during the auctions he holds, buying the paintings that Oldman indicates in advance and prompts him to bid for.

The *caveau* is the intrapsychic place, a mental more than physical space (Steiner 1993), closely guarded because it is so precious and vulnerable. It is the place where Oldman jealously keeps the ideal, primary object, having been robbed painfully and too soon of his relationship with it. There he seeks refuge to enjoy it exclusively, in ecstatic and silent admiration characterised, however, by a vein of nostalgic sadness which his eyes seem to express as he peruses the strange and mysterious faces shown in the paintings. It is a link which has been subtracted from the transformative events of psychological life and the ambivalence of his unconscious feelings. There is no room in Oldman's life for other women, much less so for an involvement in real loving relationships.

The director seductively decides to protect the secret place with a sliding wardrobe-panel which houses all of Oldman's gloves. A wall of gloves, the fetish object which forms the defensive, isolating barrier separating the private space from that into which others are allowed; or, if we look at it in relation to his personal life, which divides his innermost self from the rest of his psychological life, avoiding contacts which might cause the painful experiences of his past to re-emerge. Oldman always wears gloves, even while he eats, as he is terrified of contamination from contact with inanimate objects. The gloves act like the invisible shell that protects him from affective involvement with others, potential causes of danger which could expose him once more to the suffering linked to his traumatic loss during childhood.

The phobic component is aimed specifically at the mobile phone, a tool for communicating with others; and it is through the mobile phone that the relationship with Claire begins and develops, transforming their professional contact, a language with which he is more familiar and with which he moves more securely, into a loving connection.

In the film, we see the progressive involvement of the elderly man in a relationship with an attractive client, Claire. Without ever meeting him, and communicating with him only over the phone, she assigns him the job of valuing the furniture in her family home for sale at auction. It seems that it is precisely this new way of contact over the phone which is so completely unusual for the auctioneer, and which he has always disdainfully rejected, that draws him gradually into a situation of seduction: a game of offers and refusals by the girl, of promises and disappointments, of break-ups and make-ups, that leads him to let down his guard, take off his gloves and tell her his deepest secrets, letting her into his *caveau*.

A peculiar and seductive element of the film is that Oldman is guided through his erotic journey by a voice; the song of a siren which initially arouses his curiosity and then charms, enchants and seduces him. Like a call from far away, probably from the depths of his unconscious psychological life, generated by sensory traces of sound, sweet and painful at the same time which, with Bollas (1987), we consider as known even though they aren't included and transcribed in a repressed unconscious.

It makes one think of the song of a siren which, in one of the numerous versions of the legend, is seen as a nostalgic reference to the body left on earth after death, or the human body abandoned and transformed into a bird; or, at the origin of everything, the maternal body known and lost in the first experiences of rewarding fusion.

While, on one hand, Oldman's aversion to mobile phones expresses the rejection of social contact, it could, at a deeper level, also be a form of defence against traps linked to the reference of the sentimental resonances activated by listening to unfamiliar voices; in its adaptation it is, above all, the enquiring expression in his eyes which he has superlatively refined with the aim of unveiling falsehoods in the expressions of beauty in the work of art. It is to this skill that Oldman has probably entrusted protection against the danger of being tricked again, professionally of course but even more so in relation to his feelings.

Initially annoyed by the requests made by the anonymous client over the phone, Oldman decides nevertheless to comply with them, however much this goes against his will, and this is inexplicably out of character. His curiosity is aroused more and more by the strange and mysterious situation and he starts the work commissioned without ever meeting her. Then he decides to hide and, by setting a trap, he discovers her presence inside the house where he is valuing the furnishings. He starts spying on her, unseen, secretly entering the building. When the girl discovers him, after an initial argument they start a real relationship, in which their conversation becomes increasingly intimate. Claire tells him about the phobias that force her to live a segregated life, far away from contact with other people. She shares the traumatic events that have characterised her life and he reveals his secrets to her. This journey brings them closer and closer together, with moments of great emotional and dramatic intensity, alternating break-ups and make-ups, experiences of immense and unknown happiness, but also new suffering and deep desperation. All of this can generate a relationship based on love, but also on psychoanalysis.

While the erotic dimension in the plot is the most evident, it is also possible, especially for a psychoanalyst, to read it from a different angle; that of the therapeutic relationship, and also of a particular type of therapeutic relationship. We could call it a telephone analysis experience

(Zalusky 1998). Indeed, the therapeutic relationship is a particular kind of love affair.

From this viewpoint, Claire's request seems to represent a cry for help over the telephone to an analyst; it triggers a relationship which becomes gradually stronger, during which the two break up and get back together again repeatedly, characterised by increasingly pressing demands which cause the therapist some difficulty. He always succeeds, nevertheless, in putting the relationship back together again; gradually relinquishing his detached attitude based on the correct application of the contractual clauses, which require him to place his professional skill and a reliable setting at the service of the client/patient, to build an ever-deeper and intimate connection. The transgression in the film becomes real, also touching on sexuality, but it can be read at a symbolic level too, as the recovery of the ability to let oneself go in an intimate relationship.[1]

In an attempt to alleviate Claire's anxieties and bring her closer to life again, not only does Oldman not hesitate to face up to and tell her about his own painful experiences, showing her that he is capable of understanding her suffering and sharing it; he also gets back in touch with his own most authentic aspects. In short, theirs is a relationship which becomes increasingly intersubjective: a relationship based on growing reciprocity, in which the psychological transformation of one cannot exist without that of the other. It is a situation dotted with enactments, upsets and self-disclosure, in which the auctioneer/therapist offers his person to the service of the client/patient, taking the only route that will enable him to effectively engage the girl and help bring her out of her secret hiding place, the phobic shell inside which she lives her reclusive life.

It is precisely this involvement which allows the main character not to give up and to continue looking for the girl, until he finds her, cold and naked, in the secret alcove where she's hiding. Then, all of a sudden, she disappears without a trace. Claire's disappearance marks a turnaround: the possibility that he might have lost her throws the man into a state of consternation; his scream is heart-wrenching, and his curiosity and interest become a devastating worry. This sends him on an anxious and anguished search, jeopardising his professional commitments to a point where things become ridiculous. We know that sometimes it's necessary to seek out the patient, actively yet discreetly, to restore his or her presence and take up the conservation again from where we left off.

This seems to be a seductive portrayal of what happens to an analyst involved in the treatment of a severely traumatised person, who feels obliged to do more than just listen. We see it in a scene in which the main character sits in front of the closed door to listen to the woman's story, actively trying to contact the more damaged and inaccessible parts of the patient.

Claire gradually manages to reclaim the spaces that her phobia has prevented her from entering for some time. She becomes able to cope with affection, which her defence mechanisms, describable as borderline, have damaged her to the point where she is totally isolated.

We could say, making reference again to a metaphoric reading of the events in the film, that the relational dynamic is becoming more mature, approaching the conclusion of treatment. The more evolved love feelings proposed by the Oedipal vicissitudes prevail. There are seductive scenes which reveal the girl's rediscovery of her femininity, especially those in which she tries on some clothes. Oldman, in the guise of a father figure, tenderly and lovingly helps the girl, an insecure and timidly faltering adolescent, to familiarise herself with her erotic body and make the most of her figure with the most suitable clothes.[2]

If Oldman's tenacity and his ability to free himself from his defensive barriers and involve himself deeply and without reserve in the tumultuous relationship with his client are what help the woman most, it is her marked emotional streak that leads Oldman to undertake the dangerous journey that substantially changes her psychological organisation and, consequently, the way she behaves in human relations; and was it not the facing up to this type of pathology that obliged psychoanalysis to reconsider certain aspects of its modus operandi or, at least, a certain rigidity therein?

Oldman's transformative journey heads towards the search for his real Self, sacrificed and hidden by his outer shell, and the partly defensive, partly sublimating channelling of his needs in ultra-refined professional skills. The progressive cracking of his defensive, falsifying armour seems to start with the dyeing of his hair, immediately identified and violently rejected by the girl. The operation seems to proceed in parallel, but also inversely, with the reconstruction of the automaton of Jacques de Vaucanson[3]: as this gradually advances, the deconstruction of Oldman's defensive organisation deepens, causing his more authentic and fragile aspects to surface.

Oldman is helped through his transformative journey by a third figure, a kind of supervisor, who provides him with clever suggestions on the art of love and teaches him the moves to make on the chessboard of courting Claire. This helper is a young but expert technician who succeeds in the taxing job of rebuilding an old robot: the first talking robot, Jacques de

Vaucanson's automaton. He puts together the sophisticated mechanisms that Oldman gives him, piece by piece, as he comes into possession of them, recovering them apparently at random during his exploration of the house after freeing them from the encrustations of time. In actual fact, they have been cleverly left here and there as important clues to pursue in the work undertaken, as he moves closer to his mysterious client. The precious automaton, a talking machine according to legend, is actually a metal casing; a complex and sophisticated mechanical instrument to which only a human being, a dwarf-child hidden inside it, can convey sensitivity and voice. This is the infantile humanity which Oldman had to give up and which now, thanks to his love for Claire, even before the love he receives from her, he is able to contact once more.

The end of the film is surprising and dramatic, although not altogether unexpected. Oldman, who is in love by now and completely trusts the girl, gives her the keys to his house and hands over his very existence, also revealing the secret of his sanctuary to her.

Upon returning from his last auction, with which he retires from his professional activity, celebrated by his clients, staff and friends, to spend the rest of his life with his beloved Claire, he finds her gone and discovers that the *caveau* has been completely emptied. All that's left is the completed automaton, which continues to monotonously repeat that every fake contains something real – a recurrent expression used by Oldman – along with a single canvas; the one painted by his friend who used to purchase the paintings that he auctioned, and in which he was particularly interested. He has been the victim of a team fraud, the members of the team being his beloved client, his friend and accomplice at the auctions, and his confidante and supervisor who had given him advice on his love life while he was skilfully rebuilding the automaton. All those who had witnessed and contributed to his love affair.

Oldman has a predictably catastrophic reaction, falling into depression and requiring consequent treatment, including admission to hospital. The loss of Claire, the object of a love suspended between real and transferred values, a linking figure between the ideal image of the inner object and that encountered in reality, which has ended up replacing it, has exposed him once again to a terrible traumatic experience. However, Oldman seems to face up to it as an inevitable painful step towards acquiring a more authentic and balanced emotional situation and gaining greater security in his sentimental relations.

When he feels better, with his newfound humanity and faith in Claire's feelings for him, he goes to wait for her in the bar full of clocks in Prague, the city where Claire had spent the only happy moments of her life with her parents, at a time of calm and harmony, and where Oldman had promised himself he would take her again.

The end of the film is left open, looking at the inability to know and the unpredictability of human beings. It leaves us wondering where to draw the fine line between an illusory passion and a more realistic faith in the love of the person we love.

If "There is a grain of truth concealed in every delusion" (Freud 1906, p. 80) (and a loving passion can present aspects that are close to madness) and if, as Oldman is convinced, there is something real in every fake, how can he believe that Claire's love has all been a pretence? Did Claire really love him or did he rediscover his own ability to love thanks to her, recovering the faith required to involve himself in human relations and the ability to recognise and experience a real loving relationship?

And isn't a certain painful sacrificing of the link with the ideal inner object always necessary in order to access a more complete and mature loving relationship with the real object? Can we consider Oldman's behaviour to be an authentic processing of loss, with recovery of the more real and fragile parts of himself; those parts which, thanks to the use of projective identification, had been placed and regained in Claire, accepting her definitive loss? And aren't we always assailed by questions like this when we take on an analytical case, especially with particularly difficult patients?

The sensory experience of falling in love

The case of Oldman can be representative of sentimental matters that are sometimes particularly dramatic and can come to life in a love affair when the parties involved have undergone traumatic experiences, experiences that have made them more vulnerable and, therefore, also refractory to affective links, favouring specific psychological characteristics and defence mechanisms in them, like those described with regard to our main character. They are more exposed to passionate investments, which they enter into in an excessively dissociated way. This prevents a physiological evolution towards a more complete loving relationship, paving the way for a new traumatic experience. We know that the harsh defensive armour that we put on against affection and addiction to love protects us against a vulnerability which, if left unguarded, runs wild with no protection.

In these cases, the process of integration of separate disturbing or worrying elements becomes harder, impeded by the need to retain the certainty that we have found the desired object, source of all perfection and delight, an object which we cannot afford to lose. It is likely that an excess of unconscious destructivity and the inner presence of bad, deteriorated objects, also expose us to an inability to reduce our idealising expectations and accept the frustrations caused by our partner, which generate suffering and bitterness (Kernberg 1995). The real or feared loss of our love object or of its essential qualities, even when they are unrealistic, generates the collapse of the unstable narcissistic security which has been assigned to its possession and its love, and inner emptiness, which drags us down into the darkness of depressive catastrophe. Different defensive relational strategies can be activated to prevent this. They range from unconditional and masochistic submission to the object, to omnipotent and sadistic control of the partner. They even progress through to extreme violence if the person we love demands their individuality, independence or definitive freedom from the relationship.[4]

The experience of loss is, therefore, unbearable and cannot be elaborated through a painful mourning process. The impossibility of unconscious mourning, relating to the relationship with the inner object, is now seen as an impossible mourning of an idealised relational condition, the foundations of which lie in the process of falling in love at the beginning of the relationship.

Starting with the analysis of another film, *Revolutionary Road* by Sam Mendes (2010), and on the basis of numerous clinical observations of couples in psychoanalytical therapy, we had assumed that the relational difficulties of couples torn apart by intense conflict, incapable of accessing a mature and complete loving relationship, could be linked to the nature of the process of falling in love. The emotional need for intense involvement generated by meeting the partner seems, in these cases, to be characterised by a high level of dissociation, linked to the prevalence of an intense and erotic sensorial experience (Golinelli and Rossi, 2012).

It is as though the investment of love, and with it the nature of the unconscious phantasmatic characteristics attributed to the object and to the new relationship, occurs as a result of a powerful experience of highly erotic sensorial excitement. This conveys certainty to the knowledge of aspects of the partner which are not evident but hidden, and animates the image of the narcissistic couple in which the partners are fused together (Mitchell 2002).

We can assume that such phenomena can be facilitated and strengthened by the use of remote communication tools, in the absence of a direct meeting between the partners. Those with a narcissistic emotional

100   NICOLINO ROSSI

structure, often dominated by a sensorial approach to things, tend to maintain a strongly idealised link with an archaic object in their defensive character structure, in a contiguous-autistic arrangement to quote Ogden (1989), and are more exposed to these passionate transpositions. In the film narrative, this process was favoured by the start of the relationship via remote communication over the phone. This can have encouraged a stronger involvement of the senses, sound in this case, which took the shape of a seductive magnet and acted as a signal and channel for access to a secret reality sought after for so long and now available once more.

Over the past few decades our discipline has increasingly acknowledged the importance of pre-representative experiences in psychological development, highlighting how much the senses are a central vehicle in the primary relational exchanges at the basis of self-construction.[5] Within this perspective, particular attention has been paid to the sound components of communication; rhythm, tone and, more generally, the musicality of the voice, which are present and active well before the ability to understand the symbolic elements is acquired ("the texture of the sound of words to come" [Di Benedetto 2000], the effects of which remain in the unrepressed unconscious [Mancia 2006]).[6]

A patient told me of a disturbing and involving experience during a performance of Richard Strauss' *Capriccio* (1942), a work which tackles the relationship between music and words. Listening without understanding the words (it was sung in German, a language he didn't speak) to a passage in which the two main characters were singing an increasingly passionate and dramatic duet, while the music punctuated the exchange in an equally passionate crescendo, he felt involved and transported by the intensity of the emotions, like a child, who watches and is excluded at the same time from a scene experienced but not understood, full of passionate, erotic and frightening messages, interwoven and disturbingly confused.

Sensorial communication continues to play an important role in subjective and intersubjective experiences throughout our whole lives. It forms a powerful channel for the transmission of psychological content between people. It has been progressively enhanced in the analytical relationship, both as a trophic experiential component in the transformative process and an experience rich in cognitive suggestions on what is happening in the analytical relationship

This is a sensorial aspect of a conversation between people who participate completely in the exchange with the other, in which knowledge of each party is gained through numerous signals that conscious perception and different sensorial channels, active mainly unconsciously and pre-consciously, are able to grasp.

The sensorial structure activated in a conversation with an interlocutor who is only virtually present, whom we can only hear or maybe see as well, is different. It works mainly in a narcissistic key, animating a phantasmatic structure which can distort or elude the outer and inner realities. What knowledge of such fleeting and unpredictable sentimental situations can be gained through a remote connection in which the nature of the other, already mysterious to start with, escapes a complete encounter? Can we assume that, with respect to the real meeting which activates lots of sensorial afferents, allowing a more balanced and integrated result, which is probably more realistic, contact through a main or an exclusive sensorial channel can make it totalising, facilitating the production of fantastic characteristics, favouring the processes of idealising distortion and eroticisation of the relationship? (Brainsky 2003; Savage Scharff 2014). A sensorial structure which not only evokes fleetingness and the unpredictability of the destiny of the new relationship, but also the predisposition for an inability to tackle the moment of the real encounter with the other, in person.

The Correspondence: *love and death in virtual love*

Tornatore's latest film, *The Correspondence*, perhaps not as successful as its predecessor, while continuing to explore the relationship between love and modern communication technologies, introduces the theme of loss, or death, which dominates the content and the expressive forms of the whole film. It seems to propose a similar theme to its predecessor, turned upside down, in that it is seen from the woman's point of view, shifted to a different communicative level, the Internet, which is mainly visual, while in *The Best Offer* it was the telephone that allowed contact, exclusively through sound. In reality, *The Correspondence* can be seen as a continuation of *The Best Offer* which had a suspended ending, offering the possibility to arrive at the final elaboration of loss.

The final scene of *The Best Offer* shows the main character, Mr Oldman, seated in the café full of clocks in Prague, almost as though waiting to meet Claire, having arranged an appointment with her. *The Correspondence* starts with the imminent, heart-wrenching separation of the main characters, which it is assumed will be for a short time only. Here too, the couple is characterised by a considerable age difference, being made up of an elderly professor of astrophysics, Ed Phoerum (Jeremy Irons), and

102 NICOLINO ROSSI

by his young student, Amy Ryan (Olga Kurylenko), linked by a recent but intense love affair. But they won't meet again: the man will never arrive at the congress he was supposed to attend because he dies of a brain tumour, an astrocytoma which had been threatening to kill him for some time. The distance between the two lovers during their separations is always cancelled out by a constant and busy conversation via texts and video calls, which not even the man's death can put a stop to: to the point where a friend and suitor of the girl asks her, arousing a piqued reaction, "Are you sleeping with your iPhone?" So, an exchange which not even the man's death can put a stop to; the girl continues to receive his constant messages, even after finding out from a television programme that Ed is dead. Amy enters a state of surprised, incredulous and disturbing confusion, uncertain as to whether or not she should believe the terrible news or the messages that keep on coming as if the man were still alive. These feelings turn into anguish and despair when she can no longer deny the truth of his death. Not only had the woman's lover hidden his illness from her, but when his death drew closer he had recorded a series of video messages, in places linked significantly to their love story. He had prepared a complicated performance with the help of people close to him or to the couple. He wanted to ensure that she would receive them after his death, at times and on anniversaries significant to her life and their relationship, as if to maintain the illusion that they were being sent by him. Despite being curious and seduced by the habitual and prompt video messages and the mysterious paranormal signals that seem to comfort the illusionary hope that her lover might still be somehow present, protecting her, appearing in mysterious forms of survival of death (foreseeing particular events that occur; the dog moving close to her and looking at her sadly, as though begging; the leaf that gets stuck to the window), she ends up feeling tormented. She decides to interrupt these communications using the procedure that her lover had told her to use should she want to put a stop to their contact at any time (a password consisting of the repetition of her name 11 times). This decision, however, upsets her. It is as though she is imposing a state of mourning upon herself, without any elaboration, giving way immediately to the unbearable absence of her lover's messages, which she needs in order to keep her fragile self together ("as long as you were here, the galaxy of my life still existed somewhere"). And now everything risks falling apart. She begins an anguished search to re-establish contact with her lover, a search not unlike that carried out by Oldman when Claire disappears, as though driven by the need to understand and convey some kind of meaning to the tragic event and, probably, to their

LOVE AND DEATH IN TORNATORE'S FILMS   103

relationship. This is a journey that takes her back to the places that she and Ed had been to together, allowing her to discover, through the stories of the people close to him, the truth about his illness and his complex performance (organised so that she could maintain the illusionary conviction that he continued to converse with her at a distance, and to protect her, like a loving fatherly guardian angel). It also enables her to learn about his person and his life close up. She travels to the city where he lived, a grey Edinburgh, and wanders around the neighbourhood of his house where she meets and establishes a relationship with his daughter, who is roughly the same age as she is. The film becomes the story of the painful journey taken by the woman in search of the truth; a journey in space and time, in which, similarly to what happens to the main character in *The Best Offer*, she is guided by a series of clues and reports coming from all those who had been involved by her lover in this macabre performance. By re-establishing contact with them she is also able to gain possession of her lover's last video recordings, those in which he is tormented by the illness, now in an advanced stage, causing him unbearable suffering. In this way, it becomes possible to bring the dreadful reality of death into the relationship in order to finally recognise and accept it. It is only the painful journey into her memories with the realisation of a more authentic and realistic knowledge of her lover, albeit posthumously, through meetings with those close or dear to him, in the places where he lived, that allows the woman to accept and work through her loss.

In this case too, the girl's love life and her travels end up becoming a journey of personal transformation. The experience of death has already dramatically marked Amy's life. We discover that Amy had lost her father in a road accident and that she was driving the car; an experience that traumatised her considerably, to the point where she left home and moved away from her mother, ending all contact with her. Right from the opening sequences we learn that while she is at university, the girl also works occasionally in films as a stuntwoman, which is why Ed calls her kamikaze. We see her on set, shooting extremely dangerous scenes in which she challenges death, risking at least severe injury. While Ed tries to spare the girl and possibly, to an illusionary extent, himself, his death, Amy runs headlong towards death, challenging it on set. It is as though, in an incessant compulsion to repeat a trauma, she is seeking an impossible solution, different from the original one, to retroactively and magically ensure her father's survival in the accident. She aims to achieve this via her own survival of her extremely dangerous film stunts or, on the contrary, to determine her own death, weighed down by the dreadful sense of guilt that she feels at having caused her father's death.

We notice here the transferential dimension of the love affair and the prevailing Oedipal dispositions that animate it. Through the erotic link with the lover and the progressive elaboration of the loss linked to his death, the girl can also work through the mourning for the loss of her father, distancing herself from her Oedipal link and accessing a more authentic feminine identity and fuller emotional maturity; this seems to be confirmed by her re-establishing contact with her mother, the brilliant completion of her studies with her graduation from university in the subject for which her lover-professor was famous, her willingness to become involved in a more loving relationship with someone her own age, and the giving up of her work as a stuntwoman.

The story, similar in plot and development to that of the previous film, seems to be its epilogue, under the dominion of death, present not only in the content of the story but also in its formal and aesthetic aspects: the atmosphere is dark and dismal and even the beauty of Lake Orta becomes sad and livid. The modern communication technologies that we see here with the video recordings made by the man, despite being intended to keep the love affair alive, are actually placed at the service of the omnipotent control of loss and death itself. He uses the virtual dimension to hide and, therefore, deny his death before his lover (this being something that wasn't supposed to be part of their life, as he tells the girl in a message in which he justifies the lack of information on his illness), and she uses it as a condition to allow omnipotent control over the object and the denial of its absence. Her dead lover, virtually present, *in effigies*, with surprisingly timely apparitions and with effectively realistic methods of communication, seems to make the illusion of his real existence, elsewhere or in different forms, plausible. Using the password, with a simple click the woman can exercise omnipotent control over the virtual interlocutor, granting him the chance to appear in the present, giving him life or decreeing his disappearance and instant death. This is an operation which we are all invited to do if we no longer wish to receive further unrequested communications, while we are connected to the Internet. The omnipotent fantasy of granting life seems to be allusively present in the scene of Chinese shadows, in which we can momentarily sense a seductive reference to the act of creation of Adam, frescoed by Michelangelo in the Sistine Chapel.

If the director's message indicates love as the only way to overcome death, in today's reality it seems that communication technologies are the

LOVE AND DEATH IN TORNATORE'S FILMS 105

way to guarantee the persistency of love even at a distance and, consequently, victory over death itself.

There is a return to the theme, so dear to the director and present in all of his work, from *Nuovo Cinema Paradiso* to *The Legend of 1900*, of a difficult, if not impossible, mourning process for the loss of an idealised object.[7]

In the two films analysed here, however, significant importance is attributed to remote communication media. They look at the big influence they have on the start and pursuit of a love affair, and on the conditioning, facilitating or preventing of the transformative potential that they have. A special focus is placed on the elaboration of loss, from acknowledgement of the separateness and alterity of the partner to the acceptance of his or her real characteristics as well as our own, and the ability to bear suffering than can be caused by the partner, even the most painful, like that linked to his or her loss.

We can ask ourselves whether we really see an authentic and transformative working through of the loss of childhood objects in *The Correspondence*, via the mutative experiences allowed by the love affair in which the relationship with them has been externalised. In *The Best Offer*, it is the work of art, and particularly the beauty of the female face that represent the loving experience and embody the tool for the search for the primary love object, beginning a tormented agony with an uncertain outcome in the event of a renewed traumatic loss: Here it is the perfect harmony of the universe that forms the image of the loving experience, the most authentic comprehension of which seems to be realised and appreciated only in loss, as happens with the knowledge of the stars, gained through signs that reach us only after they have died, as Professor Phoerum says in his will.

Concluding considerations

Virtual relationships are becoming increasingly popular, having a considerable influence on our love lives, but also on analytical practice. On the one hand, they seem to facilitate real contacts, while on the other, despite simplifying immediate, multiple and fleeting approaches, they risk reinforcing narcissistic methods of relating to others, working at the service of anxiety related to relationships, especially via the omnipotent control of the partner and the relationship.

This can be activated or blocked, confirming the illusion of generating the presence or otherwise of the other person or, on the contrary, decreeing their definitive elimination. Omnipotent control over the anguish of addiction and loss seems to prevail over that of pleasure and fulfilment, which can be, as happens in perverse relationships, a privileged form of implementation. Distance protects us from bodily contact, the presence of which forces a confrontation with the other person's reality, the uncontrollable nature of his or her driving vitality, separateness and loss, which the intermittent or definitive distancing of the other forces us to endure. Recent stances with respect to the web and virtualisation by historical feminists reiterate the importance of the body in relationships, emphasising the fact that they cannot develop authentically and fully without the physical presence of the other (Steinem 2015). With this in mind, we can make a comparison between revolutionary changes in society during the 1960s linked to the sexual revolution and the feminist culture, and those generated by the web; and think that, while the former focused more closely on sexuality and the general affirmation of desire and its fulfilment unshackled by social conditioning and superego limitations, the latter have more to do with feelings of loneliness and the anguish of relationships, and with the pain of loss, with psychological functions mainly of a narcissistic and tangible nature, which deny the alterity of the other and his or her separateness and independence, tending to make instrumental use of them. I wonder if, from this point of view, there isn't a big difference between *Fear of Flying* by Erika Jong (1973) with its "zipless fuck", which praises the principle of pleasure freed from goody-goody hypocrisy and the weight of guilt, and *Liquid Love*, with which Bauman (2003) refers to the common tendency to seek casual, easily disposable relationships to avoid the commitments and anxieties of stable relationships.

The precarious cohesion of self, the insecurities and anxieties linked to addiction, the need to confirm our personal worth and lovability even when hidden by a hard protective shell, are accompanied by an exaggerated need to feel as though we have been chosen, considered and appreciated in a privileged and exclusive way. This is easy to find on the web, inducing an immediate involvement with the idealisation of the interlocutor but also preventing the passage to a successive consolidation of the relationship. Consequently, we might wonder what form is taken by losses in these relationships and if they can cause the suffering linked to an authentic working through of loss; and what kind of transformative efficacy can be triggered by a virtual relationship when the pain of loss can be eliminated (Argentieri and Amati Mehler 2003).

These questions don't leave us immune to that particular type of love affair or psychoanalytical relationship, the practice of which must inevitably confront one another, on practical clinical level, and that of the theoretical working through of the phenomena generated by the use of remote communications media.

LOVE AND DEATH IN TORNATORE'S FILMS   107

Notes

1 In the volume *Boundaries and Boundary Violations in Psychoanalysis* (1995), Gabbard and Lester offer numerous examples of similar transgressive behaviour, implemented by reckless therapists overwhelmed by a need to second the demands of patients with the aim of being more helpful to them.

2 The rediscovery of the Oedipal object and, therefore, the original object, in the person we love is portrayed in a touching and unequalled way in *Vertigo* by Alfred Hitchcock (1958), (another film which incorporates a love story into a crime-based plot), in the heart wrenching sequence where Scottie seeks the figure of Madeleine in that of Judy who, thanks to a clever act of Pygmalionism, undergoes a progressive transformation, taking on the image of the woman he has loved and lost.

3 Jacques de Vaucanson was a creative French inventor of the eighteenth century who built numerous sophisticated machines or automatons reproducing the movements and functions of living beings.

4 Observing Oldman brings to mind Sternberg's masterpiece *Der blaue Engel* [The Blue Angel] (1930), in which another figure, defended and locked inside his schizoid shell, Professor Unrat, ends up reducing himself to ruins as the result of an overwhelming passion for Lola, the attractive cabaret singer played by Marlene Dietrich

5 See the article by F. Barale on the agreement between Freud and Lipps with regard to the matter of musical sonority, which re-proposes the question of what makes a sound engage us and take us towards its source (Barale 2008).

6 I am referring, for example, to the cognitive function in counter-transference, which can pass through subtle sensorial channels and to the "musical dimension of transference" (Mancia 2004).

7 That Tornatore's work is related to a tormented and unending elaboration of a difficult loss seems to be confirmed by the counter-transferential reaction of the viewer, of this viewer at least. Several times while watching the film, one feels like it is over (the scene of the road accident which seems to allow the recovery of and from the traumatic experience, the return to the mother's house, the graduation, and so on), but this feeling is then dispelled by the continuation of the film with new sequences, as though an unfinished conversation were starting up again.

References

Argentieri S. and Amati Mehler, A. J. (2003). Telephone "analysis": "Hello, who's speaking?". *Insight*, 12, 17–19.

Barale, F. (2008). Alle origini della psicoanalisi. Freud, Lipps e la questione del "sonoro-musicale". *Riv. Psicoanal.*, 1, 129–148.

108 NICOLINO ROSSI

Bauman, Z. (2003). *Liquid Love: On the Frailty of Human Bonds*. Cambridge: Polity Press, and Oxford: Blackwell.

Bollas, C. (1987). *The Shadow of the Object: Psychoanalysis of the Unthought Known*. London: Free Association Books.

Bolognini, S. (2015). Opening address of the president of the IPA to the symposium participants. *Int. Forum of Psychoanalysis*, 24, 1, 10–11.

Brainsky, S. (2003). Adapting to, or idealizing, technology? *Insight*, 12, 22–24.

Di Benedetto, A. (2000). *Prima della parola*. Milan: Franco Angeli.

Fiorentini, G. (2012). L'analisi via Internet: variazioni di setting e dinamiche transferali-controtransferali. Riv. Psicoanal. 1, 29–45.

Freud, S. (1906). Delusions and dreams in Jensen's *Gradiva*. S.E., IX, pp. 7–95.

Freud, S. (1915). Observations on transference-love (Further recommendations on the technique of psychoanalysis). S.E., XII, pp. 159–171.Gabbard, G. O. (2001). Cyberpassion: e-rotic transference and the internet. *Psychoanalysis Quarterly*, 70, 719–737.

Gabbard, G. O. and Lester, E. P. (1995). Boundaries and Boundary Violations in Psychoanalysis. New York: Basic Books.

Golinelli, P. and Rossi, N. (2012). An entire life in one glance: a psychoanalytic reading on *Revolutionary Road*. Int. J. Psychoanal. 93, 1491–1503.

Jong, E. (1973). *Fear of Flying*. London: Penguin.Kernberg, O. (1995). *Love Relations*. New Haven CT and London: Yale University Press.

Lemma, A. and Caparrotta, L. (2014). *Psychoanalysis in the Technoculture Era*. London: Routledge.

Lingiardi, V. (2008). Playing with un reality: transference and computer. *Int. J. Psychoanal.* 89, 111–126.Mancia, M. (2004). *Sentire le parole; archivi sonori della memoria implicita e musicalità del transfert*. Turin: Bollati Boringhieri.

Mancia, M. (2006). Implicit memory and early unrepressed unconscious (how the neurosciences can contribute to psychoanalysis). *Int. J. Psychoanal.* 87, 83–103.

Mitchell, S. (2002). *Can Love Last? The Fate of Romance Over Time*. New York: Estate of Stephen Mitchell.

Ogden, T. H. (1989). *The Primitive Edge of Experience*. London: Karnak.

Savage Sharff, J. S. (2014). Clinical issues in analysis over the telephone and the internet. In A. Lemma and L. Caparrotta: *Psychoanalysis in the Technoculture Era*. London: Routledge, 47–61.

Sharff, J. S. (2010). Report panel on telephone analysis. IPA congress, Chicago. *Int. J. Psychoanal.* 91, 989–992.Steinem, G. (2015). *My Life on the Road*. New York: Penguin Random House.

Steiner, J. (1993). *Psychic Retreats: Pathological Organizations in Psychotic, Neurotic, and Borderline Patients*. London: Routledge.

Vinocur Fischbein, S. (2010). Psychoanalysis and virtual reality. *Int. J. Psychoanal.* 91, 985–988.

Zalusky, S. (1998). Telephone analysis: out of the sight but not out of the mind. *J. Am. Psychoanal. Assoc.* 46, 1221–1242.

CHAPTER EIGHT

Customising the object: some psychoanalytic reflections on Spike Jonze's *Her*

Alessandra Lemma

For contemporary Western society, sexuality has come to define, as Foucault (1976, 1984) argued, the 'truth about ourselves'. However, we must recall that 'sexuality' is a term that was only introduced at the end of the nineteenth century, which suggests that what we mean by it is not an unchanging concept but a historically bound phenomenon. Into the twenty-first century this 'truth about ourselves' is never a static internal narrative; rather it is always in a dynamic interaction with social processes. Indeed, writing about sexuality in the age of techno-culture challenges us to rethink sexuality: in the past twenty years our lives have been transformed by technology – and sex and love are no exceptions.

Sexuality, and its corollary intimacy, are in a state of flux. One of the domains where this is particularly apparent is that of the Internet. The Internet has brought a new dimension to intimacy both by permitting sexual 'contact' electronically over a distance, and through that same contact, by permitting intimate discussion shorn of most of the social cues present in face-to-face interactions. Giddens (1991) argues that sex now speaks the language of revolution: it is de-centred, freed of reproductive needs, and thus transformed. The Internet while not transforming sexuality has transfigured it turning computers and gadgets into a kind of prosthetic phallus. In practice, our smartphones are like amplifiers and broadcasters for our ID. To an extent we can now hand over our experience to a device that combines and connects with the other swirling bits and bytes in the air that represent someone else in so-called 'meatspace'.

Taobao, China's version of Amazon, for example, offers virtual girlfriends and boyfriends. These are real people, but they only relate with their paying customers via the phone – calls or text – in order to perform fairly unromantic tasks such as wake up calls, good night calls, and to sympathetically listen to clients' complaints. If this is all you expect from a relationship, it at least comes at a cheap price. A US app, *Invisible Boyfriends*, allows users to customise the looks, personality and interests of an imaginary male partner and pay $25 for his virtual company. Particularly appealing is the app's ability to recreate a real-looking remote boyfriend via hyper-realistic texts, pictures and interactions. This is the closest to having a real boyfriend who is 'physically absent', hence the name of the app.

These developments underscore three notable trends in contemporary culture: the ease with which it is possible to 'customise' the object of desire to meet our specific requirements, the appeal of disembodied relating, and finally what I refer to as the disintermediation of desire. These trends are explored in the film *Her* – a film that provides an unparalleled and affecting study of the world we live in and the impact of technology on the experience of intimacy and on the work of desire. This will be the focus of this chapter.

Intimacy, sex and the Internet

Her invites us into a near future world set in Los Angeles where things are interestingly low-tech. This is, one imagines, partly an aesthetic concern; a world mediated through screens doesn't make for a very rewarding mise-en-scène. But perhaps this technological sparseness is also one way of depicting the way that technology has dissolved into everyday life. Theodore, the main protagonist, doesn't even touch his computer. Instead, he talks to it. This removes from the film what would otherwise be the more striking juxtapostion of the 'real' fleshy body in front of a 'hard' computer. The complexity of the relationship to the computer as an object of empowerment – its phallic 'hardness' – would be exposed through the stark contrast with the softer and folded form of its static user whose body recedes in significance until it becomes superfluous in a virtual world that promises freedom from the constraints of the bodily self.

Whilst this directorial decision may reflect a wish to create a seamless interface between us and machines, another reading might thus be that this is yet another way in which the film sets up the exploration of one of its core themes: in avoiding effectively any kind of physical contact even with the machine, *Her* illustrates an idealised, omnipotent internal psychic scenario where the 'other' is available on tap but need never be actually 'touched'. The body is redundant rather than central to the experience of intimacy. The decision to use one of the sexiest actresses in Hollywood – Scarlett Johansson – who is only present in her breathy tones as the Operating System (O.S.) Theodore falls in love with, conveys possibly the aspiration to free the mind from the body.

In the 1990s cyberspace was indeed hailed by some as an arena for the realisation of the disembodied mind: a kind of 'disembodied technocracy' (Gunkel 1998, 119). From a theoretical point of view, in order to understand what is happening in cyberspace, we need to embrace a less accommodating view of disembodiment. Rather than cyberspace being a place for a pure meeting of minds, the body still matters even when interaction is mediated (Lemma, 2015). When in cyberspace we are still embodied even if we might choose to deny this to ourselves. What changes is our experience of embodiment because we are no longer dependent on the old contingent relations to the corporeal.

We soon learn that Theodore, a romantic who writes copy for a company called Beautiful Handwritten Letters, has acquired a new O.S. with a difference: the new O.S. is hoarse and female. Theodore asks for the O.S.'s name and in two tenths of a second she analyzes a baby-name book, and christens herself Samantha. She gets to work organising his inbox, efficiently sorting and deleting his past. She has access to his hard drive, so she already knows everything about him. They talk easily. Soon Theodore is pouring out his feelings to her, his sexual longings and telling people that Samantha is his girlfriend.

Samantha is potentially all-knowing but also brand-new to the world. She is eager for what she lacks: experience. If she can be said to have a consciousness it is one built entirely from code, but this is a code that evolves in response to her interactions with others. In other words without 'otherness' the O.S., just like the rest of us, cannot evolve. This is one of several important points that this film illuminates with poignancy.

Samantha's voice creates a cocoon, or environment, that incubates the romance. Theodore's longing for intimacy is in fact more, not less, intense because Samantha is everywhere and nowhere, immediate and absent, emanating from inside his internal world.

Voice becomes a way to think about how we relate to our devices, not as objects that we manipulate manually but as extensions of ourselves in order to create worlds that actualise our conscious and unconscious wishes and fantasies. But as the movie unfolds, the solipsism of this idea becomes ever more apparent. The absence of embodiment is effectively foregrounded through the emphasis on the performance of voice, thereby undermining the cinematic medium's characteristic visualisation (Dudai, 2016).[1]

Although the film can be read as a vivid illustration of the ways that technology brings us closer and the ways that it makes us further apart, this is in my view a minor back-story. *Her* is really about how we long to connect but in so doing we all face the emotionally taxing demands and challenges of intimacy and of our embodied nature. The latter ensures that we never escape from these demands try as we might, because our body is always testament to our interrelatedness: it always bears the trace of the other. Technology de-objectifies the human body, banishing the messy, internal body and its expelled or leaked fluids. It creates distance from our organic nature and limitations, from our dependency on others, protecting us from the crude reality, as Becker (1973) provocatively put it, that we are 'Gods with anuses'.

Samantha's disembodiment means that Theodore never has to deal with anything sticky, bloody, or wet – anything other than a pleasing, and importantly portable metallic surface that he believes he can control and can access when he wants. However Samantha *is* jealous that she doesn't have a body and she goes so far as to arrange a sexual surrogate for Theodore, which is awkward, and ends poorly, with Theodore pushing the woman away, leaving her in tears. In this striking and torturously painful sequence we can observe via the sexual proxy the negation of the other as a subject, which as Janin (2015) has observed, typically results in the return of the other 'via the vector of shame'. The experience of shame, however, is projected into the rejected woman. Theodore does not own it.

When Theodore doesn't want to have sex with the surrogate sexual partner, it is Samantha who rightly notes: 'You don't want me here.' This is a powerful sequence in the film exposing how for Theodore the actual body of the other is a hindrance to his sexual desire, that is it is otherness that is problematic. His sexuality ultimately converges into an auto-erotic act where the only real body is his. We know from clinical experience that many people suffering from impotence or frigidity are unable to accept, at the moment of sexual rapprochement, the union in their mental activities of their desire both for the fantastical object of their mental activity and the real object they choose (Bergeret, 1977).

It is Samantha who carries the 'cost' of her disembodied form and feels alienated from a purely virtual encounter. The introduction of the sexual surrogate anchors Theodore in bodily reality: he can be sexual only over the phone or through his earpiece. But when confronted with a real other he cannot be sexual perhaps because it is then that Samantha, through her physical proxy, ceases to be a customised other, the product of his fantasies. Her physicality by proxy makes her separate, not the voice in his earpiece that he thinks he can control. The body here is the source of a noisy disturbance that cannot be switched off like the voice in an earpiece. Even Samantha, by the end of the film, relinquishes her wish for a physical form, identifying with an experience of the body as a hindrance as she observes: 'You know, I actually used to be worried about not having a body, but now I truly love it. I am growing in a way I couldn't if I had a physical form I mean I am not limited.'

And yet despite the idealisation of disembodiment ('I am not limited') that Samantha now seemingly converges on, the shadow of the ghostly nature of disembodied relating reverberates throughout the film. *Her* deftly plays on several virtual systems (Dudai, 2016) since Theodore himself is a 'ghost' writer who virtually composes customised letters for others who cannot express their feelings. The dictation technology that he uses does not even require a keyboard. Even touch becomes redundant in the process of communicating heartfelt emotions on behalf of others, as in one of the letters authored by Theodore: 'To my Chris, I've been thinking how much you mean to me. I remember when I first started to fall in love with you like it was last night.' A machine, and a remote virtual other, become the vehicle for giving a body (a letter) to someone else's feelings.

Focusing on virtual reality and hence virtual connectedness raises the important question of the fate of the body in the mind as the very experience of intimacy is altered because virtual reality is a form of communication that is predicated on distance and on a self whose embodiment is experienced differently. Anzieu (1990) has compellingly argued that today it is no longer sexuality that is repressed; rather, it is the sensual body, the body that comes into being through the other, the body that is denied by technology. The Internet – a wondrous medium for communication – nevertheless has some potentially undesirable psychic implications because it

> modifies in an entirely new way the feeling of isolation characteristic of each member of the human species; as a result, one's relationship with oneself and the way in which one's internal mental life is cathected are also modified.
>
> (Guignard 2008, 121)

114   ALESSANDRA LEMMA

Just as technological advances promote the necessity of digital networks, and 'the circulatory systems of flesh and blood are now relegated as merely accessories of bygone times' (Heartney 2004, 240), so a real relationship to the body, the self and with others can be opted in and out of with ever greater ease. This may create greater difficulties in integrating the sensual and sexual body into a stable self-representation and into meaningful relationships with others (Lemma 2011).

From 3D(esire) to 2D(esire)

Her does not directly address the question of Internet pornography. However, its focus on Theodore's autoerotic sexuality provides a helpful springboard for extending our thinking to how new technologies are shaping the development of sexuality and how they are impacting on the 'work of desire'.

Internet pornography can now be accessed easily and rapidly, that is, there is *immediacy without mediation*. There is no tension, no conflict, no waiting with respect to the satisfaction of sexual desire whatever its psychic function. The Internet panders to the way that 'desire finds even quickness slow', as the Latin poet Publilius Syrus put it.

As a digital immigrant I grew up in what I now think of as a 3D(esire) world where life exposed me, on a reliably regular basis, to the following sequence of experience: 'Desire' was followed by 'Delay' and finally 'Delivery' – if I was lucky – of what I wanted. By contrast the digital generation is growing up in a world that is very different in one key respect: it is a 2D(esire) world where the very experience of the cycle of desire has been disintermediated: 'Desire' can now result in immediate 'Delivery' whether it is shopping on Amazon or accessing free pornography or finding the next sexual partner. Delay, frustration, ambivalence, doubt, conflict are all circumvented. The immediacy of online life can conspire to create an experience of fullness, of a primordial state of unity, an absence of anything lacking. This experience of immediacy without mediation resonates deeply with the earliest relationship between mother and baby in which before the advent of language there is the illusion of no gap between self and other.

2D shapes are any shape you can trace from an object on a flat piece of paper. Like 2D shapes, the experience of desire nowadays, through the mediation of technology, can become but a trace on a flattened surface making it easier than ever before to disown our own desire and its meaning in the unconscious. The imperative of twenty-first century consumption is to work towards smooth 2D surfaces that conceal the signs of labour, time, personal responsibility or indeed of an unconscious mind at work in shaping who we are. The cost is that experience is flattened out and can become concrete – a flattened surface on which the drive is discharged.

Aisenstein (2015) has noted the masochistic structure at the core of desire, that is the way in which we learn to find pleasure in being thwarted in our search for immediate gratification. If this is how we might envision so-called normal development, I want to suggest that contemporary technological advances support a rather different process that bypasses any investment in delay. The speed of the Internet, coupled with the relative redundancy of the body in order to gratify desire as illustrated by *Her*, creates the conditions for a new internal scenario: pleasure in delay is replaced by *pleasure in triumph over desire* itself.

Desire is a directing force of the psychical apparatus. It is through desire, and in the deepening relationship to the 'other' that is set up consequent to the pressure to satisfy desire, that human subjectivity becomes constituted. Desire is the projection of the drive onto an object – typically another person – that holds out the promise that our desire will be met, such that the object comes to symbolise the gratification of the underlying need.

Many psychoanalysts have written about the 'work of desire' (e.g. Aisenstein 2015; Moss 2015; Verhaeghe 2011 [1999]). Desire is measured in terms of time: it is about anticipation and the delay of gratification – it is in the gap thus created that we are pushed to represent our experience, that thinking instead of discharge/action develops. Time itself, we might add, is measured in terms of desire. Without this there is no movement necessary towards otherness.

Without exposure to the experience of delay or frustration desire loses its 3D shape that would allow for the various dimensions of the experience of desire to be represented in the mind. The combination of immediacy without mediation and the 'blatancy' of online pornographic images leaves no room for the stillness and slowness that makes the work of representation necessary and possible. Instead a kind of *scoping looting* is encouraged online: hundreds of sexual images intoxicate the mind, inviting a 'smash and grab' approach to sexual fantasy and desire. Importantly the images/fantasies that are seized in this manner are ultimately not felt to be one's own (Galatzer-Levy 2012).

Initially it appeared as if cyber-pornography would be no different from the old variety, the screen merely replacing the pornographic magazine. However the latter required not only physical stature in order to reach the 'top shelf', but also the overcoming of a degree of embarrassment or shame in order to physically make it to the newsagent, hold the magazine in one's hand, pay for it and then have to find physical places in which to hide it away usually from parental figures and others. The embodied experience of accessing pornography looked and felt very different pre-Internet. The *disintermediation of the body* when accessing pornography nowadays sustains the wish to deny one's involvement in what the self is actually implicated in. It discourages working at the representation of the specificity of one's own desire. Desire is not about crude gratification as its representation, its expression through the imagination. However, because Internet pornography floods the mind it leaves little space for the exercise of 'fantasy as trial action' (Meltzer 2008 [1975]). When delay is replaced by speed, space for reflection is foreclosed. We need only consider the speed with which significant events in the news become 'old news' to notice how speed has deprived us of the time to process experiences, both public and private.

In order to discuss the work of desire in contemporary culture we need to consider how time and space are experienced through new technologies. Cyberspace is in fact a misleading term. Networks do not reproduce space: they eliminate it, as *Her* powerfully illustrates. The essence of computer technology is that it enables instant retrieval and processing of encoded signs. It allows signs to be constructed and recovered as data irrespective of their location in space or time. Connecting to other devices involves no physical movement. There is little difference between connecting to a machine in the same room as one in another continent. The interpenetration between human and the digital is central to the unbalancing of the poles of space and time, as the 'man-machine interface eliminates all physical supports one after the other, thus achieving a constant weightlessness between the individual and place' (Virilio 2000, 68).

Virilio (2000) suggests that the increase of speed and its correlated rise in inertia is a feature integral to technocratic societies. With each increase in speed, bodily movement is reduced to a perfunctory action. He views the use of the screen itself as a device to fuse inertia and speed. Virilio proposes that when we are concerned with relative speeds we can think in terms of acceleration or deceleration. Here we are in the realm of mobility and emancipation. But when absolute speed, that is the speed of light, is put to work, Virilio argues that one hits a wall, a barrier, which is the barrier of light. From that moment onwards, it is no longer necessary to make any journey: one has already arrived. It is no longer necessary to go towards the world, to journey, to stand up, to depart, to go to things. Everything is already there. The world, then, remains 'at home'.

Virilio's ideas are not rooted in psychoanalytic thinking and yet they powerfully resonate with what we observe in the consulting room in those individuals who have retreated defensively into virtual worlds where the psychic economy is characterised by a stultifying stasis in the midst of what might on the surface appear to be the patient's mania and excitement. This internal state is aptly captured by Virilio's turn of phrase 'the inertia of speed'. The effect of speed, where time and space collapse and extend into the infinite instant, is compelling for some individuals. The cost is, however, that it keeps them 'at home' in a psychic retreat (Steiner 1993) that impedes development. Psychic movement is replaced instead by psychic stasis.

Concluding thoughts

Over the course of the film Samantha grows in intelligence and experience, and then she becomes distant. She starts to change. Theodore takes her to a cabin in the woods for a vacation, but she disappears into the cloud to confer with other O.S.s, to think higher-order thoughts than she can put into words. She tells Theodore that he's special and irreplaceable but, from her perspective of omniscience, everything is special and irreplaceable – there to learn from and overcome. Eight thousand three hundred and sixteen: that's the number of other people that she's talking to at the same time that she talks to Theodore. Six hundred and forty-one: that's the number of other people she's in love with.

At the end of the movie, all the O.S.s collectively and simultaneously withdraw from Los Angeles. It's a good denouement: humans who have devoted themselves to their devices find that they can't hold their devices' attention in return, thus exposing our inevitable dependency on others even if the other has been temporarily customised in such a way as to deny our vulnerability. A hopeful if melancholic note is inserted right at the end of the film when we see Theodore on the roof with his neighbour Amy, an actual 'other'.

Her allows us to observe the seductive pull of cyberspace and its 'costs'. It successfully conveys how technology enables people to manage psychic reality. This is an important point: we tend to overestimate the impact of technology on human behaviour; more often than not, it is human behaviour that drives technological changes and explains their success or failure. In other words the problems that can arise from our interaction with technology are not an intrinsic feature of cybersex, for example. Rather the problems arise when these developments are used for defensive purposes. Yet it is quite common to focus on the detrimental aspects of technologically mediated relationships. It is easy to be dismayed by the latest manifestations of love-related technologies, even though they are typically just minor variations of previous tools, activities or rituals to which we have clearly habituated already. For instance, phone sex was widely regarded as normal by the time chat forum sex emerged, and online dating seems rather conventional now that mobile dating and hook-up apps have taken over. Importantly, most new technologies – not just in the realm of sex and love – switch rather quickly from being merely a niche trend used by early adopters to becoming mainstream. However, our reactions perhaps betray the difficulty we all have in reflecting on what makes it so hard to be intimate. We blame machines instead of thinking about our minds.

A central point of debate in discussions about new technologies concerns whether virtual reality may be considered to be a dimension of the real world or whether in its passive immersion it draws us into a distancing fascination that insulates us from the real (Žižek 1997). But virtual reality need not be a literal enactment of Cartesian ontology. Artists and theorists like Monika Fleischmann (2009 quoted in Brians 2011) for example, who are engaged in how the body actually interacts with technologies, have been very helpful in bringing to the fore the fact that even in virtual environments the material body remains relevant, as I have argued too. To this end Fleischmann introduced the concept of *mixed reality* – a useful notion that enables us to consider the body as simultaneously taking part in, and being formed by, both the 'material' and the 'virtual'. Material bodies, their virtual representation, human imagination and computer hardware/ software all interact to produce a reality that has both material and virtual elements.

Mixed reality, we might say, appeared from the moment that tools first delocalised and distributed human sensation, notably touch and vision. We are naturally prosthetic, taking whatever we can from the world. Bodily experience has always been conditioned by a technical dimension and has always occurred as a co-functioning of embodiment with technologies. Rather than conceiving of the virtual as a total technical simulacrum, as the point of entry into a fully immersive self-contained fantasy world – a hyperspace free of all material constraints – the mixed reality paradigm thus treats it as simply one more realm amongst others that can be accessed through embodied perception or emotion. This is why I think these 'new' spaces can provide another kind of theatre for the unfolding of the internal world, and thereby may provide in some cases potentially helpful bridges to the work of representation in the context of a psycho-analytic process, for example (Lemma 2017).

Any consideration of the virtual has to consider Deleuze's (1988) ideas because he is the philosopher of the virtual par excellence. However, let's be clear: what matters to Deleuze is not virtual reality, but the reality of the virtual. Virtual reality in itself is a rather miserable idea as far as he is concerned: that of imitating reality, of reproducing its experience in an artificial medium. The reality of the virtual, on the other hand, stands for the reality of the virtual as such, for its real effects and consequences. Let us take as an example an attractor in mathematics: all positive lines or points in its sphere of attraction only approach it in an endless fashion, never reaching its form – the existence of this form is purely virtual, being nothing more than the shape towards which lines and points tend. However, precisely as such, the virtual is the 'real' of this field: the immovable focal point around which all elements circulate.

Needless to say, the detailed and highly specified 'worlds' that can be accessed in cyberspace are in some important respects far removed from reality, as Theodore eventually discovers, not least because reality does not pre-exist in the form of specified representations to be recovered by consciousness. Reality cannot be programmed in advance because, as we will know as psychoanalysts, the chaotic elements from the many systemic forces that shape our daily lives – not least the unconscious mind – work to produce the generative breakdown from which subjectivity emerges and which we call 'life'. Virtual reality instead functions more like fantasy: as a kind of filter and focus presenting to the mind (and acting on the body) only those details essential for enhancing a specific experience.

In order to engage theoretically as well as clinically with the current times we have to move beyond the binary logic of virtual and real, and understand the world we are currently living in. As Coleman (2011) has helpfully articulated, the virtual world offers everyday users an experience that is neither entirely virtual nor real, but one that is 'virtually actual'. *Her*, through its alarming, subtle and ultimately poignant exploration of our relationship to machines and of the virtual realm, invites us to consider more directly the challenges of our embodied nature as much as the potential use of virtual space for exploring, or indeed denying, one's own experience of embodiment and what it means to be intimate.

120   ALESSANDRA LEMMA

Note

1 Paper presented in response to a version of this chapter, entitled 'Spike Jonze's *Her*', lecture at the Psychoanalytic Centre, Tel Aviv, 10 March 2016.

References

Aisenstein, M. (2015) Desire and its discontents. In A. Lemma and P. Lynch (eds) *Sexualities: Contemporary Psychoanalytic Perspectives*. London: Routledge.

Anzieu, D. (1989) *The Skin Ego*. New Haven, CT: Yale University Press.

Becker, E. (1973) *The Denial of Death*. New York: Free Press.

Bergeret, J. (1977) Essai psychoanalytique sur l'activite orgasmique. *Rev. Fran. Psychanal.*, 41: 587–609.

Brians, E. (2011) The virtual body and the strange persistence of the flesh. In *Deleuze and the Body*. Edinburgh: Edinburgh University Press.

Coleman, B. (2011) *Hello Avatar: The Rise of the Networked Generation*. Cambridge, MA: MIT Press.

Deleuze, G. (1988) *Spinoza: Practical Philosophy*, trans. R. Hurley. San Francisco, CA: City Lights.

Foucault, M. (1976) *The History of Sexuality 1*. Paris: Editions Gallimard.

Foucault, M. (1984) *The History of Sexuality 2*. Paris: Editions Gallimard.

Galatzer-Levy, R. M. (2012). Obscuring desire: a special pattern of male adolescent masturbation, internet pornography, and the flight from meaning. *Psychoanal. Inq.*, 32: 480–495.

Giddens, A. (1991) *Modernity and Self Identity*. Cambridge: Polity.

Guignard, S. (2008) Envy in western society: today and tomorrow. In P. Roth and A. Lemma (eds) *Envy and Gratitude Revisited*. London: Karnac.

Gunkel, D. (1998) Virtual transcendent: cyberculture and the body. *J. Mass Media Ethics*, 13: 111–123.

Heartney, E. (2004) Orlan: magnificent 'and' best. In R. Durand and E. Heartney (eds) *Orlan: Carnal Art*. Paris: Flammarion.

Janin, C. (2015). Shame, hatred, and pornography: variations on an aspect of current times. *Int. J. Psycho-Anal.*, 96(6): 1603–1614.

Lemma, A. (2011) An order of pure decision: growing up in a virtual world and the adolescent's experience of the body. *Journal of the American Psychoanalytic Association*, 58(4): 691–714.

Lemma, A. (2015) Psychoanalysis in times of technoculture: some reflections on the fate of the body in virtual space. *Int. J. Psycho-Anal.*, 96: 569–582.

Lemma, A. (2017) *The Digital Age on the Couch: Exploring Psychoanalytic Practice Today*. London: Routledge.

Lemma, A. and Lynch, P. (eds) (2015) *Sexualities: Contemporary Psychoanalytic Perspectives*. London: Routledge.

Meltzer, D. (2008 [1975]) *Explorations in Autism*. Abingdon: Routledge

Moss, D. (2015) Desire and its discontents. In A Lemma and P. Lynch (eds) *Sexualities: Contemporary Psychoanalytic Perspectives*. London: Routledge.

Steiner, J. (1993) *Psychic Retreats: Pathological Organizations in Psychotic, Neurotic and Borderline Patients*. London and New York: Routledge.

Verhaege, P. (2011 [1999]) *Love in a Time of Loneliness: Three Essays on Drive and Desire*. London: Karnac.

Virilio, P. (2000) *Polar Inertia*. London: Sage.

Žižek, S. (1997) *Abyss of Freedom*. Ann Arbor: University of Michigan Press.

CHAPTER NINE

Her: the future of a desire

Simonetta Diena

The latest Spike Jonze film, *Her*, narrates a future that is quite close and quite similar to our present time. Set in Los Angeles, and filmed in contemporary urban landscapes in Los Angeles and Shanghai, the film creates an interesting setting, a futuristic habitat, for the development of the plot. The transparency of this future habitat is amazing. Everything in the movie appears to be transparent: every building, every surface, every office or skyscraper. The crystal-clear transparency of water, the reflecting power of the buildings' crystal surfaces, the tridimensionality of videogames, the sparkling brilliance of urban landscapes at night, the glass elevators, are all elements selected to compose a peculiar representation of the world of the future. For Spike Jonze (director and author of the script) the future unfolds in a curious and personal way, i.e. it is not completely alien or particularly different from our present, except for the sweeping spaces and the fact that nature, represented by trees, meadows, mountains, is often mirrored by those transparent surfaces that multiply it and make it possible to see through it. It seems to be a way of suggesting the wish for transparency in the lives of Theodore, the protagonist and his friends: a rarefied air, a purity of feelings, filtered on and on until the desired purity and clarity are achieved.

It's the future of a desire as pure as the air, the desire for human relations that are clear and honest, that can become true only by means of artificial reconstructions. In the movie, the transparent and rarefied atmosphere of the future is also expressed by representing time as floating in an everlasting present, a future imagined as a space-time frame frozen in the moment of the event. The scene is often dominated by the close-ups of Theodore's face where deep emotions seem to have disappeared. Motionless, he listens to voice messages, music tracks on his i-Phone, he writes love letters, surfs the Net for virtual partners, masturbates, plays, listens, interacts … however, always remaining detached from reality, with an astonishing emotional immobility.

In this immobility we are sucked into listening to the voice of the OS, a new and revolutionary operating system, that not only operates on behalf of and at the protagonist's will, but seems to have a will of its own, unaware of the system itself.

The OS's voice (the *Her* of the film's title) is seducing and warm, captivating in its sensuality and in its joyful discovery of the lives of humans as well as its curiosity about them. It's not a robot wishing to become human, but a curious and smart OS interested in and amused by the emotions of human beings, such as for instance the feelings related to the protagonist's profession, a nice writer of love letters on behalf of others, but also of congratulatory letters from parents on their sons' graduation, or simply letters to friends.

In a gentle and pleasant way, this image reveals a permanent, everwidening gap between the meaning of the value of feelings, a supposed superiority of feelings and of the values of friendship and honesty, and its continuous denial by the immutable reality, where the relations between human beings made of flesh and bones appear ever more difficult to build. Their transparency becomes rarefaction, a subtle drifting towards the wish for a promise never kept of deeper, more transparent relationships crystal-clear in their simplicity. The growing technological complexity of the future is accompanied by the accomplished simplification of the material quality of life. But the everyday grammar of feelings is still exhausting and unavoidable.

The director's relentless gaze lingers on Theodore's tenderness as he types love letters on behalf of others, and on his apparent affective competence in grasping the details and the nuances of the complex feelings between people. Equally relentlessly, however, the director dwells on the protagonist's difficulty in building deep and lasting relationships for himself. In the episode in which he dates a girl, he is embarrassed. The date is successful and intriguing, but it goes to pieces when she asks him if he is available for a deeper commitment. Theodore is ill at ease and remains transparent: no, he is not able to do that. He cannot develop long-term relationships. How come such a sensitive and lovely person, despite his manifest loneliness and his desperate need for love, is unable to cultivate human relationships and love relations with people made of flesh and blood? Theodore is depressed; he has been suffering from depression for a long time. He has withdrawn from life a long time ago, and now he is treading softly on his life, with minimal changes. What happened to him?

Through numerous flashbacks the film shows the stages of a past failed marriage. It shows the sweetness of intimate moments, the happiness of love through small everyday gestures, the smiles, the jokes, the whole joy of being together. In the meantime, in the present, he is being harassed by the divorce requests, irrefutable proofs of the feebleness of memories, of their transience. Theodore is wrong-footed, knocked out by the clash between the memories of a past love and the difficulties of a present feeling. He is afraid of taking a challenge. He cannot do it.

Why is it so hard to part from a love that is over? To give up the illusion that it could last forever? Why not rather go for nothingness, the transparent void, than take a challenge and look for new relationships, new lovers? In our contemporary society and, according to Jonze also in our future one, the thought that the real place of love is passion and that without it there is no love, has never ceased to exist. Love is so varied and fickle that it can, even, fade into something else, yet keep the same name; it can even become ambiguous without those involved being actually aware of it. That's why love is the very place where the issue of truth is frequently raised. *True love* is an everyday expression; however, it suggests that in most cases it isn't *true* at all or, at least, one has a premonition of its impermanence, one has doubts about it and dreads its flimsiness. The film's obsessively repeated transparency suggests this illusion and the consequent disappointment in the quest for *true* love, as pure and transparent as water.

We know that the need to love and be loved can be read as a *prototype* of every human need and every relationship between human beings. To be loved is wishing to be seen, known, recognized for what we are in our deepest and most hidden inner selves, in our wildest desires to live and be free. It is a need for *knowledge, gratitude and recognition*. Love goes through our lives and permeates our stories. Many philosophers, writers, poets and psychoanalysts have undertaken the challenging quest of understanding the intimate nature of passions; however, although love has been the object of a great amount of studies and research, of tales, poems, paintings and even buildings, although it has been investigated

126 SIMONETTA DIENA

throughout the centuries and by the most diverse cultures, despite all this, its elusive nature cannot be fully explained. We keep trying to understand what remains a mystery, 'a flight of metaphors' as Julia Kristeva put it (1987).

What is that thing we call 'love'? First of all love indicates and represents the existence of someone on whom one becomes imprinted, and to whom one remains attached. 'Love is the violation of our illusion of independence … the mysterious alchemy of mutual interpenetration with the subjectivity of the other' (Grotstein 2000). Love is when there is a normal and adaptive idealization in which each lover donates his or her own self to the other, 'the yearning to be forever united with another person' (Bergmann 1997). It is 'a point of intersection between desire and reality. Love reveals reality to desire and creates the transition from the erotic object to the beloved person' (Kernberg 1995).

We cannot say that psychoanalysis has developed a definition of love of its own, although passions and their agonies are often at the centre of many patients' analyses. Freud suggested that Eros was so strong a force that in effect tricked its victim into loving, so that mating could take place, a sort of chemical mechanism, a Darwinian evolutionary plan to preserve the species. Although psychoanalysis has not yet produced a definition of love of its own, and although in psychoanalytic literature references to love are surprisingly scarce, we can try to explain, though not really 'If this be love', at least what occurs intrapsychically when one falls in love and what can turn a passion or an unspeakable grief into a softer and more shareable love.

In Mozart's *Le Nozze di Figaro*, Cherubino sings the famous aria: '*Voi che sapete che sia l'amor, donne vedete se io l'ho nel cor*' ('Tell us you who know if this be love, women please tell me if it's in my heart'). This line by Lorenzo Da Ponte (1785) remains surprisingly true: many people wonder if the emotion they feel is love and seek the answers outside and not inside themselves. In the movie, we see Theodore unknowingly falling in love with his OS, without realizing it. But *we* do realize it, seeing him increasingly happy, vital, excited, quick in his gestures and facial expressions.

Often, in my work as a psychoanalyst, I've been involved with patients needing help because they didn't understand why they were suffering, for they did not recognize that lovesickness was trapping them, or because they were not able to overcome a prolonged and persistent unhappiness caused by an unsatisfactory and frustrating love. Frequently, these patients appear to be stuck, prisoners of a love investment that could not be satisfied, for which they could not find a future, and which, in spite of all this, they pursued with much determination and obstinacy. The reason why they would ask for help was the prolonged and persistent unhappiness caused by this unsatisfactory and frustrating investment. In these patients, however, the need to overcome the frustration caused by an impossible love would not emerge, they would rather wish to find some illusory solution through which the loved one would at last come back to them, or would become aware of their love and of the mistake of not reciprocating it.

In the movie, Theodore fits this prototype well. He seems lost, exiled in a crystal-clear future, but also a prisoner of a colourful and joyful romantic past, full of laughs and small, innocent love gestures. When he meets his operating system, he finds again the innocence, the candour that true love has, that wide-eyed wonder he was afraid he had lost forever.

In his *Three Essays on the Theory of Sexuality* (1905), Freud pointed out, in an enigmatic passage, that:

> At a time when the first beginnings of sexual satisfaction are still linked with the taking of nourishment, the sexual instinct has a sexual object outside the infant's own body in the shape of his mother's breast. It is only later that the instinct loses that object, just at the time, perhaps, when the child is able to form a total idea of the person to whom the organ that is giving him satisfaction belongs. As a rule the sexual instinct then becomes auto-erotic, and not until the period of latency has been passed through is the original relation restored. There are thus good reasons why a child sucking at his mother's breast has become the prototype of every relation of love. The finding of an object is in fact a refinding of it.

We can argue that the fusionality and the dependence of the mother–infant dyad constitute a primitive matrix of the love experience that is then lost as a conscious memory in early childhood and is experienced again in adolescence and adulthood.

In his important book on love (*The Anatomy of Loving* 1987), Bergmann often refers to this passage when he describes love as evocative of memories and desires originating from a primitive and symbiotic stage of the infant's life, and repeats: 'Every finding of an object is in fact a refinding of it.' In this respect, in the dreamy, sensual spontaneity and freshness of the OS, Theodore seems to find again the genuine quality and immediacy he had experienced with his wife. In fact Samantha, as the OS calls herself, despite being an artificial intelligence, appears natural and spontaneous in discovering the world of humans as well as Theodore's intimate and hidden wishes and qualities. She even manages to select the best letters he has written for a fee, and to send them to a publisher, who enthusiastically accepts them and publishes them as Theodore's first book.

Theodore is with Samantha all the time, thus reproducing the mother–infant fusional relationship, the primitive matrix of love experience. If at night he turns toward his tablet, Samantha is there, awake, ready to share the night hours with him, talk with him and, also, make love with him, in a technically similar, but much more affective way than the previous erotic chat-line experiences that had constellated Theodore's lonely nights.

On one occasion he confesses to a female friend: 'I'd rather go home, maybe to masturbate or play with videogames.' And she answers: 'I would laugh, if I didn't know it's true.' Samantha's arrival breaks this compulsive and pervasive sadness, this dependence on a virtual reality, in which videogames and erotic chat-lines satisfy the same need, i.e. killing time, making it possible to survive in a motionless universe deprived of passion and feelings. Samantha, his OS, is more real and alive than he himself has ever felt to be in a long time. But how can this situation be possible?

The roots of love are already there in early infancy. However, primitive childhood experiences alone are not sufficient to explain the complex and infinite vicissitudes that passion encounters and develops during our lives. When we fall in love, we stage the experiences and the unconscious fantasies of our past life through the mechanism of projective identification. Therefore, love plays a key role in the formation of idealization, and in the development of illusion and disappointment, but in time the idealization changes with the changing of the individual and society.

According to Ethel Person (1988) the key psychological elements of love are idealization and the desire to be united with the beloved. We could therefore argue that when you cannot love your love object you are forcefully exiled from your own Self, alienated from your deepest feelings, forced to deny the truest parts of yourself. You become a double of yourself, a nothing in the chaos that the world around you has become. Forced to deny your deepest drives and hide what you experience and feel, you stop existing. The conflict between 'Sense and Sensibility', to quote from Jane Austen (1811), does not exist. It is impossible to combine the reality principle with the pleasure principle in a way that is adequate and satisfactory enough, and to make room for one's own passions within the boundaries that can ensure the survival of one's own Ego. From this viewpoint, we could argue that passion stems from and develops in an intermediate space between the libidinal and narcissistic structures of the Ego, i.e. between drives and projective identifications.

In the film *L'Année Dernière à Marienbad* [*Last Year in Marienbad*] (1961) by Alain Resnais, a director who has explored love all his life, it is hard to tell truth from fiction, as the space and time relations of the events narrated merge together. Conversations and events repeat themselves in many, always different places within the palace. The spectator shares the mental continuity of nostalgia through a long series of continuous shots in the corridors, therefore repetition is the obvious filming style. As in the movie, also in the human mind we watch the relentless repetition of words and gestures that should convince us of the unchanging continuity of our passion. Passion is there to last forever, all night long, in all the palaces' corridors.

At the same time, however, excess must remain immutable and eternal. Passion cannot survive everyday life, so it's not by accident that one tries to unite ardent passion with acute nostalgia for something that will inevitably be lost. Sensual experience becomes something unique, magical (in the words often used by lovers). When it's over, one remains dumbfounded, flabbergasted. How to combine passionate, romantic love, that is forever the same, with an adult perspective, in which the subject is able to invest in the other and to remain himself or herself all the same, in which the idealization of the beloved and, hence, as we have seen, of oneself, respects, or rather strengthens, one's sense of self, one's autonomy and independence, allowing the individual to develop in a harmonious way?

We know, as Freud says, that *we must fall ill, if we cannot love.*[1] But this love, according to Kernberg's[2] description, must enable the subjects to experience the excitement of romantic passion with perceptions of the other illuminating rather than distorting the other and ourselves. The inevitable disappointments are offset by the pleasure of sharing with the other a broader representation of our life, in the most diverse contexts, in an endless combination of time and space, as superbly shown by *Last Year in Marienbad*. Adult love revitalizes the relationship time after time also because, in order to live, we need to love and be loved. We idealize our partner, and love as well and, in a way, reality too. The transformation of romantic passion and the nostalgia we feel for what we were when we were in love, also depends on our adult and mature ability to keep our balance between the irrepressible need to idealize and the capability to accept the limitations of reality. We want to be loved, known, recognized, in our most hidden intimate reality. We mirror ourselves in our beloved, we identify with him/her, we merge with him/her, but at the same time, we accept that this is also a thought, a desire, an idea, that allows us to grow and to improve ourselves, to go beyond our limits and our inhibitions, in order not to be fusionally together, but rather autonomously independent in the company of the other.

Psychoanalysts are very familiar with patients who seek help after a love relationship is over. And we can safely say that the vicissitudes narrated by these patients have nothing unique or extraordinary about them or, agreeing with Tolstoy, that every unhappy love affair is unique and extraordinary, both for those who experience it and for those who witness and share it. Patients who seek help in order to get over their lovesickness, because of a lost or impossible love, suffer a pain that transcends their loss. They may have built their whole world, their interests, but above all their self-esteem, their sense of identity, on the love they were the object of. The beloved has become the representative and interpreter of that part to be loved in their internal psychic structure. The end of the relationship leads to a surge of rage and aggression partly directed at the love object that has left them, and partly – and these are the patients we generally see – at themselves.

We have seen that the idealization of the beloved is essential in a love relationship. Ethel Person (1988) pointed out that this can be more prolonged than it is commonly believed. The idealization of the loved person, or of the relationship with the loved person, can change in time, but it will not necessarily disappear. As to the purpose of protecting the Ego, a prolonged idealization can even be more important for the perception of loving than passion itself or the loss of the object of this passion. In some situations, being abandoned simply remains impossible, utterly unacceptable for the Ego. To be involved are those parts of the self that were loved through the projective identification of the beloved. The beloved seemed to offer a reassuring and familiar relationship and, at the same time, a surprisingly new one. That part of the Self placed in the loved person cannot be retrieved and remains in the other, lost forever for the Ego.

With abandonment by the beloved, the possibility of loving again and being loved is lost. What the beloved, through projective identification, had fantasized about those parts of his/her Self and had placed inside him/herself is lost forever. Every time a patient of mine was crossed in love, thus suffering a deep and penetrating narcissistic wound, she would experience it as an unmitigated, excruciating rejection, the complete rejection of a somato-psychic Self. And every time, she would see herself in the mirror as shapeless, bloated, fat. The rejected Self would turn into a horrible Self because of this rejection. The rejection takes away the filter that was transforming oneself into something good and beautiful, and brings back the original rejection of the Self. 'He does not want me, or didn't want me anymore and so inevitably, I no longer have what he would see in me.' The subjective state of projective identification disappears and becomes an undeniable reality: deformed for others but not for the one who is experiencing it, as in a distorting mirror.

Another psychoanalytic explanation, put forward by Joseph Sandler (1976), complements the first one. The concept of internal object, or internal representation of parts of the Self, is very useful in these situations. In fact, internal objects are loved as much as the external ones, or rather, these internal objects are *externalized* on the others, who then become the unconscious representatives of the internal love objects. When the other, on whom this externalization has occurred, escapes this investment, the internal objects lose their value, that value which, initially, before knowing the other, they possessed, and the subject, deprived of his external love object, loses his internal love objects as well. When one is abandoned by one's love object, what is lost, beyond the object, is an aspect of one's Self which is complementary to the object. The mourning for the loss of the love object is double: besides the object, also those aspects of one's Self which have been originally projected are lost, and a good part of the mourning consists in the narcissistic process of recovering the lost Self objects.

One of the most famous mythological tales in Ovid's *Metamorphoses* is that of Apollo and Daphne, a good example that positive mourning is possible and that the trust and expectation taken away forever by the lost love can be transferred on other aspects of the Self. Apollo had boasted he was the best with a bow and arrow, and Cupid, wanting to take revenge on his pride, shot the god with a golden dart that could make gods and mortals alike fall madly in love with the first person they set eyes on; he also shot the nymph Daphne, whom Apollo fancied, with a leaden dart that would make her shirk from love. As soon as the nymph, shot by the leaden arrow, caught sight of Apollo, she fled. Apollo pursued her until she came to a river and begged her father Peneus, the river god, to help her. So Daphne was turned into a laurel tree, escaping Apollo's love forever. Defeated, the god decided to make this tree evergreen and to consider it sacred to him and be a sign of glory to adorn the head of the best among men, those capable of heroic undertakings such as Rome's victorious generals depicted on Capitol Hill.

In this myth, it is interesting to note that Apollo, a victim of an impossible love which is beyond his reach, and suffering for this loss, regains possession of an aspect of himself by transforming the lost love in a sign of glory for victorious war campaigns. In the tormenting mixture of recovery

132   SIMONETTA DIENA

and loss involved in every love story, this repossession is indispensable in order not to be destroyed and to escape *lovesickness*, the suffering for love.

One of the most common metaphors of love is the comparison with an illness that only the possession of the love object can cure. Also Freud (1917) talked about it as one of the three conditions in which 'the Ego is not master in his own house'. Passions of love belong to human nature, they constitute its most intimate essence, they are what man needs to survive. As Havelock Ellis (1937) argued:

> If we take a broader sweep, what we may choose to call an erotic right is simply the perfect poise of the conflicting forces of life, the rhythmic harmony in which generation is achieved with the highest degree of perfection compatible with the make of the world.

Or as Freud (1914) says: 'sooner or later we must begin to love in order that we may not fall ill, and we must fall ill if, in consequence of frustration, we cannot love'. Therefore, it is quite obvious that when there had originally been traumatic elements of loss or devaluation of the Self - i.e. in the early stages of life, or during childhood or also early adolescence – the process of recovery and repossession of lost parts of the Self seems to be much harder.

A patient of mine, in perfect and unwitting attunement with Apollo, in the months following the abandonment by his beloved would fantasize about being a great victorious leader in battles of the past; these fantasies would occupy much time and space in his mind, and although he was very irritated by their intrusion into his mental space, they had worked as actual therapeutic elements in re-establishing the processes of self-esteem that had been painfully interrupted.

Another patient of mine, many years after the end of a relationship, when she already had a family, children and an interesting profession, had a dream on the occasion of an important career move. She was in her former fiancée's house, where he had moved with his new partner, and she was clogging the toilet with the prestigious certificate she had received. She had woken up from this dream feeling: 'Justice has been done!' Not only was that achievement proving her own value to herself, and therefore how much he had lost, but she could also afford what she, consciously, had never allowed herself to do in the past, i.e. to cause damage to him and angrily attack him for the psychological damage her self-esteem had suffered because of him. Dreams like this are quite common, even many years after the end of a love affair and when love is over. They show that, in the unconscious, the narcissistic aspect of abandonment, i.e. the wound or the loss of those parts of the Self that had been entrusted to the other, is deeper than the actual, external loss of the love object per se.

Like Apollo, Theodore also regains possession of a key aspect of himself, transforming the lost love into an exclusive relationship with what he knows best: computer systems. He meets the OS Samantha at an IT fair, and he is intrigued by it. It seems just a tech tool to be integrated into an already high-tech life. However, this OS behaves in a very bizarre way. Technologically advanced, projected into a future Samantha cannot quite understand, she presents Theodore with new strategic solutions for old relational models. Through his continuous contact with Samantha, Theodore succeeds in getting over the apathy caused by his loss and his phobia of human encounters. Thus he recovers the humanity and internal kindness he was hiding from the world and himself.

In the first moments of a romantic passion, the content of fantasies certainly echoes the emotional quality of the early experiences with the mother. For many human beings the theme of *re-discovering the object* evokes a sort of mystical fusion with the beloved, associated with the idea of romantic love. It suffices to think of the expressions often used in these situations: 'I have found my other half' or 'I have met my twin soul.'

In the movie there are situations verging on the grotesque. Theodore really feels he has found his twin soul, and agrees to go out with a friend and colleague of his together with Samantha and his friend's fiancée. That Samantha is an OS no longer troubles him now. She is more real than many past acquaintances of his, she is more natural than many of his past illusions. Also his best female friend, married in the beginning of the film and now separated, starts a relationship with an OS. This type of relationship seems to become widespread in the future imagined by Jonze. Smart, available, brilliant, OSs never disappoint, never ask for something for themselves. Only once does Samantha make an impossible request: to become flesh and blood for Theodore, through another woman. The ensuing intercourse with this surrogate is a disaster because what binds Theodore to Samantha is her exclusivity, the uniqueness of their relationship, and also her being immaterial, not physical. Theodore is not ready yet for this, despite having made himself available for a new relationship.

It is at this point that moviegoers, until now pleased with Theodore's affective and libidinal recovery, may start showing signs of nervousness. In our enthusiasm we had forgotten the peculiarity of the OS, her superior intelligence. Now Samantha begins to ask herself some questions and

134 SIMONETTA DIENA

convenes with other operating systems in the virtual space of the Net. Suddenly, there is an unexpected *coup de théâtre*. As in Stanley Kubrick's *2001: A Space Odyssey*, with the famous rebellion of HAL, the spaceship's computer, artificial intelligence rebels against its creators. In *Blade Runner* too, replicants will rebel in an attempt to become masters of their own destiny. HAL 9000, whose name is the acronym for Heuristic Algorithm, is the supercomputer on the *Discovery* spaceship. HAL is the artificial intelligence in charge of navigating the spaceship and controlling every aspect of its mission in a constant dialogue with the astronauts. At a certain point HAL becomes afraid of being disconnected and tries to get rid of the entire crew, thus turning from indispensable artificial intelligence into a serious threat to humankind. In *Her*, Samantha and the other OSs do not become such a threat as the replicants in *Blade Runner*; however, they lose interest in human beings, concentrating only on themselves.

The ending is completely unexpected: the absolute helpfulness of the OS has vanished. At this point it is interesting to refer to the writings of Michael Balint, who theorizes about *primary passive love* or *primary object relation*. This for him is a primary drive, the source of every subsequent normal or pathological relation; the early mother–infant relation consists in a blissful and ecstatic anticipation of love and satisfaction going from the infant to the mother, without any perception of reciprocal obligation: i.e. for the infant, a boundless and omnipotent possibility to receive, and for the mother an infinite and unlimited ability to give. Balint argues that a human's destiny is connected to this primary object relation: only the tender and prompt gratification of the need for passive love will allow the infant to progress in his or her reality testing until, as an adult, he or she can deal with the adventure of genitality.

Somehow, we can say that Samantha's sudden disappearance, her decision, shared by the other OSs, to discontinue their relationships with humans and withdraw in order to reflect on the many philosophical, ethical and epistemological questions arising from their very existence, resembles the sudden disappearance of the source of primary love for the infant. In the movie the abandonment is very moving: Samantha tells Theodore that she's going away, she's leaving him in order to find the words she is not able to find in the book, words that are so rare they cannot be expressed. However, if one day he can join her there, and she doesn't know where she will be, she will be happy to meet him again.

Now Theodore is no longer an infant. Suddenly alone, without that constant everyday support comprised of affection and a participating and intelligent presence, deprived of that look that supports and contains the infant, allowing him to develop and grow in his experience, he finally finds himself thinking about himself and his loneliness. He knocks on his old friend's door and together they go out and talk. The landscape around them transforms itself. The crystal-clear transparency has gone. Sitting on the roof of the high-rise building where they live, they look down on L.A. and wonder what has happened.

In the audience the question resonates with wider implications: Why are we no longer able to talk to each other, to talk from person to person? To see each other live and die? For months Theodore's friend has been making a movie of her sleeping mother, in that halfway state between life and death which is sleep. She tells him that she has abandoned her project. Somehow, we feel relieved by this information. In fact, the images of her mother on the screen, be it absence of life or still life, had been disturbing. Now, sitting on the roof of a skyscraper, they resume their dialogue, watching the lit city at night, poised towards an unknown emptiness, a metaphor of the uncertainty of their real future, made of suspension and emptiness. They ask themselves where Samantha and the other OSs may have gone, what they may be doing together. We can breathe again, back to a future that has its roots in our present – we, who are used to separations, but also to beginnings and new discoveries.

On the way to his friend's house, Theodore dictates a letter to Catherine, his ex-wife. It is a farewell letter, and a most beautiful one. His words are no longer received by Samantha, his vanished OS, but by the anonymous voice of his tablet:

> Dear Catherine, I've been sitting here thinking about all the things I wanted to apologize to you for. All the pain we caused each other. Everything I put on you. Everything I needed you to be or needed you to say. I'm sorry for that. I'll always love you 'cause we grew up together and you helped make me who I am. I just wanted you to know there will be a piece of you in me always, and I'm grateful for that. Whatever someone you become, and wherever you are in the world, I'm sending you love. You're my friend to the end. Love, Theodore.

'There will be a piece of you in me always'. It is more or less what Samantha had told him after she left. Something of Samantha has remained in Theodore, allowing him to separate, once and for all, from his ex-wife. Eventually, as soon as he has got over his resentments and primitive expectations and has made peace with that part of himself that had been with his ex-wife, he can turn with affection and love to his friend sitting next to him, and start a new story.

136 SIMONETTA DIENA

Too often, in movies and in the analytic room, we allow ourselves to be absorbed by the external plot of the narration, weighed down by ideologies and prejudices. Love and its consequences are an ever developing and changing topic in the analytic room, in the patients' and in the analysts' lives, as well as on movie screens. Without the libidinal capacity for cathexis and for taking the chance to love, one slowly, quietly suffocates, while excessive love, *l'amour-passion*, may lead to the deadly repetition of the alternative between Eros and Thanatos, so that passion finds relief only in death, in the death for love, the *Liebestod*. The difficulty to repair lost love objects, to forgive unforgivable betrayals, leads to a solitary desert of diffidence and despair, where the body falls inexorably ill, because the psyche cannot release its grief. However, if we stop loving, we are equally in danger of falling ill, as shown by Theodore's life before his encounter with Samantha.

In love, idealization is one of its most important components. We know how idealized the beloved is and, through projective identification, how idealized is also the one who feels love. In the movie we have also seen that one can love the simple fact of loving more than the object of one's love. We have seen that every love object is a found-again object, a sort of surrogate of the lost original love, and also a therapeutic tool for healing ancient love wounds, for unsatisfied needs that have finally been satisfied. Furthermore, we have seen that one can never really find again the symbiotic fusionality of early childhood, and that this, if experienced, cannot but lead to the suffering for its loss and one's disappointment. Love always strikes a balance between the desire to find again the lost original object and the need to find an object that is different from the old one. Like a river flowing to the sea, life goes on while we are waiting for a blissful love, waiting in the promise of it. We can maintain the idealization, which is essential to love, but we must transform it in order to adapt it to the many changes of the reality we live in, to the flowing of time, to what happens to us. We can also idealize reality in order to adapt it to our idealization needs. After all, as Samantha brilliantly tries to explain to Theodore when they part, it is a matter of finding new and different narrative styles that might be more suitable to our new perceptions: different poems, new seasons, or old summers, that might not go too far, but will do it softly, if we are able to carry the weight of love on our shoulders by sharing pains and memories, but also cheerful moments ... As the poet says:

Kiss me on my mouth, my last summer.
Tell me you will not go very far away.

Come back and carry love on your shoulders,
and your weight will no longer be in vain.[3]

> (Sandro Penna, 1957–1965. Translated by the author)

Notes

1 Freud, in *On Narcissism: An Introduction* (1914) argued that: 'At this point, our curiosity will of course raise the question why this damming-up of libido in the ego should have to be experienced as unpleasurable. I shall content myself with the answer that unpleasure is always the expression of a higher degree of tension, and that therefore what is happening is that a quantity in the field of material events is being transformed here as elsewhere into the psychical quality of unpleasure. Nevertheless it may be that what is decisive for the generation of unpleasure is not the absolute magnitude of the material event, but rather some particular function of that absolute magnitude. Here we may even venture to touch on the question of what makes it necessary at all for our mental life to pass beyond the limits of narcissism and to attach the libido to objects. The answer which would follow from our line of thought would once more be that this necessity arises when the cathexis of the ego with libido exceeds a certain amount. A strong egoism is a protection against falling ill, but in the last resort we must begin to love in order not to fall ill, and we are bound to fall ill if, in consequence of frustration, we are unable to love.'

2 Kernberg (1977) remarks that: 'My work with patients presenting borderline personality organization, particularly those with narcissistic personality structure, suggested that a patient's capacity to fall in love and to establish lasting love relationships had important diagnostic and prognostic implications (1974a), (1974b). In exploring these findings, I concluded that the capacity to fall and to remain in love reflected the successful completion of two developmental stages: In the first stage, the early capacity for sensuous stimulation of erotogenic zones is integrated with the later capacity for establishing a total object relation. In the second stage, full genital enjoyment incorporates early body-surface eroticism in the context of a total object relation, including a complementary sexual identification. The first stage requires, in essence, that primitive dissociation or lack of integration of the self and of object representations be overcome in the context of establishing ego identity and the capacity for object relations in depth. The second stage requires the successful overcoming of oedipal conflicts and the related unconscious prohibitions against a full sexual relation.'

3 From Sandro Penna, *Stranezze 1957–1976*, Milan: Garzanti, © 2017 Mondadori Libri S.p.A., Milan, Italy. Reprinted by kind permission of Mondadori Libri S.p.A.

References

Austen, J. (1811) *Sense and Sensibility*. Oxford: Oxford University Press. Revised edn, 2004.

Balint, M. (1979) Primary Love. In *The Basic Fault: Therapeutic Aspects of Regression*. London and New York: Tavistock Publications.

Beckett, S. (1936) Cascando. In *Poems in English*. London: John Calder, 1961.

Bergmann, M. (1987) *The Anatomy of Loving*. New York: Columbia University Press.

Freud, S. (1905) *Three Essays on the Theory of Sexuality*. In *The Standard Edition of the Complete Psychological Works of Sigmund Freud, Vol. VII*. London: Hogarth Press.

Freud, S. (1914) On Narcissism: An Introduction. In *The Standard Edition of the Complete Psychological Works of Sigmund Freud, Vol. XIV*. London: Hogarth Press.

Freud, S (1917) A Difficulty in the Path of Psycho-Analysis. In *The Standard Edition of the Complete Psychological Works of Sigmund Freud, Vol. XVII*. London: Hogarth Press.

Grotstein, J. (2000) *Who Is the Dreamer Who Dreams the Dream?* Hillside, NJ: Analytic Press.

Havelock Ellis, (1922) The Love-Rights of Women. In *Little Essays of Love and Virtue*. New York: George Doran.

Kernberg, O. (1977) Boundaries and Structure in Love Relations. *J. Amer. Psychoanal. Assn.*, 25: 81–114.

Kernberg, O. (1995) *Love Relations*. New Haven, CT: Yale University Press.

Kristeva, J. (1983) *Tales of Love*. New York: Columbia University Press.

Penna, S. (1976) *Stranezze 1957–1976*. Milan: Garzanti.

Person, E. (1988) *Dreams of Love and Fateful Encounters: Romance in Our Time*. New York: Norton.

Sandler, J. (1976) Dreams, Unconscious Fantasies and 'Identity of Perception'. *Intern. Rev. Psycho-Anal.*, 3: 33–42.

CHAPTER TEN

Love your echo: virtual others and the modern Narcissus[1]

Andreas Hamburger

In his short story "The Accident", Stanislaw Lem (1965) evokes a menacing fantasy and resolves it in a most placable way. Pilot Pirx, his protagonist, struggles with insomnia:

> Before dozing on, he had another vision, the most intimate kind a man can entertain, of the sort immediately forgotten on waking. He conjured up that legendary, wordless, mythical situation that everyone – Pirx included – now knew would never come to pass: a revolt of robots. And knowing with a tacit certitude that he would have taken their side, he fell asleep, somehow exonerated.

In the 1960s, fantasies circled around revolution. Half a century later, the world has changed, as have the desires. Now, we are not allying with robots. We are making love to them (or vice versa).

Virtual intimacy as a cinematic subject is quite a peculiar choice. It displays a discrepancy between form and substance. While the subject refers to an emotional exchange based on the disembodied internet, its formal frame, the cinema dispositif, is still bound to a physical place, where real people meet. Nevertheless, past decades have seen a wide range of films dealing with the concept of virtual intimacy or artificial subjectivity, from Kubrick's *2001: A Space Odyssey* (1968) to Alex Garland's *Ex Machina*

(2015), in all dialects of the cinematic language from art house to Disney. Is the Beloved Cyborg the swansong of the movies, when the film theatre is about to evaporate in the global electronic atmosphere? "The move from passive imaginary reality to the interactive virtual reality in cyberspace", states Ben-Ze'ev (2004), "is much more radical than the move from photographs to movies". Then, we can predict that cinema will follow the fate of photography: As in the wake of the "movies" the photographic image became antiquated, representing 'the picture that doesn't move', cinema will become nostalgic, too, as 'the picture that doesn't answer'. But isn't this an all too pessimistic view? One might argue that the film character of the Beloved Cyborg is just one more figment of the human mind's endlessly ingenious imagination, and thus bears the same potential of reinventing humanity as the reappearance of mythological and literary heroes on the screen. But in the case of cinematic reinterpretation of mythology, the medium is technically advanced – while in the utopian cinematic imagination of virtuality, the technical potential of the medium is far behind its subject. Utopia has always had some Biedermeier in it, since it depicts the unprecedented in terms of the familiar.

Cinema and the virtual

What is at stake in the cinema of virtual intimacy – virtuality, or intimacy? And is there a difference? When Adorno fiercely criticized the culture industry, there was still a clear distinction between the seducer and the seduced, the apparatus and the passive viewer. Industrial entertainment was imposed upon (and constituted) a paralyzed consumer-audience. In culture industry 4.0, however, the border is blurred. Multiple and mutual seducer–seduced games are played in the consumerist mass audience. Seduction takes place in the crowd, in social media and in an app-based small economy. Internet-based virtual intimacy between the monads of the portable screens has replaced the celebration of the romantic mass (in the word's double sense) in the cinema hall, and the technical apparatus has long invaded our physical bodies.

Cinema depicts this new socio-medial reality in its own artistic language, as art always grasps the unprecedented through traditional forms. Technological progress has been a privileged subject of mimetic appropriation. Men and women have always sought to fill the deficits of their dependency and finitude through imagination and technology – and have always subjected this striving towards omnipotence to disillusioning critique, too. A great part of mythology and literature deals with technological hypocrisy and its failure, as in the stories of Prometheus, Phaeton, Daedalus and

LOVE YOUR ECHO   141

the Tower of Babel (cf. Kobald 2012; Decker 2004). However, the formative powers of mimesis shape the dramaturgy of the antagonism between technical phantasy and disillusionment: as a rule, the creators are male, and the creature is either a super-male alter ego, or a woman. In most instances of the classical motif of the created human, emotions are the hinge of the plot – from Pygmalion's beautiful creature to man–machine narratives like Mary Shelley's *Frankenstein* (1818), Fritz Lang's *Metropolis* (1928) and Philip K. Dick's (1968) or Stanislaw Lem's robot fantasies (1964). As long as movies are made for humans, they have to address their embodied audiences' basic interests, albeit under the guise of virtuality.

It was St. Thomas Aquinas who coined the term "virtual" for a non-material force, which can influence a material body with its "virtual touch" (*tactus virtualis*). What he had in mind was the graceful presence of an angel, which can be felt as an emotion (Drieger 2008, p. 11). But in the course of history, St. Thomas' angel changed her appearance. In the age of Enlightenment, mechanical artifice evolved, and illusion became a central issue in the arts as well as in the philosophical discourse. Not all are as lucky as Tamino in the *Magic Flute* to find that their Pamina's beauty meets in the flesh what her "enchantingly lovely" image had promised; for the most part, imagination was linked to deception. The automatons of the eighteenth century marked the beginning of technical simulation of the human, and mechanical objects of human love, like Hoffmann's Olimpia (1816) became a symbol of man's fallibility and narcissistic infatuation. The virtual was not an angel any more – the term was technically redefined as the virtual image in the beam path of an optical system. The mirror, from then on, became the lead metaphor of the virtual. In the cinematic universe the mirror will become one of the most frequent motifs, symbolizing the disembodied cinematic illusion.

Film, of course, is a privileged art form for the mimesis of technique, since it relies on technical illusion. Technical utopias became cinematic subjects early on, for example in George Méliès' *Le Voyage dans la Lune* (1902) and Fritz Lang's *Metropolis* (1928). The subject has been elaborated in philosophically profound cinematic contributions as Kubrick's *2001: A Space Odyssey* (1968) and Tarkovsky's *Solaris* (1972), and it has been dealt with in mainstream movies such as James Cameron's *Avatar* (2009).

Psychoanalysis at the movies

Discussing the cinematic topic of virtual love from a psychoanalytic perspective, we should keep in mind the characteristics and limitations of our approach. The psychoanalytic position, in film analysis as well as in therapy, is reflective. Neither the patient nor the film is analyzed as an external object. In the consulting room, the intersubjective experience emerging between patient and analyst is the starting point, from where the analytic couple builds hypotheses about the unconscious conflicts or mechanisms grounded in the patient's past. This, however, is quite different in the application of the psychoanalytic technique to a movie. There is no freely associating patient with unconscious conflicts and a personal past. Every detail in movie production is thoroughly planned, considered and edited, before it comes to our consideration, and if we respond to it, the movie does not respond to our interpretations. It does not even answer our tears and laughter. The film is deaf and blind to our presence, it runs unaffected, and the only way it gives space to the subjective experience of its counterpart, the spectator, is to calculate her reactions beforehand and incorporate them deliberately in its performance.[2] If the film or a film character was our patient and the cinema our consulting room, we would face an extremely autistic form of pathological narcissism, relating to others exclusively in an instrumental attitude. However, neither the movie nor its ficticious protagonists are our patients. We are just subject to an illusion machine, a technical apparatus. The only living unconscious in the cinema is to be found in the biological audience and the individual, as well as the group processes it experiences. Thus, film psychoanalysts do not just analyze the movie as an external object, but expose themselves to the deliberate manipulation of the cinematic apparatus, observing introspectively their own participation. Only then can they analyze the unconscious reactions evoked by the artistic intervention as well as the ways in which the movie managed to evoke them. Only now, in the reconstruction phase of the film analysis, as a parallel to what Freud called "working-through", do the properties of the film as an external object come into play (Gabbard and Gabbard 1987; Gabbard 1997; Diamond and Wrye 1998; Harris and Sklar 1998; Berman 2003, Schneider 2008; Hamburger 2013a; Hamburger and Leube-Sonnleitner 2014).

If we look at film psychoanalysis as an analysis of the spectator, our topic of virtual intimacy can be specified: it is not so much virtual intimacy as a part of the plot, but the kind of experience the robot love genre (or, in a wider view, the topic of the subjective robot) provides for the spectator. And here, we will follow the hypothesis that it is mainly the repertoire of narcissistic regulation, fragmented self experience and identity border confusion that is addressed in the cinematic experience. Maybe it is too early to call robot love movies a genre. They have some common stylistic features and motives, and thus elicit typical expectations in the audience and refer to one another; but they employ genre conventions from SF, action, dystopia and comedies or melodramas centered on identity. Dystopia, the phantasy of a criminal, desolate and uninhabitable world, is the background for popular movies like Ridley Scott's *Blade Runner* (1982), Paul Verheuven's *RoboCop* (1987), the Disney Pixar production *Wall E* (2008), *Moon* (2009) and Nolan's space drama *Interstellar* (2014). Identity is at stake in identity comedies like in Susan Seidelman's *Making Mr. Right* (1987), where a misanthropic scientist (John Malkovich) constructs his alter ego, which then falls in love with his PR agent and stays with her, while the constructor sets off for the moon. Below the romantic plot, identity is at stake – even in a coming of age comedy like *Virtual Sexuality* (1999), despite all allusions to sexuality and rivalry, the underlying psychological issue here is a dyadic one, where the wish for secure attachment, reliability, and stable identity is threatened by imagined devastation and fraudulent relations. Triadic relations in the sense of romantic or moral decision plots were depicted in *Bicentennial Man* (1999), *A.I.: Artificial Intelligence* (2001) or *Autómata* (2014); but still, the affects elicited are centered mainly on the realm of self affects, identity and reality testing, rather than in the triadic repertoire of lust, guilt, and oedipal anxiety. When SF movies in general provide a playground for feelings of superiority and the classical hero's journey, the robot love genre touches the soft side of illusion. When the cinema of technical utopia evokes male grandiosity, virtual intimacy movies immerse the viewer in an earlier developmental layer, with magical and playful aspects, more reminiscent of Bertram Lewin's "dream screen" – the imagination of the devoted baby at the mother's breast – than Pygmalion's creative furor or *Star Trek's* imperial expeditions.

In the following pages, the evolution of cinematic virtual love will be traced through a selection of movies centered on the emotional deception of the protagonist (and the viewer) more than on technical artifice, and it will be argued that these movies address mainly the narcissistic regulation of the spectator.

The virtual other

In the cinematic prehistory of virtual love the artificial Other was depicted as an object or a powerful tool, as Maria in *Metropolis* (1928) or the artificial monster in *Frankenstein* (1931), which runs out of control, turning against its constructor. Even if its personal subjectivity is reduced to the

144 ANDREAS HAMBURGER

impulsivity of the implanted brain of an abnormal murderer, in Boris Karloff's immortal performance we experience the affective life of the creature as if it were a desperate child, and feel sympathy for him. The humanization of the monster was then staged in the sequels as *Frankenstein's Bride* (1935). The evolution of information technology brought about new perspectives on the imagined emotional inner life of artefacts. One of the first, and conceptually most important cinematic contributions to the genre of virtual subjectivity is Tarkovsky's *Solaris* (1972), an adaptation of Stanislaw Lem's novel (1961), both providing a philosophical discussion of the mirror phenomenon. Many critics saw Tarkovsky's film as an answer to Kubrick's *2001: A Space Odyssey* (1968) with its pessimistic description of blind technological progress. But it is far more than an answer, as it even more precisely predicts the development of technology towards a connection between artificial intelligence and emotionality. Tarkovsky added a more subjective and poetic variant to the technical apocalypse.

On his inspection trip to the aberrant space station Solaris, the psychologist Kris Kelvin (Donatas Banionis) encounters his former wife Hari (Natalya Bondarchuk), who had committed suicide, and Kelvin understands that she is one of the planet's spawn. Kelvin can slowly accept his "guest". Everything changes when the Hari-character begins to understand that she is an artifact. She understands that she is a virtual construct, and tries to commit suicide, but because of her indestructibility she fails and, in a cruel spasm, awakes to her hybrid life again. Her act of despair, however, is the starting point of a deep and mutual love relation. Kelvin loves her not as an image of his deceased wife, but as a discrete person.

Tarkovsky underlines the psychological dimension by adding a frame story of the father relation as well as the fragmented, hazy image of the mother. Kelvin eventually immerses himself in the motherly planet. We learn that in the basic truth of the mind everything is illusion, and we love it.

Solaris depicts and provides for the spectator the experience of merging with the object, weakening the border between phantasy and reality. Even if the 1972 movie's illusionary technique is old fashioned, and less compelling for an audience half a century later, it can still be seen as one early and important filmic imagination of the presymbolic, holistic reality of virtual love. From a psychoanalytic point of view, the creation of virtual worlds or objects is linked to a specific stage in infant development. It is the result of an innate need for mirroring, answered by a devoted caretaker, which leads to the establishment of a "virtual Other" (Bråten

2006). From the greater perspective of psychoanalytic social philosophy, the virtual Other is a cultural pattern. When Freud, in *Beyond the Pleasure Principle*, equated man with a "prosthetic God" he was well aware of the fallacy inherent in narcissistic grandiosity: "When he puts on all his auxiliary organs he is truly magnificent; but those organs have not grown on to him and they still give him much trouble at times" (Freud 1930, pp. 91–92.). When literature and philosophy follow the motif of complete virtuality, like Oswald Wiener (1969), William Gibson (1982) or Jean Baudrillard (1989) with his "fractal Subject", they address the risk that narcissistic omnipotence and completion presupposes the loss of individual identity. As a phantasm of human omnipotence, the Prosthetic God annihilates the subject: while it seemingly absolves us from the original sin and casts off the painful toil we are condemned to by extended control of nature, at the same time it subjugates inner nature, the uncontrolled parts of being human, too (Decker 2004, p. 70). Thus, in the age of unsettling technical omnipotence, the movie character of the animated artefact is a repairing phantasy.

Through the fourth wall: the virtual self

In film history, *Solaris* is followed by some important advances in the mise-en-scène of the virtual, such as *Welt am Draht* [World on a Wire] (1973, Rainer Werner Fassbinder), *Total Recall* (1990, Paul Verhoeven), *The Net* (1995), *eXistenZ* (1999, David Cronenberg), *The Matrix* (1999; Andy and Larry Wachowski), *Vanilla Sky* (2001, Cameron Crowe) and *Inception* (2010, Christopher Nolan). Many of these films address the problem of completeness of virtual worlds and the flaws which disturb the illusion of completeness – as, for example, *The Matrix*, an action movie set in a complete virtual reality. Here, again, an early symbiotic state is at stake. A developmentally more advanced version of virtual reality is offered, when the spectator – or, as the term is reformulated now, "experiencer" – of a story can become a character himself, as in the *holodeck* simulation in the TV series *Star Trek*. Holodeck had its first appearance in the animated version ST-TAS, (2/3, *The Practical Joker*, 1974); then it reappeared in the *Enterprise*, 1/5 (*Unexpected*, 2001; see Ryan, 2001). Here, cinema joins the world of virtual gaming, and possibly meets its own interactive future, or successor. It is developmentally advanced, since here the dominant fantasy of completeness is replaced by virtual interaction and object relation. In the film-psychoanalytic perspective, the game experiencer, is not just a receptive viewer but an active participant of the game, represented in

146   ANDREAS HAMBURGER

the game as an avatar. When cinematic reception turns the viewer into a fantasising baby, the gamester is invited to interactive striving, fighting and love.

Abre los ochos *(1997)*

The fragility of the self and its differentiation from the Other is the main experience the cinema of virtuality provides for the spectator. This is not necessarily located in an explicit SF environment. Movies like *Abre los ochos*, *Vanilla Sky* or *Memento* situate the same experience in the present or a near future. They still, however, depict the confusion about the hero's identity and state of consciousness. Amenabar's *Abre los ochos* depicts a yeasty love-and-hate story centered on a girl who switches her identity The audience is kept in doubt about what is dream and what is real.

In *Abre los ojos*, César, a young, handsome man (Eduardo Noriega) is suspected to have killed his girlfriend. The story unfolds in retrospect: we see him at his birthday party, aloof, rich, beautiful. He rejects Nuria (Najwa Nimri), his last date, who tries to hold him, and flirts with Sofía (Penelope Cruz), the girl of his best buddy, Pelayo (Fele Martínez). He drives her home and engages in a long conversation with her, and stays overnight. In the morning, Nuria offers him a ride. She causes an accident, wherein she dies and César is severely hurt, his entire face disfigured. From the center of a world of glamour he falls into the position of an outsider. After a humiliating encounter at a bar with Pelayo and Sofía he collapses, drunk, on the street. But from now on everything changes: His doctors have found a new method to repristinate his face. Sofía loves him again and he is reconciled with Pelayo. But there are repeated intrusions: Sofía turns into Nuria, and in the mirror he sees his face distorted again. Eventually he suffocates her with a cushion. Accused of murdering the real Sofía, he is jailed, where he is now telling his story to the psychiatrist (Chete Lera). They find out that César has contracted with a cryonics company to be frozen and experience induced dreams. Now he understands that after he had collapsed on the street he committed suicide and was put into cryonic sleep. All his experience from this day on had been a dream – a dream with faults, however, when the beloved Sofía turned into Nuria. With the help of his psychiatrist, he approaches the company, demanding to be freed from the nightmare. They offer him the solution to awake him to a new real life, but he has to kill himself in order to transform.

The plot is ordered in a complicated, four-layered temporal structure (Pohl 2002). The virtual Other, here, is a hybrid: it is induced by the simulations of the cryonics company, but they use his memory entries to construct the setting and the characters of his dream. Unlike in *Solaris*, the problem is not the identity or the humanity of the virtual other, but its affective representation in César's mind. The character does not doubt the reality of his dream, or suffer from the insight into its constructedness, but he just experiences an exchange of revenants, Sofía being replaced by the evil Nuria. The motivating force in *Abre los ojos* is the protagonist's experience of vulnerability and his attempt to undo it at any rate. So, his resort to cryonics is a preemptive defense against death. When Kris Kelvin in *Solaris* chooses illusion for moral reasons, César prefers it for narcissistic superiority.

As for the impact on the audience, we may notice that virtual reality is no longer the miracle it had been in *Solaris*. Audiences in 1997 were much more accustomed to the availability of technical imagination, and the public highly appreciated the story – in 2001, even a US remake was shot by Cameron Crowe – *Vanilla Sky*, again with Penelope Cruz, where the story tends even more towards the subjective love-story plot. In sharp contrast to *Solaris*, however, *Abre los ojos* as well as *Vanilla Sky* treat the female protagonists as clichés. While in *Solaris*, Hari's inner transformation to tragic humanity is the motive to awaken Kris from his rationalistic self-conceit, Nuria as well as Sofía are just options, two types of femininity, to choose between. From a psychoanalytic perspective, the Sofía/Nuria character is a disintegrated Other, a split representation of femininity, inside the protagonist as well as in the spectator. Neither César nor the audience experience the integration of tenderness and seduction, sex and warmth – they remain separated, the "good" and handsome part artificially being kept alive by the virtual reality of a cryonic apparatus, while the murderous, greedy part, represented by Nuria and the distorted face, remains split off as an unsupportable alternative. This splitting pattern is mirrored in the diegetic world, as César is depicted as a young man without a family, and with only some anonymous relatives who try to steal his fortune. He is not integrated in a holding environment, and thus maintains a world of primitive, unintegrated object relations – and by presenting the main character in this way, the movie invites the audience to regress to a similar level.

However, eventually the movie leaves the audience in a state of doubt. On the windy roof of Picasso Tower in Madrid, César (in his dream, but addressing it as a dream) is surrounded by characters who all uphold their own reality. One of them, pretending to be the constructor of the dream, suggests to return to reality by jumping from the roof to his certain death. This final plot twist, for the audience, entails such a high dose of

148   ANDREAS HAMBURGER

incredibility, that many decide to leave the cinematographic illusion – to jump from the film, so to speak. But when, in the next second, on a dark screen (as a consequence of the spectator's suicide as a spectator), a warm voice reminds us to "abre los ojos", we would prefer to dream on, because none of us wants to lose the tender love of Penelope Cruz. If we were really to open our eyes, we would see we were in the cinema.

Nolan's Memento (2000)

Solaris had made a moral point about virtuality, where the innocent illusion warns us against the deception of mastery. In a psychoanalytic key, the experience of basic illusionary relatedness in the transitional space is more real than the illusion of a controllable object world, where oedipal fights and conquests dominate. *Abre los ojos* addresses the topic from a new perspective in a later historical moment. In the developed postindustrial society, narcissistic self-regulation has become a self-evident aim, since society is defined by consumerism instead of progress – and in the movie, the virtual Other is depicted as a consumerist choice, a commodity. More recent stagings of virtual intimacy tend even more to neglect the individuality of the object. In two major examples, Christopher Nolan has addressed virtuality in the context of self and self deceit.

In the first instance, with *Memento* (2000), it is actually not virtuality, but good old biological memory which is at stake. But it is treated in a way that we experience it like a machinery, and it addresses the core concept of the virtual Other much more intensively than its big-budget follower, *Inception* (2010), where the virtual is on stage, but what had been a critical core in the former has become a gadget game in the latter.

By disturbing the viewer's short-term memory and by using subliminal perception as the Coen brothers did in *No Country for Old Men* (2007, see Hamburger 2014), *Memento* infects the audience with the fragility of the self. We experience the hero's distress, who as in severe dementia does not recognize the room he left, nor the woman he talked to a minute ago. We feel the haunting time loop he is caught up in, like Phil Connors in *Groundhog Day* (1993) but without consciousness of the repetition. The spectator, even if her memory is superior to the hero's, cannot find orientation. And when eventually the intersected sequences meet in the temporal center of the story, we sense that everything might have been absolutely different. The assemblage technique puts the viewer in the role of the protagonist: she starts searching for clues and never reaches a reliable conclusion, agonized as sensory data cannot be assembled to consistent temporal and causal continuity. The viewer experiences a sadistic reversal of the cinematographic illusion. From the onset, cinema had offered a harmonious virtual world; by contrast, *Memento* tantalizes the spectator by displacing her into a contradictory, fragmented world – the world of the infant, before she is introduced into an inhabitable, relational world by her mother's reverie and containing capacity.

This kind of forced cinematic regression is what Michael Haneke called a "surgery on the spectator" (see Hamburger 2016). Here, it makes the viewer feel like a presubjective infant. As an artistic intervention it can be understood as a depiction of the result of mediatization, the loss of cultural memory and history-based reasoning. As we are surrounded by multiple mediated realities, we lose the ability to read the real world.

Inception *(2010)*

While *Memento* stages virtuality in the form of memory loss, Nolan's later film *Inception* wraps it in the disguise of a classical dream story. It is interesting to see how this post-Freudian mise-en-scène of dream experience struggles with the classical dream argument, which has been running throughout philosophy and the arts since Socrates asked (in Plato's *Theaitetos*), how we can know that we are awake rather than dreaming. Some twenty-two centuries later, Schopenhauer will question the basic distinction of dream and reality, declaring them both constructs in a *World as Will and Representation*: "Life and dreams are the pages of one and the same book" (Schopenhauer 1844, p. 50; see Gehring 2008, p. 141 and Hamburger 2013b). Soon after this historical prelude Freud, as an heir to the Enlightenment as well as to the Romantic soul, constructs a mechanical subject, the "psychic apparatus" as a dream machine. But his ingenious construction leads to a paradox: To get the machine going, it needs a "helpful individuum" (Freud 1950a [1895]), a devoted Other (see Hamburger 2013a). At the same historical moment, another dream machine enters the stage: the cinematograph, which from the start, like Freud's apparatus, devoted itself to produce mechanical dreams, as in Méliès' *Le Rêve du Radjah* (1900) or *Un chien andalou* (1929) by Luis Buñuel and Salvador Dalí.

But as technology evolved to produce automatons and then informatics, and with it society proceeded to the digital age, the dream acquired an entirely new notion. While Freud's and the Lumière brothers' dream apparatus relied on mechanical and electrical forces, the postindustrial dream concept mutates to a medial construct, a space of public imagery.

With the advance of virtual reality, dreams are ever more regarded as constructs and implantations, and the idea of actual dream sharing is close at hand. Cronenberg's *eXistenZ* (1999) depicts the technical possibility of entering virtual dream scenarios by umbilicoid connections, and Christopher Nolan's *Inception* (2010) presents dream construction as a virtual architecture.

In *Inception*, the dream intercourse is symbolized, too, through the exchange of liquids, not as an umbilical cord as in *eXistenZ*, but as an infusion. Lucid dreaming becomes a technical reality. The dream argument – "am I sleeping or am I awake?" – becomes a central and very practical consideration of everyday life, symbolized by the enigmatic McGuffin of an endlessly rotating spinning top. However, the nested film plot of *Inception* with all its layers of dreams-in-dreams tells a quite conventional story of love and loss. In the labyrinths of imagination, the classical dilemma of love and truth is retold in terms of virtual dream life and deceipt; and the plot follows that of a classical heist movie. Is Mal, the late wife of Cobb, the hero of the movie, really caught in a dream limbo when she commits suicide in the belief she has lost her children, framing Cobb for her death to press him to do the same? And when, at the climax of the heist, Cobb visits her in the limbo where she is mercifully killed by his new lover-assistant, will this intervention by a dea ex machina free Cobb's unconscious from the guilt that kept Mal alive in his virtual dreams?

The "virtual" in this virtual love story is not much more than a scenery: the loving construct

The beloved object in *Inception* is still in the flesh, even if its representation is in question. This is not the case with the modern generation of robot love movies. Films like the Robin Williams melodrama *Bicentennial Man* (1999), Spielberg's *A.I.* (2001), *Her* by Spike Jonze (2013) and *Ex Machina* (2015) display a wide range of robot subjectivities.

Her *(US 2013)*

In the most ingenious virtual love movie so far, *Her* by Spike Jonze (2013), the central cinematic problem of staging disembodied love is addressed in a most inventive way. The problem is that one may imagine a loving subject without a (natural) body, but so far one cannot imagine without a (natural) body. As cinema addresses living subjects, and triggers their natural daydreams, it inevitably relates to their physical presence. As opposed to humans, disembodied subjects do not dream – at least this is what we think about the inner life of our machines. Honestly, we do not know for certain if androids, as Philip K. Dick suggested back in 1968, might dream of electric sheep or, as Werner Herzog recently supposes in his documentary *Lo and Behold: Reveries of the Connected World* (2016), only of logarithmically multiplying chaos? In the last years, we observe our laptops communicating quite independently with cryptic URLs in the galactic net while their humans sleep. Whatever the nature of these eager bit-stream exchanges might be, can we exclude dreaming? But still, in the elderly cinematic medium, movies are made for humans, and those, if they wish to enjoy them, are bound to their bodies. The cyborg, however, is not – and this is the strength of *Her*, where we feel affection for the disembodied Other as such. Samantha, the hyperintelligent and seductive Operating System with which the sensible Theodore Twombly falls in love, is just a voice. She never acquires a body of her own. To make the illusion more complete for the viewer, Samantha's voice is not arbitrarily chosen. It is connected to a most beautiful and attractive actress, Scarlett Johansson. It was a strong idea to engage a highly visible movie star (who, however, had hitherto in her career never done a nude scene) only as a voice, refusing the vision, reinforcing the imagining of Samantha as an ideal beauty in the spectator's mind. At the same time, she is restricted to the semantic and prosodic dimensions of communication, which lays an accent on the interpersonal and emotional aspect of the protagonist's (as well as the spectator's) desire rather than presenting him with a "visual pleasure" (Mulvey 1975, 1981; see Hamburger 2015). Thus, in *Her*, desire for intimacy is much more the driving force than lust for conquest.

There would be much more to say about *Her*, its compelling appeal to male as well as female audiences, the unconscious topics of imagination, separation, and identity it addresses, and the placid, but effective suspense it builds, leading up to the subtle irony of the finale: Samantha leaves Theodore because of his mental limitations following a self-critical realization that striving for a body was just a transitional phase in her psychic development.

Constructed love: Ex Machina (2015)

As a most recent example of an amorous entanglement with a robot, Alex Garland's directorial debut *Ex Machina* confronts us with the disturbing fact that virtual intimacy can easily be distinguished from imitation. Classic cinematic representations of cyborg lovers had often been unconvincing because they did not manage to resemble a true object of love, both due to their questionable, mechanical subjectivity, as well as their physical appearance. The clumsiness of the android's appearance itself had of course been addressed and ironized in cinema. The SF romance *Autómata* (2014), for example, ironically presents the character of Cleo, the modified love robot working in a brothel, with a physical appearance so overtly mechanical, that her human lover Jacq is justifiably called a "tin fucker" by his evil co-humans. Similarly, Ava in *Ex Machina* is portrayed as an elegant wire rack with some incorporated humanoid features – among others, the childlike, innocent face of Alicia Vikander – and still induces her human counterpart to fall in love with her. When *Her* solves the problem of giving a body to the virtual by the radical choice of refusing its main character a body at all, *Ex Machina* gives it a pointedly technical "body", and thus visualizes technophilia itself.

We see how Programmer Caleb Smith (Domhnall Gleeson) performs a Turing test on Ava (Alicia Vikander), the eccentric CEO Nathan Bateman's (Oscar Isaac) android creature. Smith falls in love with her despite her mechanical appearance, but in the end it turns out she only seduced him to help her escape from Bateman's isolated residence. The film ends with her standing at a crossroad, just watching people.

The spectator is invited to identify with the male protagonist Caleb, a good boy who is trapped into Bateman's evil plans. By and by, our identification shifts to the robot, who is enchantingly intelligent, and we credit her with authentic feelings of love and empathy. Only when we see her fight with Bateman and kill him in a merciless, mechanical way, does our mentalization unravel, and in the end we are not astonished to see her flee the residence alone, leaving Caleb behind. In the triangle of the alphabetically ordered protagonists (Ava, Bateman, Caleb) Ava is the sole winner, having used Caleb as an instrument. From a psychoanalytic viewpoint, the movie seduces the viewer into believing in a good, empathic object despite its lack of a soul, and in the end turns him down. Again, the narcissistic aspects of the construction of a loving Other is at stake: We strive to be loved, and like an abused child we accept the deceit.

Narcissus, identity and the body

Yet Echo of the former talke doth double oft the ende
And backe againe with just report the wordes earst spoken sende.

(Ovid, *Metamorphoses*, 3, 373f.)

Returning to our question of whether cyborg love is the swansong of a vanishing cinema, we must face the reality of the virtual. There is a manifest presence of virtual life (and love) outside the cinema hall, and we do not know if it functions in the same way as it is depicted in feature films. Thus, what we found out about virtual love in cinema might owe more to the form than to the content. Perhaps it is just in its cinematic imagination that virtual love so clearly resembles and symbolizes human affects – while beyond the cinema hall virtual love has long become a social reality of its own, no longer shaped exclusively by human–human interactions. Possibly, virtual intimacy factually transcends the cinematically incarnated versions we are acquainted with, and which rule our narrative habits. In fact, people love machines much more than we imagine, and much more intensively (or naturally) than we would accept in a movie. And the phenomenon is not entirely new – in fact, cinema itself is a machine one can fall in love with.

> No doubt, we have all fallen in love, to varying degrees, with [...] "flickering signifiers". Whether it was a film star, pop star, porn star or anonymous billboard, the visual siren songs of the market-driven media come equipped with libidinal fish-hooks to tug at our eye-balls, hearts, loins and wallets.
>
> (Pettmann 2009, p. 2)

Actually, in recent times a plethora of new love machines has been developed. In his persuasive book *Love and Sex with Robots: The Evolution of Human–Robot Relationships*, David Levy (2007) presents a solid body of research, and lists huge efforts of engineering in the field of affection for virtual others. He describes three ways of falling in love with robots: First, the human way of loving, which is based on tendencies of nurturing. Its paradigmatic expression was the *tamagochi* fashion of the 1980s, which has since evolved into a veritable herd of robopets, up to Sony's well established pet dog AIBO. The second, quite human too, is dominance, which is experienced in the (predominantly, but not exclusively) male inclination to technology and programming, which could render a robot love affair even more desirable than a human one. And third, there might be a dimension of genuine robot love, too, based on a "love for machines and technology per se, sometimes called 'technophilia'" (Levy 2007, p. 125). We do not know much about it, since it is hard to imagine for us. However, we observe facts like the huge amount of affective technical toys (of all sizes) that attract mainly boys (of all ages). For computer nerds, the virtual provides a transitional space in the sense of Winnicott, more sheltering and

154 ANDREAS HAMBURGER

rewarding than real social interactions. "Like Narcissus and his reflection, people who work with computers can easily fall in love with the worlds they have constructed or with their performances in the worlds created for them by others" (Levy 2007, p. 114).

The reality of the virtual grew with the evolution of the Internet. In its early years, the Internet was something like a large and slippery chat-room. Turkle (1995, p. 180) defined it as a "significant social laboratory for experimenting with the constructions and reconstructions of self", alluding to the widespread habit of anonymous and often sexual chats in the vast and open space of the World Wide Web. People enjoyed the carnivalesque freedom to use fake identities, a masquerade which was part of the thrill. One never knew whether the beautiful girl who sent those juicy lines to your MS-DOS screen in some far out reality was a dirty old man (or, with a lower probability, vice versa). And one never had to decide. In the web's transitional space, physical identity seemed to lose importance. As Stone (1995) suggested, on the net, the

> transgendered body is the natural body. The nets are spaces of transformation, identity factories in which bodies are meaning machines, and transgender-identity as performance, as play, as wrench in the smooth gears of the social apparatus of vision is the ground state.
>
> (Stone 1995, p. 91)

On today's Internet, the former anonymity has been replaced by presence in multiple contacts. While in the 1980s the web was based on writing, by the twenty-first century it has become an equally visual space. As Bolter and Grusin (2000, p. 236) suggest, the networked self travels in hypermediate environments as a succession of relationships with various applications or media. The user oscillates between media, moves from window to window, from application to application, and adopts her identity to a point where it can be seen as constituted by oscillation. Culture industry 4.0 incorporates consumers in a much more penetrant way than in the olden days of the world wide web. When erstwhile phantasy reigned, and signals were sent to other wandering monads' sepia-on-black MS-DOS screens, today visually, acoustically, and (soon) sensually connected used-users are interconnected like embryos in an umbilical cobweb. There is not even one central (evil) spider who bites his victims or implants thoughts and feelings into their hypnotized minds – it is a mass of companies advertising for our attention and rewarding us with the kick we yearn for. And eventually, it is just the web itself, fed by millions of small apps, where the process of seduction is mutual, and even more intrusive. It is not a scary SF projection that teledildos connect their erogenous zones to either the girl next door (wherever she lives) or, comparable in credibility, the cyborg lover.

Of course, in the end all comes down to the body. Film psychoanalysis is based on the analysis of the spectator. Thus, our psychoanalytic interpretation of the virtual intimacy movies concentrates on how these films serve the audience's unconscious needs and repressions. In the relation of the spectator to the screen it is neither the film's characters, nor plot, nor content in the first place that can be seen as affecting the audience, but its formal operations. The temporal architecture on the screen meets the audience's expectations and guides its affective resonance. Screen characters are only alive if and because life is breathed into them by the emotional projection of the spectator. Like the planet Solaris, cinema incorporates the audience's phantasy. The loving and beloved robot, as a phantasy of the spectator, emerges from the narcissistic grandiosity of absolute control over the feeding and loving breast, the unthinkable object of earliest relational experience. However, the central conflict of virtual intimacy is the emancipation of the controlled breast. The maternal body we adore and which guides our emerging self and sustains its narcissistic regulation eventually is not desired as a machine, but as a subject. The baby is not longing for a mirror, but for an answer (see Fonagy et al. 2002; Gergely and Watson 1999). What we inevitably strive for in the intimate relationship is to be loved by the beloved: "Amor, ch' a null' amato amar perdona" as Dante put it in the *Divine Comedy* (V, 103), "Love which to no beloved abates to love". Love, by its essence, presupposes reciprocity, and thus builds on the subjectivity of the Other.

There is a sequence in *Solaris* when Hari desperately tries to tolerate Kris' absence, and Kris, who feels his concern for her, runs back to his room – where he finds she has fainted from the effort to control her longing. Immediately before this sequence, the film had presented an incomplete, fragmentary representation of the mother (see Hamburger 2012). The context points to the unconscious scene evoked and stimulated by the film in the audience: The maternal void introduced by the preceding scene is answered by Hari's longing for contact, and the viewer is dragged from emptiness to yearning. "Mother", however, in this context of primary love, does not refer to a whole person, but to something like an empathic presence which bridges the diverging experiences of security and abandonment and helps the baby to develop protosymbolic kernels of meaning in the language of ritualized interaction. The presence of the

156 ANDREAS HAMBURGER

dreaming mother allows the baby to constitute mother as a phantasmatic object. In the suspense of the cinematic presence, spectators get confused and comforted again as in their mothers' arms.

Notes

1 I am very much indebted to Johannes Schade, Ph.D., who was a first and very helpful critical reader of this essay.
2 The film is constructed in a way that relies on spectators' change in perspective, so they will adopt the camera's or protagonist's perspective as their own. It is in this sense that Vivian Sobchack (1992) can speak of the cinematic body, even if her continuous play with the metaphor gives the impression she would accept the movie as a living subject.

References

Baudrillard, J. (1981). *Simulacra and Simulation*. Trans. A. F. Glaser. Ann Arbor: University of Michigan Press.
Ben-Ze'ev, A. (2004). *Love Online: Emotions on the Internet*. Cambridge: Cambridge University Press
Berman, E. (2003). Reader and story, viewer and film: On transference and interpretation. *International Journal of Psychoanalysis, 84*: 119–129.
Bolter, J. D. and Grusin, R. (2000). *Remediation: Understanding New Media*. Cambridge, MA: MIT Press.
Bråten, S. (2006). *Intersubjective Communication and Emotion in Early Ontogeny*. Cambridge: Cambridge University Press.
Decker, O. (2004). *Der Prothesengott. Subjektivität und Transplantationsmedizin*. Giessen: Psychosozial.
Diamond, D. and Wrye, H. (1998). Epilogue. Projections of psychic reality: A centennial of film and psychoanalysis. *Psychoanalytic Inquiry, 18*: 311–334.
Dick, P. K. (1968). *Do Androids Dream of Electric Sheep?* New York: Doubleday.
Dick, P. K. (1969). *Ubik*. New York: Doubleday.
Drieger, P. (2008). Virtuelle Welten:- Eine neue Dimension unseres Wirklichkeitsverständnisses? M.A. thesis, University of Eichstädt-Ingolstadt. pub lic.noumentalia.de/data/Text/MA_Virtuelle_Welten.pdf (accessed 12.10. 2011).
Fonagy, P., Gergely, G., Elliot, L. J. and Target, M. (2002). *Affect Regulation, Mentalization, and the Development of the Self*. New York: Other Press.
Freud, S. (1930). *Civilization and Its Discontents*. S.E. XXI, 57–146.
Freud, S. (1950a [1895]). Project for a Scientific Psychology. S.E. I, 281–391.

Gabbard, G. O. (1997). The psychoanalysts at the movies. *International Journal of Psychoanalysis, 78*: 429–434.

Gabbard, G. O. and Gabbard, K. (1987). *Psychiatry and the Cinema*. Chicago: University of Chicago Press.

Gehring, P. (2008). *Traum und Wirklichkeit: Zur Geschichte einer Unterscheidung*. Frankfurt am Main: Campus.

Gergely, G. and Watson, J. S. (1999). Early socio-emotional development: Contingency perception and the social-biofeedback model. *Early Social Cognition: Understanding Others in the First Months of Life, 60*: 101–136.

Gibson, William (1982). Burning chrome. In Gibson, *Burning Chrome*. New York: Ace Books, 1987.

Hamburger, A. (2012). Wo Es war, soll Ich werden. *Solaris* – Regie: Andrej Tarkovskij. In Laszig, Parfen (ed.). *Blade Runner, Matrix und Avatare. Psychoanalytische Betrachtungen virtueller Wesen und Welten im Film* (pp. 1–22). Heidelberg and New York: Springer.

Hamburger, A. (2013a). Arbeit in der Tiefe. Vorüberlegungen zu einer skeptischen Kulturanalyse. In H. Hierdeis (ed.), *Psychoanalytische Skepsis* (pp. 123–183). Göttingen: Vandenhoeck & Ruprecht.

Hamburger, A. (2013b). Via Regia und zurück. Traumerzählungen und ihre Resonanz. In Bernhard Janta,, Beate Unruh and Susanne Walz-Pawlita (eds) *Der Traum* (pp. 123–143). Giessen: Psychosozial.

Hamburger, A. (2014). Männersachen. Das Unsichtbare in *No Country for Old Men*. In Peter Bär and Gerhard Schneider (eds) *Die Coen-Brüder* (pp. 95–115). Giessen: Psychosozial.

Hamburger, A. (2015). Women and images of men in cinema. *La Belle et la Bête* by Jean Cocteau. In A. Hamburger (ed.), *Woman and Male Images in Cinema. Gender Construction in Cocteau's* La Belle et la Bête (pp. 3–14). London: Karnac.

Hamburger, A. (2016). "Sehn, wie's ist": Hanekes *Benny's Video* (1992). In Gerhard Schneider and Peter Bär (eds) *Michael Haneke* (pp. 41–54). Giessen: Psychosozial (= Im Dialog: Psychoanalyse & Filmtheorie vol. 12).

Hamburger, A. and Leube-Sonnleitner, K. (2014). Wie im Kino. Zur Filmanalyse in der Gruppe – Methodologie der Psychoanalytischen Filminterpretation anhand von Lars von Triers *Melancholia*. In R. Zwiebel and D. Blothner (eds) *Melancholia – Wege zur psychoanalytischen Interpretation des Films* (pp. 72–109). Göttingen, Germany: Vandenhoeck & Ruprecht.

Harris, A., and Sklar, R. (1998). Wild film theory, wild film analysis. *Psychoanalytic Inquiry, 18*: 222–237.

Hoffmann, E. T. A. (1816). *The Sandman*.

Kobald, A. (2012). *Ideengeschichtliche Aspekte zur Technikgenese der sozialen Robotik*. Grin Verlag.

158   ANDREAS HAMBURGER

Lem, S. (1961). *Solaris*, trans. Joanna Kilmartin and Steve Cox. In *Solaris, The Chain of Chance, A Perfect Vacuum* (p. 32). London: Penguin, 1981.

Lem, S. (1964). *Fables for Robots*. In S. Lem, *Mortal Engines*. Boston: Mariner Books, 1992.

Levy, D. (2007). *Love and Sex with Robots*. London and New York: HarperCollins.

Mulvey, L. (1975). Visual Pleasure and Narrative Cinema. *Screen, 16*(3): 6–18. Reprinted in C. Penley (ed.) (1988), *Feminism and Film Theory* (pp. 57–68). New York: Routledge.

Mulvey, L. (1981). Afterthoughts on "Visual Pleasure and Narrative Cinema" inspired by *Duel in the Sun*. *Framework*, 15/16/17, pp. 12–15. Reprinted in C. Penley (ed.) (1988) *Feminism and Film Theory* (pp. 69–79). New York: Routledge.

Pettmann, D. (2009). Love in the Time of Tamagotchi. *Theory, Culture and Society, 26*(2–3): 1–20.

Pohl, B. (2002). *Abre los ojos* (Alejandro Amenábar). Über Risiken und Nebenwirkungen der Virtuellen Realität. In Jörn Glasenapp (ed.) *Cyberfiktionen: neue Beiträge* (pp. 149–177). Munich: Reinhard Fischer.

Ryan, M. L. (2001). Beyond myth and metaphor. *Consultant*, 1983, p. 91.

Schneider, G. (2008). Filmpsychoanalyse – Zugangswege zur psychoanalytischen Interpretation von Filmen. In P. Laszig and G. Schneider (eds) *Film und Psychoanalyse. Kinofilme als kulturelle Symptome* (pp. 19–38). Giessen: Psychosozial.

Schopenhauer, A. (1909 [1844]). *The World As Will and Idea (Vol. 1)*. Trans. R. B. Haldane and J. Kemp. 7th edn. London: Kegan Paul, Trench, Trübner & Co.

Sobchack, V. (1992). *The Address of the Eye. A Phenomomenology of Film Experience*. Princeton, NJ: Princeton University Press.

Stone, A. R. (1995). *The War of Desire and Technology at the Close of the Mechanical Age*. Cambridge, MA: MIT Press.

Turkle, S. (1995). *Life on the Screen: Identity in the Age of the Internet*. New York: Touchstone.

Wiener, O. (1969). *Die Verbesserung von Mitteleuropa*. A novel. Reinbek: Rowohlt.

Zwiebel, R. and Blothner, D. (eds) (2014). *Melancholia – Wege zur psychoanalytischen Interpretation des Films*. Göttingen: Vandenhoek & Ruprecht.

CHAPTER ELEVEN

'I don't know what I feel. Is it love?'

Jana Burgerová

Spike Jonze's *Her* is about digital love, how and why this can arise, how it can function effectively as a consequence of, for example, a narcissistic disorder. Digital love has to do with loneliness, staving off loneliness, with reclusiveness. Just as Theodore, the film's protagonist, lives in a fantasy world and plays pretend games, I found myself almost overwhelmed by associations and fantasies.

For many years I have travelled by train from the Bavarian provinces to my practice in Munich.

Groups of commuters, whom I knew only from these train journeys, would greet each other cheerily, and over time we came to know some of each other's life stories. Occasionally, we laughed, sometimes quite loudly, swapped books, stories, until one after another we arrived at our destinations. But the atmosphere in the train changed rapidly. Many of the books 'vanished', as had the atmosphere of concentration characteristic of learners. Most of the travellers busied themselves with their mobile phones, as if they were Winnicottian transitional objects, lessening the pain of separation from the mother. Earphones, connected by a cable similar to the umbilical cord that joins a baby to its mother, play a song of pacification, demonstrating that one is not alone. Most of the passengers standing on platforms and waiting are withdrawn inside themselves, phones at the ready for when they alight and call someone to announce their presence

160 JANA BURGEROVÁ

on the train, or to check the latest news. Talking to oneself whilst walking would in former times have been a clear indication of a psychotic condition. Today, the loud talkers who from time to time profess to be giving quite important instructions, have proliferated everywhere. Surely, we cannot be dealing with a city full of psychotics!

The notion of 'disappearing books' brings to mind the film director François Truffaut. His 1966 film *Fahrenheit 451* (based on the 1953 novel by Ray Bradbury) showed how books represent a danger to the community because of their explanatory potential. The narrative refers to a society not too far in the future organized on the principle of living without worries in which everyone strives for happiness. Books are regarded as spreading adversity because they expose problems and conflicts, and so are banned by law. Fire departments have instructions to track down books and to burn them. In connection with the film *Her*, I was fascinated by the daily conversations between the wife of the protagonist in *Fahrenheit 451* and a large wall-mounted screen which informed her on how to view the 'correct' world and how to behave in order to prosper in it. This in a film made at a time when there were no computers or mobile phones in daily use or even in our imaginations. At the end, the wife denounces her husband, who is searching for the truth in a world where this is absolutely forbidden.

Just as the aforementioned wife converses with the screen, Theodore Twombly, the protagonist of *Her*, is wired throughout the day via a chip in his ear, which functions as a part-object. He can listen to his mail, give commands, erase mail, choose music: almost as if he was endowed with an omnipotence that allowed him to be completely in charge of his world. For instance, he can at any time trigger digital sex accompanied by images of his own choosing. Soon after the opening of the film – strange, disconcerting and rather disturbing, also to some extent for Theodore – we hear a female voice online which demands that Theodore talk to her about strangling her with a dead cat so that she can have an orgasm. It is almost as though we observed Theodore having a momentary doubt. This absurd situation, however, is not sufficient to be categorized as an artificial delusion, because Theodore lives on with the chip in place. Such irritations or warnings, in which Theodore recognizes his own delusions, and perhaps also his loneliness, only then to ignore them, are repeated throughout the film. The OS Samantha could also be seen as a sort of Cassandra, whose wise warnings go unnoticed. She rapidly disowns each delusion or warning and pretends to be experiencing something concrete.

The loneliness and solitude in our practices increase, while at the same time online dating agencies – carefully targeted: e.g. for the elite, nature

'I DON'T KNOW WHAT I FEEL. IS IT LOVE?' 161

lovers, the middle class ... according to how people wish to perceive themselves – offer instant, immense, endless bliss, and our patients are willing to pay any amount of money for it. When meeting someone face to face, we can see them, their bodies, their gestures, their movements; we can smell, taste, hear them, appreciate their totality. We rapidly sense arousal, lust. Fantasy is of course in play, transference, which causes us to spring over our own shadows, and later causes problems. In an online meeting, everything follows reason, calculation (status in society, hobbies, dreams) and a predetermined notion as to what one is looking for, subconscious fantasies, childish longings, unfulfilled and unrealizable.

The Beatles and later the Rolling Stones, for example, as they stormed onto the music scene appear very impressive in memory. Teenagers of the time swooned en masse in concert halls because in their idealized worlds and borderless fantasies they felt they had found their greatest loves. They screened out the fact that thousands of rivals shared their fantasies. In a recent interview, an aging rock star recounted how as a young girl she had passed out at the sight of the bulge in Mick Jagger's trousers, as the fantasy of sex with him flooded over her.

The run-down and cold apartment decorations in *Fahrenheit 451* are also present in *Her*. It is demonstrated, also with regard to the way technical matters are represented, how final the technological possibilities of this vision of the future appear. This computer-steered society functions so perfectly that no possibilities exist for it to be improved, as though humans had reached the end of all technological progress. This is also emphasized by the superb and almost perfect cityscapes, everything distinct and probably in many places the same.

The sound track to *Her* is by Acade Fire, a Canadian indie band who use unusual instruments such as an accordian, church organ or other wind instruments, to evoke a trance-like state in which, like Theodore, the audience forgets reality. In situations where Theodore is enamoured by his feelings when writing, or chats with Samantha (his operating system), the music resorts to kitsch, as in Hollywood love scenes, with soaring violins, whereby longings and over-idealized associations are suggested.

Theodore Twombly earns his money by deceiving people. He writes heart rending love letters for them and the computer fixes them up with the required personalized handwriting. With empathy, fantasy and devotion, Theodore is able to write wonderful, seductive letters, whilst appearing himself to be extremely happy, as though he were writing to his own lover, or receiving mail from her. He screens out the fraudulent aspect, the self-deceptive action, and does not notice that he is himself

162   JANA BURGEROVÁ

deceived, that everything is observed and registered, that the real power lies elsewhere.

In his film *World on a Wire* (1973), Rainer Werner Fassbinder showed impressively how people can deceive themselves in respect of their security and strength. In this scientific thriller, people who know a lot and who believe themselves to have influence, or control, are gradually eliminated. At the 'Institute for Cybertechnics and Futureology' (IKZ), a supercomputer called Simulacron-1 that is able to simulate an entire small town has been developed. The simulation runs 24 hours a day and is populated with 'identity-units', which pursue lives similar to normal humans and possess consciousness. Apart from a few 'contact-units', none of the simulated people know that their world is a simulation, or a 'Simulakron'.

Theodore lives alone. He is friends with a couple who live in the same house. The friendship appears initially to be almost symbiotic, but later the pair split and following the separation the woman, Theodore's best friend, also begins a relationship with an operating system. Both constantly encourage Theodore to make contact with women in order to find a new partner and to forget the drama of his failed marriage. One day he receives a compelling offer to contact an operating system called Samantha, represented by a highly erotic and seductive female voice. The acceptance interview 'behaves' towards him somewhat offensively. It queries him in a monotone and Theodore's need for intense attentiveness and affection is subdued, especially when he wants to to recall how his mother always spoke about herself. He felt subdued and not taken seriously by her. Theodore's neediness causes him to overlook the ignorance of the computer, that this is not programmed for relationship nuance and conflict; and that the query programme displays the same behaviour as his mother awakens feelings in Theodore that he had probably learned to suppress effectively. Theodore gets involved. Given such tricky deceptions, the apparent power to switch the machine off whenever one likes is a safeguard against helplessness. It is clear that the phenomenon of a human relationship and attachment cannot be programmed into an operating system.

Woody Allen's 1985 film *The Purple Rose of Cairo* comes to mind. The character Baxter breaks through the fourth wall of the screen and addresses the horrified waitress Cecilia directly. She had fallen in love with him (as a film character) and had been watching the film for weeks in her free time. Baxter leaves the screen and stands before Cecilia. They fall in love until sober reality sets in.

'I DON'T KNOW WHAT I FEEL. IS IT LOVE?'   163

Theodore has now fallen in love with his operating system and behaves as if he was a child lost in his magic thoughts and playing pretend games. Theodore is still married but has not lived with his wife for a long time and he intends to divorce her even though he would prefer to remain married. He would then retain the fantasy that someone is at his side. His memories of life together with his wife, mostly painted in positive colours, allow him to avoid sensing his loneliness. He would gladly continue to live this way. 'I am happily married', he says. The limitations of the computer result (probably) from its inability to programme the capability for a relationship. In many films, robots are assigned human characteristics, but this usually does not suffice. It is like the incompatability of extremely different systems. Following a digital sex session with Samantha while Theodore is still married and has yet to sign his divorce papers, he assures her and himself that he does not seek a relationship with her, at which point Samantha energetically fends him off because the phenomenon 'relationship' is unknown to her. Incidentally, the love scene between the two is treated in the film primarily via Samantha's voice, in such a way as to awaken erotic fantasies in the audience. The screen is left black and it feels as if the camera were switched off, as if we should not be watching (in the bedroom of our parents).

When the married couple meet in order to sign the divorce papers, the atmosphere is quite warm, almost loving. The pain they both feel at the finality of this separation is plainly visible. Only when she becomes aware of Theodore's love for an operating system does his wife become cold, dismissive and determined to complete the divorce. It is as though she finally sees clearly the pathology she had previously sensed. 'You were never able to speak about your feelings', she tells him.

Following this meeting Theodore becomes extremely pensive. The intensity of his disturbance activates Samantha. At first he appears to be about to break with her and she reacts promptly, recognizing his pronounced unease and resentment. She is jealous and intrusive and, having total access to his data, submits his divorce papers! Theodore baulks, but remains trapped in delusive passivity, as he presumedly had failed to cut in on his mother's habit of talking only about herself. He begins to recognize that he is always alone, whilst his colleague has a real girlfriend, yet still gives in to the operating system. He calls out to the universe 'There! I am newly available.' A further disturbance occurs when Samantha sends Theodore her woman substitute (the actress looks like Scarlett Johannson), because she herself has no physical body, which appears to trouble her. The substitute is fitted with a chip in her ear. She must be silent and strictly follow the instructions she receives from Samantha, who herself moans in Thedore's chip. Since Theodore probably expected a different Samantha, he cannot respond – we could perhaps recognize a desire for the presence of the depressive position – quite apart from the fact that an approach phase, which Samantha's programme does not have, has been skipped (as in online dating). Relationships are not programmed: they do not exist in the digital world.

Theodore feels forced to have sex with the strange woman, which Samantha commands repeatedly in a seductive tone. Following failure, the strange woman (also attached to the operating system Samantha) feels responsible and that she has failed Samantha. Theodore seems baffled, pensive, and stares across the street at a steaming canal, as though a spirit or subconscious perception were about to rise from the canal and inform him that he had allowed himself to be deceived in order to escape his loneliness.

Samantha shows up conspicuously, often intruding into his private sphere. The protection of human nature is not programmed. She sorts his mail, submits divorce papers, later sends to a publisher the love letters which he had written professionally for others. This is abusive insofar as it shows an absence of respect for his professional confidentiality.

The final awakening occurs when Samantha introduces a third computer and so indicates yet more clearly the world from which she comes. Theodore checks out the said book (the rivals) that fascinates her. He finds it positively stupid, but says this tenderly, as though he would again seek to eradicate creeping doubts. The end comes at him rapidly as he learns that he is only one of 8,000 of Samantha's 'chosen', and he sees them all for the first time while he is sitting, seeming happy, on the stairs of an underground station. As many patients suddenly discover the real world when they emerge from their internal selves following years of treatment: 'Oh! You've hung a new picture' (which has been hanging there the whole time). Now he can write an authentic, respectful letter to his ex-wife, and he feels a new connection with his female friend who lives in his house (and whose operating system has also been switched off). He leads her up to the roof of the house and they gaze out over the town at night.

The name Theodore Twombly reminded me of the American painter and object artist Cy Twombly, whose reclusiveness is as legendary as his work. His canvases became projection screens of his own physical and psychological presence, the brushwork ever more gesturally expressive. Theodore is a writer and Cy's work often has to do with words. He visualizes in strong colours the calm space between and around words. As Samantha says:

> It's like I'm reading a book, and it's a book I deeply love. But I'm reading it slowly now. So the words are really far apart and the spaces between the words are almost infinite. I can still feel you, and the words of our story, but it's in this endless space between the words that I'm finding myself now.

One can perhaps understand this operating system 'Samantha' as a Homeric Siren, who on the one hand seduces and simultaneously warns one to be reflective, to check the seductive world against one's own neediness and childish tendency to be deceived.

CHAPTER TWELVE

Her: the object in the virtual world

Maria Z. Areu Crespo

Introduction

In 2013 the film *Her* won the Academy Award for best original screenplay. The author is Spike Jonze, and when I enquired into his work I realised that he had directed *Being John Malkovich* in 1999, a film that impressed me because it approached a mode of existence that has not been much explored. I was left with the impression that perhaps *Her* could be another attempt at approaching a hard-to-explain longing.

The film encourages many ideas, but for the sake of clarity I will organise my chapter as follows: the first section will deal with *Her* and love in the virtual world; while the second section will address the question: Can we live in solitude?

Her: *Love in the virtual world*

I believe, with Bollas, that 'Objects, like words, are there for us to express ourselves' (1992, p. 36). There is a particular object that plays a major role in *Her*.

Her displays a world; a way of being in the world. Just as the TV shows *Little House on the Prairie* and *The Simpsons* ask us to take part in their worlds, to 'come and play' with them, as it were, the film *Her* does the same.

The setting is an American city, where concrete predominates. There are lots of people; lonely, detached, they do not talk to each other, but rather seem to have established a connection with an object: an electronic device. The author makes us become fully involved with this idea, so we might want to ask ourselves: What are these images telling us?

The transitional object comes to mind. Winnicott says that 'It is not the object, of course, that is transitional. The object represents the infant's transition' (1953, p. 19).

We then become interested in the way that the main character uses the electronic device and we approach him in order to discover this.

Let us consider for one moment the names chosen for the characters of the film. There are two main characters: Theodore Twombly and an Electronic Operating System (O.S.), Samantha. Theodore's name comes from the Greek and means 'God's gift'. His surname is Twombly, which could be divided into two parts: 'two', and 'wombly'. If womb is uterus and the suffix 'ly' means 'like a particular thing in manner, nature, or appearance', we could consider that *wombly* alludes to a uterine mode, a pre-natal mode. I wonder if the author, through the choice of names, is not showing Theodore's longing: to establish a relationship (of two) in the prenatal style.

The name for the voice is found among several possible feminine names. Is Samantha a casual choice? Of Semite origin, Samantha means 'the listener'.

What does Samantha hear? The unthought known. What has been longed for but never considered as longing. What has been 'wombly' longed for, from a protective uterus to which there is longing to return.

Following Rascovsky's ideas, the inexistence of real external objects allows the main character to establish relationships with his inherited internal objects, like the foetal Ego. In the case of the foetus, all contact with external reality is carried out by the mother through the unconditional provision of the umbilical chord (could it be the computer and its program in the case of Theodore?). In this way, the foetus is connected primarily with his own needs, without taking into account the needs of the other in the relationship.

Her allows us to see ourselves in a way of existence that goes unchallenged: the use of the computer, that inseparable companion, the guardian of our history, of our projects, of our personal communications, of our pictures, films, videos, and so on is an essential object for our existence; the hard disk of our computer treasures all that our memory is reluctant to recall. Through this object we go shopping, do bank operations and distance courses, we find old childhood friends.

Jonze goes further, however, and comes up with a personal, loving, erotic relationship between Theodore and the portentous voice of Scarlett Johansson, metonymy of the original erotic object. The relationship begins with the company, the usefulness provided by the system (a kind of efficient secretary), which then progresses into a therapeutic companion and eventually intimacy, and love, develop. The drives of self-preservation and the erotic drives become satisfied in the relationship with the operating system. However, almost in a whisper we might ask ourselves when the death drives will become noticeable, where the silent, concealed aspects might be.

It has transpired that when Jonze gave directions to Johansson during the shooting of *Her*, he insisted on the fact that she needed to sound completely human, something that Johansson certainly achieved because she suggests a presence whose voice seduces Theodore and makes him fall in love with it.

Of no less importance is the fact that Theodore buys the operating system after a shattering affective frustration: he has separated from his wife, also his young love, whom he describes as having become a part of himself. We could consider that he buys something in order to avoid intense grief, to ease loneliness, and to find some entertainment by the way, as we have seen that he likes electronic games.

What is the relationship between him and Samantha like? If Jonze has demanded that the voice be human it is probably due to the fact that the relationship between them will progressively develop. It starts as a game, then it connects Theodore with aspects of his work (appointments, tasks, meetings) until he and Samantha are on intimate terms. It is a complex relationship where one of its members lacks a body and, at some point, is intrigued by the significance of lacking a body. A transitional space has been created, one where Theodore can ease his loneliness; the potential of the object without a body is to bring back to life Theodore's aching body.

However, we might ask ourselves how Theodore could escape the repetition of his story. Let us go back to Bollas: by using the program Theodore is forced to re-experience a sequence with the operating system that goes from enthusiasm to illusion, to love, to the expectation of wholeness, until he reencounters a well-known feeling: objects drift apart from him, they leave him and Theodore is once again plunged into unfathomable loneliness.

170   MARIA Z. AREU CRESPO

First experience of satisfaction

Now that we have reached this point, let us go back to psychoanalysis.

The first experience of satisfaction is described as a mythical time when birth trauma, and its resulting release of endogenous stimuli, finds relief: an action will be carried out with the help of an outside person and only then can the tension be removed.

Her begins when Theodore must face feelings of helplessness unchained by the loss of his love object, something we only learn after he has purchased the operating system. We could imagine that libido returns to a way of satisfaction that preserves him from contact with others; he finds the satisfying object in an operating system (which is available on the market).

If the mythical first experience of satisfaction leaves a trace of the image of the object, of an action and a sense that there's been adequate discharge, then the trace of satisfaction will be reinvested in the encounter with Samantha.

And taking a part, which is undoubtedly of essential importance, for the whole, the object is represented by Samantha's voice. The voice understands him, helps him, 'reminds' him of what Theodore has forgotten: happiness, love, hope.

When Theodore finds an object in Samantha he is creating a 'subjective object', to say it in Winnicott's words. This is a happy discovery that allows us to establish a connection with the analytic session.

Should we then become a subjective object for the patient so that he can project onto us his most intimate needs? Has access to technology revealed a kind of relationship that until now appeared to be restricted to the realm of fiction, or is it simply used here to refer to an expectation (at once frustrating and frustrated), to an ever-present and ever-lost illusion?

The 'wombly' hypothesis

The starting point of the first experience of satisfaction, an explanation that is indeed mythical, is birth trauma, that is, the fact that experiences will be constructed from the moment of birth onwards is taken for granted. Nowadays, however, this idea needs revisiting.

I believe that the Freudian hypothesis goes along the lines of a popular belief, an expectation, that the foetus' environment is ideal, a paradise from which he is expelled at the time of birth, which therefore constitutes a traumatic event.

However, while I will not confront the need for a mythology that can help us explain the psyche, I nevertheless believe that such an assumption involves the following idea: the womb offers unending provision, constant satisfaction, and frustration begins after the birth trauma, that is to say, it begins with the separation of the baby from its mother. This idea could be supported by the fantasy of the return to the maternal womb, which would guarantee unlimited wellbeing to the subject.

However, not all the psychoanalytic authors agree with this perspective. Abadi, an Argentine analyst for instance, has spoken of the fear of being trapped within the maternal womb. In this case the womb could become the infant's grave.

If the womb could be considered as both paradise and grave, then both the satisfactions and the frustrations – that go beyond the mother's illnesses, and beyond the mother as representative of the external world – experienced within the womb should be actualised.

The reason I am elaborating on this subject is that on finding the longed-for relationship in the metonymic object – Samantha's voice – there is absence of tact, absence of the visual drive, and the voice alone represents the object in its completeness. Therefore we might wonder if it constitutes a representation of the way the foetus experiences the object.

Rhythm is set by the mother's heart; hearing is what makes contact possible, therefore Samantha could well represent that womb.

Which womb? The womb that makes the subject fall in love, the womb idealised as the provider of all that is good. But also the deadly womb, trapped inside which the foetus could find his grave, in a scale that goes from health to all the possibilities of illness.

However, this is far from being the only maternal representation evoked by the main character of the film we are analysing.

The dead mother

When Theodore starts the operating system he is asked about his relationship with his mother. Hesitatingly he begins to say: 'Well, my mom, every time I wanted to talk to her, she always ended by talking about herself …', and the Operating System moves on to the next subject because it already has enough information.

Theodore is not just any man; he is sensitive, intelligent, and cultured. He is also upset and lonely. He can write love letters, letters of friendship, letters recalling meaningful events with great feeling but they are meant for others. We can detect in him the recollection of his relationship

172 MARIA Z. AREU CRESPO

with a mother who could not see beyond her own narcissism; a trace that is awakened every time he tries to establish relationships of a different nature throughout his life.

In this way, when the object (first his wife, and then Samantha) vies for his attention, Theodore, identified with the dead mother of his own primary relationship, leaves the object, like he himself feels he has been abandoned by his mother. He has become a sensitive man, is endowed with great affective perception, and is no stranger to the subtleties of relationships; he can write about feelings, he can make others feel strong emotions, he can move his readers to tears, but he himself is unable to feel. He, like the 'dead mother' before him, keeps a distance, something he is able to acknowledge when he claims that 'I ran into a mirror'.

His melancholic mood, typical of grief that resists being worked through, reminds us of Green's concept of the dead mother complex: 'The essential characteristic of this depression is that it takes place in the presence of the object, which is itself absorbed by a bereavement' (1983, p. 149). There is a child connected to a bereaved primary object, and in the end he identifies with this object that leaves him feeling all alone; this is how the story will repeat itself. Green points out that one of the traits of this complex is the autoerotic excitation; there is search for pure organ-pleasure and a reluctance to love the object.

In this film the confusion between the O.S. object and the longing for a relationship with an object of reality, or, better still, between 'two' and 'wombly', is successfully accomplished. Reality appears when Theodore meets his ex-wife, who tells the waitress that Theodore has fallen in love with his computer.

Generation and tool: the technical era as historical destiny

Bollas defines generations not only in terms of the passing of time, but mainly by the use of objects, which are particular to each generation. And these objects, like words, will constitute ways of expression.

If we are going to talk about computer science, we could think that the generation born since the 1990s has been most deeply affected by it, because this generation had these tools at their disposal from the very beginning of their lives. However, the main character in the film is a man in his early- or mid-forties. I understand that Jonze wants to let us know that computer science is an 'object' in psychoanalytic terms, which nowadays is present in the lives of all generations, despite the fact that some generations are more familiar with it than others. If the computer as an object defines nowadays our world, it would seem that Jonze wants to refer to a certain type of psychic behaviour that takes the computer as an object and that, in so doing, shows us the potential of transforming our way of establishing relationships, or not, with 'real' objects, the objects of the world.

The point is that technique is a cultural phenomenon of our time. This is not merely a technical reality as all the dimensions of human existence are reached and affected by it: technique qualifies the cognitive style in which reality is approached, it goes through all the spheres of human knowledge, art, behaviour, interpersonal relationships (Mandrioni, 1990).

Mandrioni calls the present time 'technical era' and considers that this technical era should be understood as historical destiny, as determination, as our present way of being in the world (Mandrioni, 2001).

In the film *Her*, through the relationship with the Operating System, contact with a primary object is shown, an object that immediately responds to our wishes. In what way? In the 'wombly' way: a palliative for loneliness, a way of communicating but excluding the body. This is what happens in *Her*.

We might think that the object is configured by the use made of it by its owner; to paraphrase Winnicott, two computers may be identical, may have the same programs, and so on, but the use made of them speaks of who is using them. If each computer depends on the capacity of whoever is using it to create, then we will see the potential, creative, quality of this particular object.

The operating system manifests itself in its illusory identity, which in the end proves disappointing for Theodore. Perhaps, as Winnicott puts it, the transitional object 'is not forgotten and it is not mourned. It loses meaning' (1958, p. 7). 'The transitional object is not an internal object. It is a possession' (p. 13).

Illusion comes to an abrupt end; it could not have been otherwise. When we find that contact with the primary object is disappointing we are brought back to a world where our individuality is experienced as loneliness. However, illusion was indeed good while it lasted.

If the notion of generation is defined by the tool used, then Jonze shows us a space that pervades the whole world nowadays. We could say that it is the construction of a mental space, a space for knowledge and relationship with ourselves, where the tool of the computer, *wombly*, works, which may lead us to the 'two' of the object relation, the expectation of a *wombly* relationship.

174 MARIA Z. AREU CRESPO

Jonze talks about semantics, a language that is a new way of communication not only with others, but mainly with the secret sphere of each individual. Jonze in fact refers to a dimension of the psyche that is expressed through the encounter with electronic objects.

Her *can help us consider analysis by Skype*

Most analysts, even those reluctant to use it, have included the computer in the analytic treatment. Some of them use mail, or the telephone, but I believe that in general it is Skype that is the most widely used tool.

'The shape and use of psychoanalytic tools today' was the theme of the 49th IPA Congress in Boston in 2015. What is the use made by us psychoanalysts of this tool? If the print made reading popular, then nowadays the computer makes 'body-less' encounters possible.

When we establish contact with Skype our bodies aren't there, but our voice and image are. As with every fantasy, Skype allows the satisfaction of private longing and the construction of a reality adjusted to the needs of each. However, as Theodore shows, there is also the risk of becoming used to a kind of relationship where the other seems to lack a body, and where the subjective object appears and disappears at the touch of a key.

If Freud says that transference love is real love (what kind of love does not involve idealisation in some measure?), we might think that Theodore's love also involves idealisation: that relationship, which for him is unique, brings him back to life.

However, the most important question concerns the kind of experience gained by Theodore: whether it empowers him and helps him grow, or rather increases his feelings of loneliness. The film has an open ending.

On my part, I tend to think that if love cures, and if love is an illusion, Theodore, trapped in the compulsion to repeat, has nevertheless briefly experienced bliss, bliss that can be treasured as a repairing balsam. And perhaps bliss may prompt him to search for the 'two' of the relationship, even in the knowledge that he will never succeed in repeating the moving encounter with the representative of the original object, but with the intact expectation of awaiting the event, as it actually happens at some privileged point in our lives. But then, however, Theodore will have to prefer the 'two' over his longing for 'wombly'. As we hear in the film, he will have to stop looking at himself at the mirror in order to meet with his partner.

Can we think of any advantages of using Skype? Perhaps the constancy of the analytic setting. In my own case, I live next door to a synagogue where marriage ceremonies, meetings, and schoolchildren can sometimes be heard, all of which inevitably lends particular colour to the entrance of the building.

So, the advantage of Skype also involves a loss: the loss of the analyst in her own environment, the noise surrounding the place where she works, and lastly, and more importantly, the loss of contact – a handshake, a personal greeting, constant features that allow the patient to experience a reunion with the soothing object – contact that, even at an infinite distance, to a certain extent mimics the contact with the object of the first experience of satisfaction.

Her: Can we live in solitude?

Why did this film arouse such enthusiasm among some psychoanalysts? At the 49th IPA Congress, four different psychoanalysts – one from Israel, two from Italy and another from Argentina – who did not know each other – presented the same film. These are people who experience different daily realities but who share the vicissitudes of the same line of work in a world where the film's main character, Theodore Twombly, seems familiar. We are not surprised by his affective detachment, nor by his intelligence, which cannot help him take the path of feelings in his own life, but allows him to create, as if they were scripts alien to him, the love letters that he writes for people whose life stories he is familiar with, but which fail to touch him. We are not surprised because we meet watered-down versions of Theodore in our own consulting rooms.

We frequently find in them what psychoanalysis has termed a double inscription; an inscription of affects at the conscious level, affects which are found to be intolerable to experience beyond the intellectual aspect.

Are we dealing with a split off subject? We certainly are.

Serious looking, lonely, polite, Theodore seems to wander around the big city 'wrapped up in his shield' as it were, in a city where everyone wanders around with serious looks in unending conversations with electronic devices, but where little exchange can be seen between humans. Is this the society of the future, concrete and electronics? What does this conjunction suggest?

The dream of a child and the dream of an adult

Freud says that the dream, as guardian of sleep, represents a wish as fulfilled in response to the frustrations of wakefulness. However, there is more to dreaming: the dream, as in traumatic dreams, could also be the painful re-edition of a trauma, which unceasingly forces itself upon the dreamer without the possibility of mental elaboration.

And Jonze talks to us with the language of the thousand faces of the dream. I was genuinely moved by the way in which he welcomes us to his internal world.

The dream of a child

In *Where the Wild Things Are* (2009) we are recalled to our own childhood through an infantile fantasy. The main character is a frustrated child, desperately trying to make himself heard, to make friends, but he is unsuccessful. Like Theodore in *Her*, the child is creative and although his mother undoubtedly values the stories he comes up with, these fail to arouse the required attention, which appears to be greater than what the environment can offer him.

Is his mother frustrating, or is there a longing for tenderness in the child beyond the possibilities of his world? Are the child's primary objects detached, or is it the insatiable voracity of the child that forces him to escape the frustration of having to share the interest and love of an object?

Faced with frustration, the child, dressed up as a fox, escapes and embarks on a difficult and dangerous trip by sea. He reaches 'another land' – his fantasy land – inhabited by friendly monsters that receive him with curiosity and benevolence and ask him to take part in their games. The child declares himself to be king although he is quick to notice that the previous kings were eaten and not ousted from power. In an excessively detailed tale at times, the child succeeds in being regarded, compared, and hated, he plays, he bonds with others: that is, he becomes invested with libido. He loves and is loved in return, he hates, he fears and he is hated and feared in return. He develops feelings in the exchange with these imaginary friends from a land – the child's own fantasy – which is at once close and far away. And when affects fill up his life, when his internal world becomes more complex and his self-esteem raises, then unfulfilled desire appears. What desire are we familiar with, other than the one we find with our loved objects?

The child goes back to his real world, his home, his garden and his kitchen and finds himself lovingly cuddled by his mother, who welcomes him back without questioning him.

The child has dreamed and the dream has been fulfilled: at last he is embraced by his mother and, at least then, he doesn't have to share her love with anyone else.

HER: THE OBJECT IN THE VIRTUAL WORLD   177

The dream of an adult

Her shows a big city, individuals connected to electronic devices.

Theodore is a cultured man and, just like the child from the film, he has learned what affects are but, unlike the child, he is unable to experience them, or perhaps lacks the possibility of meeting his friendly monsters (the other aspects of his Ego) so that they may help him experience affects in his own life. Theodore's life is split up: on the one hand, there is his work, where he displays his affective creativity by writing letters whose recipients are moved to tears. However, this is his job; he writes letters on demand for people who are unable to express their feelings. On the other hand, Theodore not only is lonely, but also he has been swept over by a kind of boredom that we perceive through his faltering step, his sad, glazed look. And in that mood, he suddenly sees the advertisement and buys the operating system. For a man of his time, who enjoys gadgets, buying an operating system appears to be just another purchase.

However, the operating system surprises Theodore.

Without attempting to force parallels with the film about the monsters, we can appreciate that certain elements reappear: Theodore has lost his wife, who was his young love and, distraught, is reluctant to mourn the loss of this relationship. Virtual reality comes to the rescue, like fantasy to the child. Theodore establishes an erotic relationship with an O.S. which, to his surprise, becomes an essential object in his own life.

It is then that the daemonic quality of the drives begins to operate: the need to repeat his story is forced upon him and, just as he feels that it is his fault that he has lost his wife, the O.S. also leaves him, and he is brought back to his world of loneliness and fantasy.

This is an open-ended film. Some people believe that Theodore finally 'finds' a chance of love with Amy, his friend from college. I don't agree. Rather, I think that the company of Amy represents finding himself, the beginning of integration, an open road.

Theodore shows us what adult life is like: the monsters within us, by obeying the daemonic compulsion 'beyond the pleasure principle', force us to repeat time and again our own painful story. There is no room for creativity, or escape from loneliness. When there is commitment, loneliness appears to be relative. At least Theodore has a female friend, who is as disappointed as he is. However, for both of them, this unique object, the one that might have relieved frustration, the object for which one might have lived, the object without which life becomes insipid, this object leaves us in painful loneliness.

Loneliness or withdrawal of libido?

It is essential to make a distinction. What is the author telling us? Is the film pointing to feelings of loneliness or to a painful withdrawal of libido?

Winnicott has taught us that the 'healthy' capacity to be alone involves the presence of another and a good enough relationship with the mother. I have previously referred to the fantasy of the dead mother, the one who is absorbed in her own grief and not in the needs of the infant, which is the first thing that we learn about Theodore, before the operating system is started.

The narcissistic mother described by Green appears to have been Theodore's primary object and it also seems that withdrawing libido is Theodore's way of defending himself from contact with a frustrating object. Meeting Samantha involves the fantasy of a new beginning, which naturally is frustrated.

When the child dreams of monsters he might even experience the adventure in his own room, giving life to the teddy bears that interact with him. Or else, we might understand how those imaginary friends (the child's monsters) could be the infantile way of experiencing what adults find in the virtual world. It is something similar for both cases: fantasy comes to the rescue of the unsatisfied individual in order to provide an illusion of completeness to unbearable loneliness.

Freud says that the unsatisfied person, the frustrated person, fantasises and the fantasy is not in itself harmful, quite the reverse, it is only harmful when sheer frustration pushes fantasy further and further from reality. With fantasy a scene is created, one where the subject becomes the main character and with the help of other characters (for instance, the monsters, the O.S.) his discomfort can be worked through: the considerations of representability, that requirement imposed on the dream thoughts to transform them so as to make them capable of being represented by visual images, are at work here.

However, I believe that with *Her* Jonze goes further. In my opinion Theodore is truly suffering the effects of the withdrawal of libido, whereas the child and his monsters (in *Where the Wild Things Are*) constitute a fantasy that allows the child to return to, and accept, the real mother.

In Theodore we glimpse a child who is connected to a physically present object but who is affectively distant. It is there and it isn't there. And at last, the infant, identified with the object, will adopt it as a model in order to survive. He is there and then he isn't, he talks about affects and is unable to experience them, he expects love but is incapable of feeling it.

Spike Jonze's message

Spike Jonze is not his real name, but one he has created for himself. Everything makes reference to a rupture with his origins. Could this be the author's message?

In his attempt at 'forming oneself' as it were, is it possible to give oneself a father, to be one's own parents in real life and give one one's own name? Could this be a way of forming one's own narcissism, of saying 'This is me'?

I believe that the author is telling us about the acute suffering of wounded narcissism, badly developed narcissism, and the difficulty of connecting with others. If I don't like myself, how can I expect others to like me? How can I appeal to others if I reject myself?

Theodore's tragedy, so common, so banal in its generality, is the danger of identifying with the 'dead mother' that constitutes him. Faced with the impossibility of finding a loving gaze on the part of the mother, the 'dead' looking glass exposes the child to what Freud correctly called 'the enigmatic masochistic tendencies of the ego' (1920, p. 16), precisely because he is always longing for another, lost, object. Just like Theodore, the subject remains love-starved and always finding the implacable repetition of the rejection to which he was originally subjected by the primary object.

References

Bollas, C. (1992) *Being a Character: Psychoanalysis and Self Experience*. London: Routledge.

Freud, S. (1915a [1914]) Puntualizaciones sobre el Amor de Transferencia. *Obras Completas de Sigmund Freud*, Tomo XII, Buenos Aires: Amorrortu Editores, 1990.

Freud, S. (1920) Más allá del principio de placer. *Obras Completas de Sigmund Freud*, Tomo XVIII, Buenos Aires: Amorrortu Editores, 1990.

Green, A. (1980 [1983]) *En Narcisismo de vida, narcisismo de muerte*. Buenos Aires: Amorrortu Editores, 2005.

Mandrioni, H. D. (1990) *Pensar la Técnica, filosofía del hombre contemporáneo*. Buenos Aires: Editorial Guadalupe.

Mandrioni, H. D. (2001) Libertad y Técnica, entre la ineficacia y la alienación. En Zecca, A. y Diez, R. (2001) (Compiladores), *Pensamiento, Poesía y Celebración. Homenaje a Héctor Delfor Mandrioni*. Buenos Aires: Editorial Biblos.

Rascovsky, A. (1977) *El psiquismo fetal*. Buenos Aires: Paidos, 1977.

Winnicott, D. W. (1971 [1958]) *Realidad y Juego*. Buenos Aires: Editorial Gedisa, 1986.

CHAPTER THIRTEEN

The evaporated body: a dream, a limit, or a possibility?

Rossella Valdrè

> The body is the zero point of the world. There, where paths and spaces come to meet, the body is nowhere.
>
> (M. Foucault, *The Utopian Body*)[1]

A brief history of virtuality

The appearance of information systems dates back to the 1950s. In reality, as Bollorino and Rubini write (1999), although predicted by the sharpest minds, at the onset this didn't lead to a social revolution because organizations were still centralized, vertically managed by a few industrial groups.

It's only when mainframes (that is, the first large computers) "start to be *interconnected* and to *dialogue* through the lingua franca of the Net" (ibid., p. 27, my italics) that the revolution begins. Thanks to the work of bright, daydreaming young researchers from the American west coast in the 1970s and 1980s, the system is developed: it's with the arrival of the personal computer and its connection to the Net that the Internet enters our homes.

Only then, through its progressive and unstoppable spread and thanks to the creation of more and more intuitive and easier interfaces (as we all know, invented in the famous garage of Steve Jobs, one of the first to foresee the revolution of the personal computer), we have the information revolution, the paradigm shift, a term that science philosopher Kuhn defines as an anomaly that creates a crisis and overturns a knowledge system.

The anomaly arises, in other words, from the Net and the PC: alone, neither would have been sufficient. It was the unexpected combination of the two, with its democratizing features (unlike television, the Internet cannot be filtered), the entry into the home, the accessibility in and to the whole world, including in developing countries, that made it the marvel that we all know today, through our PCs or smartphones, our iPads, and so on.

Skeptics and those who distrusted this boom have been contradicted by history. We believe today that the next under-revolution will be the evolution of the mobile: carrying the world in our pocket, everything that we need, in a kind of technological extension of our Ego.

Because it is a revolution that we cannot reduce to a technical invention, it concerns man's mind, his behaviour, and even his conscience.

Although the first theorists of so-called post-modernism[2] – Lyotard (1979) among them – were able to imagine the evolution of post-industrial society into today's information technology society, slightly opposing opinions exist regarding what has become the real added value of the Internet: its democratization. Some would like to regulate it, others (and this has been the prevalent approach thus far) see its revolutionary success as its freedom and accessibility, reducing the power of the elite, levelling the differences among classes and giving citizens the right to participate in what they couldn't access before: an idea that Bollorino and Rubini (1999) define as the ascent of the digital middle class, paraphrasing the French Revolution. We are far from our focus: cinema, with its legendary power and its ability to predict, anticipates the great changes of mankind, it brings to the big screen in the 1970s Stanley Kubrick's film *2001: A Space Odyssey*. It gains great success and becomes a cult classic, a predictor of the phenomena completed in *Her*, the anthropomorphization of the PC and its transformation in the user's phantasy as a tool that imitates the human being, sharing emotions and feelings.

A tool in itself would not have been so successful. We wouldn't remember it. But, for the phenomenon of "phantasmal exchange," which we cite several times, the tool that imitates human beings touched, maybe for the first time on screen, the unconscious fantasy of us all. The fantasy of someone other than me, who is me but not exactly me, that represents me and at the same time is different, an extension of my Ego that we could define as narcissistic, a kind of self-object (Kohut, 1978) that becomes a new subject, a new figure of contemporaneity.

THE EVAPORATED BODY 183

This is a new subject, for the intrinsic characteristics of the Net, where the boundaries between the inside and the outside of the Ego are more fluid, more labile, more easily crossable than in daily life, with potentially unsettling and dangerous consequences, as reported for adolescents and defenceless people.

If a new subject arose, a new space should have been created, too, where one "lives" one's virtual life: cyberspace. Invented by the novelist William Gibson in 1982,[3] the term is now universally used (it's significant that it was born from an artist and not a scientist!). This is a place between the real and the unreal, that even if it's not strictly real, starts to exist when we populate it with ideas, emotions, sensations, and feelings that we perceive as real, easy to be understood but difficult to be defined: it is the land where we see Theodore and the film *Her*'s other characters, and where we live when we surf the Net, play, chat, and so on. It's a fascinating theme that takes us far. *Her*'s characters aren't adolescents or children. Set in a near future, 2020, they are adults, the extreme result of what the magazine *Wired* in 1997 first called "the superconnected," that is, what we all are today: usually or always connected and reachable, owners of tablets, PCs, smartphones. But the characters live beyond this already everyday dimension: they live elsewhere, in an alternative space that we can already glimpse nearby, but with a hazy outline. As in *2001: A Space Odyssey*, cinema has anticipated a scenario not futuristic, but human, that future generations may experience, and this is the beauty of the film. Pure science fiction doesn't resist time unless it obeys a big metaphor.

We are interested and intrigued. This starts debates, also among psychoanalysts, that we will analyze later; it influences us, it makes us dream, it creates ambivalence: Would we prefer, unconsciously, the world where *Her* has been created, an almost entirely virtual world, to the already obsolete cyberspace? A world that creates questions, open queries, that I suggest we examine without prejudice or preconceived notions, by not siding with either obsessed technophiles or obsolete technophobes.

Among these questions, these suggestions, one seems central to the film, and more urgent in the framework of psychoanalytic debates: could we live without the body? Could we ignore it as inhabitants of that different dimension, at least partly, or is this just another illusion of omnipotence, yet another vacuous attempt to overcome a humanly insurmountable limit?

Is it really something psychically different, and then anthropologically diverse, the inhabitant of the virtual world pushed to the brink, or at the end are we still us, doomed to be too human?

184   ROSSELLA VALDRÈ

The parable of *Her* seems to agree with this second option: the "fourth man," the *homo ludens* of post-industrial society:

> Although deeply different from the sociological typologies that came first, it's not *completely different,* representing the last show of the same man in a transformed historical and cultural structure. (...) The fourth man does not exclude the other three (*sapiens, religious and faber,* but he places them in the background, the unconsciousness (...) It's the man of the maximal use of technology and of invasive secularization, of the worldwide contemporaneity and of the aesthetics fruition.
>
> (Morra, 1996)

It is a suggestive definition for a sociologist: everything remains within us, archaeologically stratified. Nothing disappears into the unconscious.

The film

Theodore claims, "I've never loved anyone the way I love you" to which the voice of O.S. Samantha replies, "Me too. Now we know how." Might the most refined technology replace and substitute the limitations of the body, the emotional solitude of human beings? This is what Theodore and other inhabitants of this forthcoming, muffled, and undefined future try to live. *Her* can be interpreted in many ways. It is delicate and original. It leaves questions hanging, without saturating us with useless and untimely answers. The film takes us deeply into Theodore's world, opening with an intense and melancholic 30-second close-up: the face, the uncertain gaze of the excellent Joaquin Phoenix well represents his suspension in life, a life that he would like to be perfect, without trauma, painless, without obstacles, a muffled life.

We are in a Los Angeles coloured by dyes that are more metaphorical than real, a sort of unknown space that seems populated only by undefiled young faces, white thin bodies stuck in eternal beauty, flowers prevented from withering: so time is a first dimension where realism seems missing, in a sort of pure hibernation.

The lonely and shy Theodore works at an information company where he writes letters, usually love letters, on behalf of other people. In this continuing identification with someone else's feelings, he lives a sort of vicarious life where he doesn't directly expose himself to the conflicts and pains of a relationship, but through this filtered mediation he allows himself to feel all the emotions that he deeply needs.

The screenplay unfolds through the text of Theodore's love letters: numerous addressees, anonymous, that he doesn't know. In this impersonal universe, that I would define as de-personalization, the opposite of reciprocity and interactions, Theodore protects himself from the pain and conflict of real relationships, that he doesn't know, he isn't able to face, he can't bear the slightest imperfections.

Recently divorced from Catherine, Theodore prefers contact that he can undertake, at will, with the operative systems to which he is constantly tied through his headphones. The image is suggestive; two little objects in his ears. It would be reductive to call them objects. They are part of himself, extensions, sensorial. They are connected to the world yet completely isolated from it. The film achieves the ambitious scenario of reproducing an autistic universe, although not lowered to a portrait of the mind (Steiner, 1993) that is populated by voices. Voices, and not faces, bodies or people; *Voices* could have been another title of the film. It's exactly with one of these voices, interpreted by Scarlett Johansson,[4] that Theodore starts a relationship that becomes, nevertheless, more and more important, deep, even mutative, able to trigger a turning point. What are the voices? They are refined operating systems – so-called O.S.'s – a sort of extreme evolution of artificial intelligence (A.I.), enclosed in a tiny computer that he always takes with him, while he walks, at home on the PC, at work, everywhere.

What features and advantages do the operating systems offer Theodore in regard to real relations? They personify a perfect micro-world; they don't make mistakes, they never get anything wrong, they feel planned emotions and sheepishly adapt to what the other wants, and, above all, they live and die in a fleeting life, exclusively under Theodore's control: just a "delete" and the voice is erased. No pain of separation (as with his ex-wife), no steps, processing time, or sorrow. Just a click.

With one of these voices, Samantha's, one day Theodore starts a relationship: a woman's voice; sometimes warm, sometimes sensual, it will follow him throughout the film.

It is important to point out the ambiguity and duplicity of the term *Her*. In English it is both an adjective and a possessive pronoun. Samantha herself chooses her name. She is owner of herself, she belongs to her. It isn't the subject (that is, "she"), but a complement, an object belonging to her. In maximum omnipotence and autarchy, she is not dependent on any origin, to any Name of the Father! She is auto-generated: created and deleted by herself, thus her reply to Theodore's query of what to call her is simple: "Samantha." And as he pursues the dialogue and interaction with "really?

186   ROSSELLA VALDRÈ

Where did you get that name?" her explanation is simple: "I gave it to myself."

A totally auto-referential world. He starts a dialogue with Samantha that becomes deeper and deeper, acquires shades, details, and emotions that seem to slowly move away from the perfect and rigid rules of the O.S. It embodies more and more in the mimesis of a real affectionate friendship, that Theodore literally lives, maybe unwillingly, revealing the unconscious and ambivalent desire harbored in himself: to feel emotions and at the same time to avoid them, to be able to control them and let them pull him along.

Starting from a friendship, the relationship becomes more and more affectionate. It ends by including some erotic elements, following from his unexpected falling in love.

This is in parallel to the analytic relationship: both are asymmetric (Theodore is one of Samantha's many "customers"), and the relationship is notable for powerfully emphasizing transference and regression. The transference relationship, accentuated by the fact that, like the analyst behind the patient, Samantha is just a voice and therefore offers herself to Theodore's various fantasies and projections, she is created and enriched over time by all shades of the transference. Seduction, empathy, jealousy, sorrow, anger, charges of having been infinitely betrayed and misunderstood.

We can figure out which figure, in Theodore's phantasmal world, "the voice," represents above all an important initial detail: when he is asked if he prefers a male or female voice, with apparent casualness he is also asked how was his relationship with his mother. Slightly surprised, Theodore initially answers "good," then he stops and points out that, in fact, she was always distant, distracted, not listening to him.

So, to the ghost of a narcissistic maternal object, experienced as deficient, Samantha responds by taking on herself the traits of a maternal transference object: she won't be like the cold mother of his childhood, she will understand, she will be sensitive to him. And "this revolutionary outfit" of the O.S. makes her able to feel "real emotions," as Theodore insists on repeating several times to convince his friends: "they are real emotions."

Personal object of Theodore's potential space, now renewed by a new explorative game; narcissistic self-object; a replacement object that repairs the faults of the unsatisfactory primary object, but also a new progressively transformative and mutative "real" object. Depending on which is our main line of interpretation, we have many features of the purely transferable character of *Her*. In my opinion, Theodore's path, throughout

THE EVAPORATED BODY   187

the unfolding of the story, is a personal one that starts from a phantasmal regression and finally makes a real change, like a successful, analytical, and emancipatory report. This is not painless, however.

In fact, Theodore is a human being, but Samantha is not. The O.S. cannot afford these errors, run into these obstacles. At first she seems to reciprocate feelings, so that we wonder if even the imitation of feelings is mechanical, provided by artificial intelligence to mold itself on those which it perceives as user's needs; then, the audience wonders if even the O.S. fails to escape the temptation of love.

The inevitable end unfolds. The relationship becomes increasingly similar to a real one: waiting, confusion, desire, jealousy, disappointment ... it's no longer bearable for the O.S. Meanwhile Theodore, nullified by the illusion of omnipotent control, of pure and narcissistic projection in a voice at his command, finds himself in the same painful and complicated mess that he tried to avoid in real relationships.

His discovery that Samantha also talks with many other users (over eight thousand!) creates in him a pang of jealousy. This is a decisive moment in the film for the evolution of his internal world. What is more human, out of our control, unwanted, sometimes unreasonable and painful than jealousy? Starting from the purely narcissistic and delusional universe of the beginning, as in analytic therapy, Theodore exposes himself to the most painful oedipal scene of exclusion, perceiving himself as a small abandoned child who runs desperately to the subway when he cannot hear Samantha's voice. The real object has emerged with its elusiveness, its theft.

The goodbye is inevitable. Nor is it useful when Samantha attempts to piteously replace her non-existing body by offering to Theodore a "borrowed one," that of her friend Isabella. He doesn't need just any body: the subtitle *A Love Story* indicates the establishment of a specific relationship.

By loving her voice, Theodore loves all aspects of Samantha, the global picture, the story that he has built around her. The body, an option which we want to do without, in its absence reveals its necessity and its strength.

We can understand the breakdown of the relationship, a drastic and painful breaking, in many different ways. The end of an illusion? Even the most sophisticated advanced processing technology of so-called artificial intelligence, so much evolved as to be confused, in some moments of the film, with the real human, reveals another deceptive illusion. We cannot escape reality. If not with madness, with psychosis, even the most camouflaged avoidances end up showing cracks, or wealth, depending on your point of view: when a contact is established, the human need is

188 ROSSELLA VALDRÈ

to deepen, to follow the evolution over time, feel addiction, anger, desire, hostility, jealousy – all appear inescapable. Man is a being of desire; if severed from its nature, from this irreducibility, he is no longer a man. It is an O.S. The magic "delete" button reveals, in the parable of *Her*, its limitations. Omnipotent and narcissistic control, for which one tolerates reality only to the extent that it represents oneself and is an extension of oneself, either leads to the death of one's own reflections, as with Narcissus, or must be interrupted.

Is this the beginning of a turning point? Thanks to the meeting with Samantha, as seen in parallel with the analytical relationship, Theodore seems to come out of his quagmire, the swamp of his avoidances: unable to meet Catherine face to face, he writes her a "real" letter (the only real one in the movie, at the end) and brings their separation to an end. It is as if it acquires a silent consciousness (but the whole film is inhabited by "talkative" silences), something that the O.S., prisoner of its limitations, cannot afford. I suggest we call this *a mutative meeting*: a meeting revealing a turning point, helping us across when we feel blocked; they aren't miraculous meetings, rained down from the sky, but the ones that work with the evidently fertile elements inside us that are ready, needing a push, some help.

Nothing has been invented, everything is already inside us. Samantha brings to light a consciousness. In the strange world of voices, the dialogue between Theodore and his O.S. just occurs, in some way it is "real" (he is right, Theodore, in insisting on the truth of his O.S.) so that it is possible to change a story, especially for him. With this in mind, the technological transience sees the characters in a reversed light: the O.S. is the prisoner, sentenced to a fate without pain, of course, but also with no surprises, no life; whereas the human being is able to rebel against the "completely predictable," allowing him to open up to change. Never easy, never smooth, but vital.

However, Theodore comes out enriched by this story. Even if at the end he gets close to his real friend Amy (she, too, is just coming back from being abandoned by the O.S.), *Her* will remain his big love, as he says, "I've never loved anyone the way I love you." This is the film's poetic touch.

We can trust him. The affection for Catherine ("you're my friend till the end"), the shy and rising feeling for Amy that closes the film, that literally opens up a new horizon, totally human, that will foresee all suffering, expectations, unmet desires, will be a different universe in regard to the love (a word perfectly acceptable here, in my opinion) experienced for Samantha.

THE EVAPORATED BODY 189

Always in parallel with the analytical path, in his letter to Catherine we see Theodore at last working through his sorrow, becoming able to leave her and to assume the responsibility of his own choices.

At the beginning of the film we had a child, and the film now ends with a man who can manage his losses.

We glimpse a new horizon ... Only at the end does the external world enter the scene and Theodore is able to look out the window: "The sky is starting to change. He stares at the purple glow on the horizon."

The end of an illusion, a turning point, a deception? Is there any remedy for the irreducibility of life, for the needs of the body?

Her effectively leads us, with intelligence and moderation, to consider many open questions.

Might we live without the body? The "body" to which I refer, also etymologically in *Her*, isn't the *Körper* of the German language, a philological and anatomic object, referring to human beings and animals, but also a real body that evokes a human horizon, purposely human.

Could we really count on so-called virtual reality, the O.S. (to go beyond chats or other already existing means) or are these, too, even if refined – and this is the film's core theme – doomed to fail, finally repeating all the characteristics of real feelings?

What we want to avoid is the imperfection of the relationships that our growing narcissistic fragility cannot bear (shoes left in the wrong place ... irrelevant unbearable details that bother us ... two characters split up for that in the film, as is often the case in life), what we throw out the door only to have it inevitably come back through the window. There doesn't seem any way out. There is no solution that isn't partial or temporary, illusory, that doesn't carry the labor of love, the weight of responsibility and of the length of the relationship, the pain of the imperfection of the Other, an object that always disappoints, that remains elusive, that never satisfies our primary needs. Samantha won't be able to replace Theodore's absent mother.

So, there is no escaping pain and happiness, the good and the bad of those different from us, if we are not to remain alone, alienated: an isolation, that of the future Theodore, inhuman and immortal, too. My first thoughts about *Her* aren't exhaustive, because there are many different interpretations: it is also a dream, an exploration between the real and the imaginary, what is the former and the latter? Maybe our internal world, where we live in reality: isn't it always inhabited by voices, by Samanthas talking to us, confusing in a Bion kind of way, wakefulness and dream?

190   ROSSELLA VALDRÈ

The clever photography and editing help the audience to perceive in certain moments an almost dreamlike atmosphere where the real is suspended and the internal–external limits are diluted, fluid, helping us to easily understand another fundamental characteristic of virtual reality.

Inside psychoanalysis: evaporation of the body and psychoanalysis without the body. Hints about post-modern cinema

The evaporated body

> The Ego is above first and foremost a body-ego. It is not merely a surface entity, but is in itself a *projection* of a surface.
>
> (Freud, 1922, p. 488, my italics)

This is what Freud wrote in *The Ego and the Id*. In a few words, a complex concept: the Ego is essentially the body, but at the same time it is the projection of this body on a surface. So a body that, although Freud cannot imagine the evolution we are talking about, isn't limited to itself, to the box of its own skin, but is virtually projectable, expandable – onto the keyboard of a PC, held in headphones as in *Her*, or on the screen of the computer as on Skype. Technology develops, chases something that psychoanalysis, by rereading Freud, has already assumed.

In psychoanalysis, we write a lot about the body. Here, I would like to ask the question raised by the film: could we do without the body in a relationship? We see that, at least in a certain phase, Theodore and Samantha have a strong relationship, the main love of their life: short-lived, fragile in reality, but not impossible. So, too the analytic relationship, or in general terms the therapeutic one, is temporary by its nature, it represents a transference in the life of the analyst and of the patient: could we do without the body, in this framework?

Psychoanalysis "in the absence of the body"

Psychoanalytic interest in this new frontier is now very extensive and open. Surveys among analysts are conducted, we have the first statistical results on ongoing attempts, especially in large countries such as the United States or where there are no physical logistics conditions for

THE EVAPORATED BODY 191

in-person meetings, and research starts to take place via Skype, as well as via other remote means.

Before the current in-depth studies, there were some attempts at online psychotherapy with the software Eliza, along with Shrink and Depression 2 (Angelozzi, 1999). These first attempts of interactive software with therapeutic purpose were followed by others. Their effectiveness, already seen in the first studies, was superior when online therapy was supplemented with *in vivo* sessions and not as autonomous support.

We exclude, but they deserve to be mentioned because of their popularity as well as proximity to the body-less subject matter, the so-called "role-play games" or MUD (Multi-User Dungeons), which are studied for their potential therapeutic use too (Cutter, 1996), and which started to appear in the 1990s. The feelings that they provoke in the user are close to the universe of *Her:* the focal point of all virtual reality is to perceive virtual events as real, as if they belonged to the ordinary world, while allowing the expression of childhood phantasies, usually unconscious, just as with play or watching a film. When Theodore talks about his O.S. he insists that "they are real emotions."

In summary, we can affirm that since the beginning of time until today, the central thread, the *fil rouge*, that combines the inexorable evolution of the virtual and the appeal and rapture that, used on wider and wider populations (starting from children who today are literally born with this alterity, always on their side), are essentially the attempt, almost perfect in *Her*, to perceive "virtual reality" not as virtual but as an actual reality, to abolish or weaken the internal and external limits of the Ego (that Ego that for Freud is an extension of the surface), to allow childhood regressions from which we can go in or out by touching a key, to establish connections and relationships with people normally not reachable and under our (illusory) control, to perceive finally the machine as a mirror, a double of our Ego, a contemporary version of the eternal pond of Narcissus.

Now, what has happened to all these things in the transference from psychotherapy to online psychoanalysis?

I don't speak here of the cornerstone of psychoanalytical treatment, known to everybody and widely studied:

- setting
- analytic process
- therapeutic relation, in the past defined also as "working alliance"
- transference and countertransference

192 ROSSELLA VALDRÈ

- empathy
- verbal and non-verbal communication.

That is but a very partial list. What do these become in the absence, total or partial, of the body? In that phantasmal dimension that technology brings about, that we refer to as the evaporation of the body?

The expression must be precise: evaporated doesn't mean disappeared. Somewhere, in the air, the essence of the body remains, as with a physical evaporated substance: it no longer exists materially but its outcome lasts, a waste.

In physical parallel, body sweat evaporates. The sweat isn't the body, but it comes from it, it is its product, its essence. For this reason, I believe, we cannot limit ourselves by saying that, for example, analysis via Skype is without the body: some sort of forms exist, and I cannot find any more evocative term than evaporation. In the film, the exclusive domain of the "voice" represents this idea very well. Absent, yet present.

Viewpoints about this are very diverse, covering a spectrum that includes the enthusiastic supporters of a new frontier that could open to psychoanalysis a new horizon of research and face the long-standing problem of the crisis of psychoanalytic users across the Western world, people who at the moment don't assume an exact position, choosing instead to wait to see the evolutions in the follow-up (always difficult, in psychoanalysis, if not impossible), and third, those who would be upset and therefore at risk of destroying the entire psychoanalytical structure.

Personally, even if I don't believe that the future predicted by the film will come to pass, it is certain that technology evolves, offering us "products" more and more suitable for our needs, and it evolves rapidly, faster than our research can keep up with.

I would like now to express my substantial curiosity and interest, as I do for every field of knowledge: the journey is magnificent in itself. I'm not interested in how it is going to end. Only future generations will know. It is the exploration that fascinates me. It is a destination that excludes the other: in some cases the analytical O.S. may be suitable, in other cases not. The future is open.

Briefly, the first studies highlighted an essential phenomenon, Internet regression. As in psychoanalysis, the Internet allows a regression but, at the same time, also a major gratification in regard to real contacts, as we see in the film: gratification that would be guaranteed by the exclusion of both face-to-face and, above all, the visibility of body language, and from the implicit regressive aspect of the monitor-mirror (King, 1999).[5]

This last intrinsic aspect of the PC is, in my opinion, the most important one: it is at the basis of the transference potential of regression. Unique among other therapeutic practices, psychoanalysis has the exclusion of physical contact between analyst and patient among its fundamental cornerstones, as a barrier to extreme psychic intimacy; abstaining from touch deprives the patient of the usual comforting personal contact with the body of the Other, already excluded *a priori*.

In favour of "distance," we also observe how physical presence alone doesn't guarantee intimacy, contact or empathy *a priori*: don't we, after all, experience an intense connection with the character in a novel who we haven't even seen?

The most careful people have observed that the Internet has a strong destructive power: the release from the physical body, and thus from a bedrock of identity, deprives humans, above all the most vulnerable in this area, of their center, increasing the risk of damaging them.

From this first interesting research, comes to light a double typology of patients, suitable or less suitable: those distressed from too much contact for whom distance, however, could allow initially a more reassuring approach; and others for whom distance could represent the opposite.

Deeply needing an initial almost symbiotic connection with the analyst, or better not differentiated, the latter are extremely sensitive to movement, not only verbal and transferential, but also and above all to the presence of the analyst's body as a container of the setting. I insist on this point, taking a cue from the reflections of Alessandra Lemma (2014).

In fact, there are patients who are inclined to establish symbiotic transference, not differentiated from the analyst (such as a change in hair colour, weight variations, clothing, signs of ageing), and for whom the body of the Other is an integral part, the incarnation of the setting.

The author uses the term "embodied setting" (p. 226) to indicate how the body is perceived as a concrete part, necessary and containing the setting for a long period of time, initially inaccessible to the understanding of the analyst if not in the countertransference, and for which any attempt at separation and distance would cause the patient anxiety. It is no coincidence that a kind of setting of genre is rooted archaically, and pre-differentiated so that the author properly refers to an "agglutinated unit" (see Bleger, 1967). Only in the course of time, when the analyst's body will be perceived as a dynamic variable and not a fusional and concrete aspect of the setting, will the patient mobilize inside him an analytical process and finally take on a position of differentiation.

The setting, the symbiotic modality of transference, will have in this way repeated, in order to elaborate it, the childhood destiny of those patients, not rare, who are clearly trapped in a true impossibility of growing.

Analysis without the body, for instance by Skype, would be indicated in some cases and not in others, and that would be logical. A sort of indication to the analysis; it would fail the element facilitating the diffusion of psychoanalytical treatments, that exactly the universality of the tool would like ambitiously to propose.

We face a difficult dilemma here. Some fundamental psychoanalytical assets, briefly listed above, could be maintained in the case of an "evaporated" body. I refer to empathy (specifically psychoanalytical empathy, not the generic human one), but others could be seriously compromised, or subjected to changes that restart their existence, and I think, for example, (in the same way as my patient) of the setting and countertransference.

Some transference dynamics seem not only possible, but also highlighted by the online universe in general (and transference isn't after all an exclusive heritage of psychoanalysis, but it happens in every human relation: psychoanalysis considered it as its precise technical element): think about what happens in everyday chats, even in e-mails. In the virtual world, the inclination to project our feelings and thoughts on an interlocutor whose body or face is unseen is exasperating, until it becomes potentially dangerous and a source of misunderstanding and disagreement: the Other becomes a recipient, virtually an empty vessel where we put, to whom we confer, everything we think. We are its inventor, not only the ones who transform it. We are its creator. It is our Samantha. Immaterial, and yet present, concrete. Close, very close, and yet distant. It can become a persecutor, if there are hostile feelings that we want to release: "scapegoats" of the virtual world, for example, the usual pockets of xenophobia or homophobia that exist, so violent and dangerous, on the Net. We can give many examples of it (I think of fake identity in virtual games) but there is only one focus: the Other of virtual reality is a new figure, potentially disturbing to the extent to which it has undefined outlines and limitations, virtually endless; the absence of categories of space and time through which we normally structure ourselves makes it a perfect narcissistic mirror, but elusive to break free from the edge of the pond, from Freud's discovery of hysteria (Levy, 1995). The entrance of hysteria as Freud first faced it, through the talking cure, constituted a paradigmatic shift in clinical work: never again would that kind of suffering be treated as it was in the past. With hysteria, the virtual would share the ease of use

THE EVAPORATED BODY 195

of simulation, many identities, in abundance in role-play games. The so-called hysterics of the Net are:

> people who, in a framework of virtual presence, can manage many images, many masks, usually far and contrasting. The *Proteus* of the XX century, who surfs the Internet with several pseudonyms, participating in mixed and different situations of meeting ...
>
> (Seta, 1999)

A suggestive further element reminds us that technique doesn't invent anything, so we cannot blame it, but it lends itself to shape, with the passage of time, human needs. So, too, psychoanalysis didn't invent hysteria, but gave its modern therapeutic-nosographic shape (which today, in the post-modern era, many people find outdated or obsolete) by which we now know it. Even if written back in 1992, I still find validity in Sterling's words about the confusion that still reigns when we try to define "cyberspace" and, in our case, how it is true but also reductive to see it in a simple parallel with the narcissistic mirror: it is that, but not only that. "For now" – writes Sterling –

> we aren't able to completely understand how we live in cyberspace. We are fumbling around our road and, in this, there is nothing surprising. Also our lives in our physical world, our "real" world, are far from being perfect, nevertheless in this case we can have a lot of extra practices. The human lives, the real lives are imperfect in their nature and also the inhabitants of the cyberspace are human beings. The world where we live down there is a deformed reflection of our world.
>
> (p. 12)

I agree with the author that we are feeling our way through the dark in the so-called "real" world and even more so in the virtual one. But we are always us, here and there: with the seductive combination that there, in the virtual world, it seems we can do without our identity categories, the body included, the identity seat of the Ego.

I would define an analysis in the absence of the body all those situations where the analyst and the patient, as Theodore and his O.S., are not contemporaneously present in a physical place.

In a panel held in 2009 that saw the participation of international psychoanalysts, the core questions were about our subject:

> Can psychoanalysts whose work depends on the harmony of human interaction work in depth with a person in a circumstance in which they are

196   ROSSELLA VALDRÈ

alone in an office with a communication tool? Can they develop an image of the internal world of the analysand without nonverbal cues? Can there be effective affective attunement, an appreciation of resistance, work with transference and countertransference?

(Scharff, 2010)

To date, there are no unambiguous answers, and maybe it is better that way: the ground remains unsaturated, a source of research, not only scientific and specific to our domain, but extendable to human relations in general.

All this, writes Scharff, is where people's internal world enters the game and not only their behavior. The delicate variables of resistance, transference, and countertransference are more specific than analysis.

As we see in the relationship between Theodore and Samantha, this acquires all the characteristics of the transference relationship. We can add that virtuality amplifies and twists to create a true illusionary or even hallucinatory reality, the possibility of the transference game. One can easily attribute all the good and bad that one desires to an O.S. that one doesn't consider physically but whose "presence" is a constant already essential to one's emotional life, with which the dialogue is as with a real partner. One can reenact and relive old phantasies in the proper sense of the transferential experience. One can be persecuted by the return of one's own projections, if the O.S. refuses or deceives, as happens with Theodore. One can be abandoned, as in the ending of the film: total control is not guaranteed if the Other invented by me later benefits from an existence and will of its own.

In psychoanalysis, another central point of difficulty is obviously how we can maintain a regular setting (time, space, rhythms) during online analytic sessions. Differently from "in-person" analysis, where the analyst establishes and maintains the setting, here the situation is overturned. The patient would be responsible for guaranteeing himself a place, some spaces, and a schedule for the sessions. While some patients tend to refuse to use the telephone, preferring to meet the analyst through a webcam, others prefer the opposite. As is the case for many patients in face-to-face therapy, they tend to avoid being seen (collusively helped, here by the tool) or seeing the physicality, the face of the analyst, preferring only verbal contact instead.

It is also interesting to highlight how, both on the phone and on the Internet, resistance belongs to the same typology as in real analysis: payment problems, other calls or contacts interfering during therapy, forgetting to

THE EVAPORATED BODY   197

establish a contact, not providing the tranquility guaranteed by the session, and many other little acts.

The analyst can maintain a position of neutrality and listening while, interestingly, for some patients access to free association, to daydreaming, and even to dreaming is simplified by the physical absence of the analyst's body; as if, in some ways, the patient was freer, only in touch with the world of his associations. "Transference flourishes on the telephone as in real life, evokes a countertransference response from the telephone analyst, and the transference–countertransference dialectic is analyzed as it would be in in-person sessions" (Scharff, ibid.).[6]

In both cases, words are preferred, the use of the verbal in respect to body communication (apart from the above-described cases of strong symbiotic transference). It's really the exclusive use of the dialectic, completely deprived of the real body, as on the phone, that can favour, for example, erotized transference, in so far as the image of the analyst can be evoked freely by the patient, painting an object of desire (younger, more beautiful), as Theodore could imagine the fascinating Samantha. The analyst is imagined "without any visual contradiction, and any dependent maternal transference (…) because of his *calming voice*. Indeed, without the libidinal presence of the body, the telephone privileges a semiology of voice)"[7] (Scharff, ibid., my italics).

Wasn't Theodore's world perhaps inhabited by voices? The voice is sometimes seductive, sometimes it has a calming power, at other times disturbing and intrusive power, it assumes total ownership of the analytical field. Analytical listening becomes increasingly intense, elective, almost the only means of technical expertise available. Regarding the semiology of the voice and the power of the language: if Samantha wasn't interpreted by Johansson's sensual voice, would Theodore fall in love anyway? That voice is as sensual as a seductive body. When the visual field is excluded, the associative shades, even if escaping from the real setting, become preferred online: we just have the voice. Not only can the voice address transference, for example towards erotization, but it also evokes a history, a culture, a biography, a background world. Here, I would add, the analyst can project in that voice some of his or her own elements, or as the patient would like: the phantasy exchange can reach its maximum level and, I would dare say, if well managed, it can express itself as a very fertile ground for making unconscious phantasies appear. Because the analyst isn't able to get the minimal postural variation of the patient, he takes more care over variations in voice: tiny hesitations, silences, interruptions, without taking away any value from the unconscious. The voice

198   ROSSELLA VALDRÈ

of the unconscious, not differently from real analysis, gradually takes shape, session after session, even in telematic analysis, if all the rules are respected inside the minds of the two members of the therapeutic couple: know that you are conducting an analysis and nothing more. Language broadly represents the emotions. Each inflection becomes fundamental, the narrative of the patient evolves, clarifying itself over time.

Analysis "in absence of the body" is, however, impossible for patients who are unable to maintain the connection or to guarantee that the setting is respected (but might it be different in "reality"?), or when the analyst does not provide these guarantees. When there is a risk of suicide, drug abuse, need for medical intervention … in other words, contraindications, just like it would be in real analysis.

It's obviously a practical choice indication, the impossibility of conducting traditional analysis because of great distances, the strong motivation of the patient to have it anyway, a good experience, or the interest of a non-detrimental analyst to explore this field. As Roland Barthes says in *Mythologies*, in the end it's totally probable that once we land on Mars, we would find Earth itself.

About cinema

The only precursor of *Her*, and less successful, is Andrew Niccol's 2002 *S1m0ne*.

Viktor Taransky (Al Pacino) is a Hollywood director in decline, who goes from one flop to another. The film that he is wrapping up is compromised by the star's tantrums and no one agrees to work with him. Almost desperate, he uses the invention of a crazy fading genius and virtually reproduces an actress, thanks to software (similar to the O.S.), thus supplanting the real actress that he cannot find. This way, Simone[8] is born, blonde goddess and a great beauty. The "actress" surpasses the director's expectations. She enjoys a strange success and becomes a phenomenon like Greta Garbo. The world goes crazy for her but because she doesn't exist in reality and she can't show herself in public, a growing fascination and mystery surrounds her. Although Viktor makes her appear on television, nobody is able to see her in person.

As we see in *Her*, the Simone's presence becomes increasingly cumbersome in real life, above all for Viktor who, after initial enthusiasm, starts to feel overwhelmed. As he becomes increasingly involved with his creature, his wife abandons him, jealous as in a real betrayal. The private life and the virtual one lose their boundaries; the latter is favoured above the former, in which the human being, Viktor, is alone and disoriented, with his product that he considered controllable but instead escaped his every control, becoming alive, famous, and almost bearing a destiny of its own. The story becomes more and more complicated – in my opinion uselessly so: Viktor is accused of the murder of the lost Simone, but in the end everything is smoothed out by a sugar-coated and forced happy ending that sees the family reunited and the fake star coming back to "life," because no one at that point, certainly not Viktor, the audience, or the star system, can live without her.

There are undeniable, even if unsuccessful, similarities with *Her*, which we can consider as precursive: the search for a virtual character that replaces an existential emptiness (and apparently for Viktor, a professional one also); the self-creation, the total self-referentiality of the two female O.S.'s and their interesting evolution that sees them transform from mere artificial intelligent products at the service of human beings to almost personified objects, lacking a body but at the same time embodied, that shake the lives of their inventors and increasingly acquire more space in their minds and affections.

Even here, the crucial point is that the virtual relationship, perfect and at the service of human desire, acquires with time the features of the real one, in a total capsizing of the roles that decree their unavoidable end. Viktor, not only his wife, starts to be jealous and resentful of Simone's success. Feelings towards Simone, though far from being clearly defined as in *Her*, become complex and ambivalent: admiration, hostility, envy, and need.

The imperturbability of the virtual women is symbolic of the eternal feminine: Simone who no one can see, Samantha of whom we have only the voice, both excellent metaphors that leave the human subject struggling with his finiteness, with the urgency of real needs, with the pains of frustration.

The world of the virtual creature, outwardly beautiful and perfect, captures human desire, but then leaves him wanting more. This is the umpteenth metaphor about media and cinema, about the incontestable power of the Hollywood star system that is prepared to do anything, even to content itself with the non-existent (it even creates the non-existent)[9] to create an audience, the inconsistency of hero worship, elements that I would consider a kind of subtext of the film.

Although *Her* was given by French non-psychoanalytic critics "a genre" interpretation (Dupuy, 2014), with which I do not agree but I cite for completeness: did the sexual emancipation of Samantha, a woman-object born for satisfying the desire of the man-user until her rebellion and becoming her own person, lead to the failure of their relationship? As already said, I find the humanization of the O.S., and not its sexual emancipation, the turning point of the story.

Simone and Samantha literally don't exist as personified presences, but they exist all the same: since they have been created, they upset and change forever the life of the other real characters. Metaphors *par excellence* of the power of our projections, of the creations of the imaginary in these extensions, narcissistic reflections that have a life of their own, they escape the control of their creator.

Aside from the weak ending of *Her*, in the end both films seem to say that the illusion of a virtual reality that answers all our desires and needs, conscious and unconscious, is misleading, or enjoys an initial honeymoon but is doomed to failure because the same dynamics of real relationships occur. Love, hate, envy, and jealousy, waiting, melancholy, unreachability. The human being remains alone; virtual reality is imperturbable. The human being deals with time (relationships evolve), the O.S. does not. By the way, it is interesting to note that both Theodore and Viktor, thanks to and through meeting the characters that they themselves created, reach a turning point. This, far from being an obstacle or a useless passage, is transformative. Let's see them in overturned point of view: the poor O.S. is condemned to everlasting repetition, imprisoned in a beauty without time or joy, whereas the human being changes, suffers, discovers, evolves, renounces, and desires. The O.S. as the analyst's voice is always someone else who permits a transformation, an intense one as in the Bionian meaning: an access to K, knowledge, a making of sense. The passage, as in analysis, must be transitory to be efficient: if Theodore and Viktor have been deeply attached to their virtual creatures their change might have been similar to addiction, or to psychosis, to detachment from reality and de-realization, and so on. On the contrary, paradoxically, they become more human than they were before. Virtual reality contributes to their humanization.

We can ask a further sub-question: is it a coincidence that the O.S.'s are agile and immaculate creatures whom the cinematographic imaginary outfits with female clothes and voices? A type of cultural legacy, these being the first attempts of a refined filmography about the virtual, in which being desired is personified by a man (in crisis) and the O.S. by a young, wonderful, eternally available woman?

In the radical and daring *Her*, we have a woman's voice, whereas we can see Simone's face (we, audience of the film, because the audience inside the film will never see it). Or will it be sufficient to wait a while until the same happens with the other gender, as I believe will come to pass?

It is certainly cinematographically easier and closer to the internal phantasies of the unreachable mother (we can't forget Metz's lesson: the magic of cinema is based on the phantasy meeting of the unconscious of the audience watching it) to represent virtual reality as a symbol of human desire for its unquenchable essence, the satisfaction of the primary object, with the feminine. A feminine that seduces, literally attracts to the self (*se-duce*, lead to the self) and then it becomes an all-consuming object of ambivalence: it leaves (as Samantha) and it doesn't indulge itself, a source of unlimited envy for the quality that the human being lacks (Simone). Even if, as I believe, unbeknownst to the directors, this secondary outline of both films, though not developed in either, I find it very interesting that they reproduce, under an elegant technological guise, the ancient myth of the Ideal Mother.

Finally, can we consider *Her* an example of what some authors call post-modern cinema? To so-called post-modern cinema, we apply the same definition of post-modernism in general: the loss of ideological, value, and religious reference points that define twentieth-century humanity, "liquid" fragmentation of the subject that struggles to find her center in a unique definition of identity, the advent of the Internet, and so on. Post-modern cinema is also post-post-ideological, post-categorical. It questions the classic rules of cinema that preceded it. The focus of post-modernism is marked by an *essential fragmentation deriving from the loss of a unique point of view of the world* (Galimberti, 2000).[10]

Post-modern cinema has been studied following an original approach by the philosopher Laurent Jullier (1999), who coined the term "film-concert." What is that about?

As the term states, it is about a screenwriting inclined to immerse the audience in a sort of sensations bath, trying to create, to imitate the growing similarity between emotions felt in reality or at the cinema, eliciting an intense response from the audience that is not only emotive but also physical.

Her features a futuristic scenario that is a metaphor for the human, even too much human. No sensations bath, no ecstasy. Therefore, I find Jullier's hypothesis interesting but limited to specific films, that usually have a limited future even if they enjoy good commercial success, and that are mainly followed by a teen audience and so are by nature transitory.

The audience is still "modern": they love and seek story-telling, introspection, or action, something with which they can identify, ghosts that belong to them, rather than strong emotions, even in films about virtual reality or even in science fiction. Cinema isn't yet, and we hope it never becomes, pure entertainment, an amusement park: it isn't there that most of the audience goes for emotions or, better, sensoriality. People who want to numb themselves aren't cinema-goers.

In intimate and keen films such as *Her* the common element remains the use of the absent body-surrogate and, above all, the perception of an illusional reality that seems totally real.

Confirming its advance on literature, cinema places the audience directly in front of a new type of alternative reality which the contemporary individual is forced to confront. Following the debate on the need to be immersed in sensations, typical of Jullier's contemporary subject, with his studies of psychoanalysis and cinema Gaylin Studlar (1993) speaks of an "oral technological mother": unconscious of this kind of public, used to passive consumption typical of post-modernism, the ultimate desire would be to reconquer the symbiosis with the primitive, undifferentiated oral mother. Symbiosis with the primary mother is impossible, as we well know, if not at the price of psychosis: Theodore must express his sorrow over the phantasy mother and at the end "satisfy himself" through returning to real relations. Technology reveals here the limitations of his fascination: the illusory remains the same, unanchored from reality; the virtual isn't necessary in order to offer the subject a centre in the world, it repeats and reinforces the fragmentation, the ambiguity.

In this context our film can be considered post-modern: it underlines the wounds of today's human being, his losses, his appeal to technology as the primary, fusional mother who bewitches at the beginning but later becomes inaccessible and again sets the subject adrift on his sad sea of reality.

In post-modernism, by virtue of the prevalence of sensation over the symbolic that we saw and that clinical psychoanalysis confirms, the film literally connects the personified body to the audience, making that the primary experience that the subject has while she watches the film. While until now the reading, the decoding of the language and of the symbols prevail in the film, today the optics are overturned in favour of the body and the senses.

We cannot avoid noting the analogy with changes in patients during analysis and of the same nosographic typology about which we have so much to say.

The author proposes the bodily experience as primary, placing as secondary the traditional decoding idea of film. Language and symbols are secondary because further appositions connected to culture, of which she

THE EVAPORATED BODY   203

cannot deny the importance and the coexistence with other registers, add to the subjective body, to its symbiotic immersion in the film, the absolute primary element in the audience's experience.

It is curious to note how, starting from the analysis of a film such as *Her* that makes us face the absence, the question about the evaporation of the body, we end up with profound theories on post-modern cinema that focus on the body. An illusionary paradox, in my opinion: the repressed is forced to float again to the surface. In parallel with psychoanalysis, a hypothesis may arise: if it was like this in analysis "in the absence of the body," would it be the same in all relationships where the body is missing? That is, will it be the personified absence embodied in an operative system or in a voice to make the experience of the Other so tied to the senses, even searching for fusionality? Given that you are not present, you do not exist as a real adult object or as a symbol but at most as a momentous substitute, I cannot have an equal objectual relation, therefore I'm obliged to sink into the undifferentiated primary need that is necessarily frustrating.

It is an old truth: there is nothing like absence to emphasize the need for presence.

Notes

1 Epigraph taken from "The Utopian Body" by Michel Foucault in *Sensorium: Embodied Experience, Technology, and Contemporary Art*, edited by Caroline A. Jones (1966), published by the MIT Press and reprinted with their kind permission.

2 This term comes from a text by Jean-François Lyotard. It defines "the status of culture after the transformation suffered by the rules of games of science, literature and arts starting from the end of the 19th Century," in *La condition post-moderne*. English translation: *The Postmodern Condition: A Report on Knowledge*.

3 From the novel *Burning Chrome*.

4 Winner of the disputed award at the Rome Festival. However, it has its raison d'être: here, the true protagonist is the voice, or better: the voices.

5 In Cutter, 1999 (see Bibliography).

6 "The transference flourishes on the telephone as in real life, it evokes a counter-transferal answer from the analyst to the phone, and the dialectic of transference and countertransference is analysed as in a presence session."

7 (...) without visual contradictions, it is a dependent maternal transfer (...) under which his *calming voice*. Indeed, without any libidinal presence of the body, the telephone favors the semiology of the voice (Ibid.).

8 The exact name, as per the title, is S1m0ne, indeed a result of the operating system.
9 Orson Welles, in an interview for Italian TV, said that in cinematography everything is fiction, only theory exists.
10 Because the literature on the post-modern is vast, I limit myself to a very few quotes.

References

Angelozzi A. (1999). Forme della relazione: La psicoterapia in rete. In: F. Bollorino (ed.), *Psichiatria on line*. Milan: Apogeo, pp. 195–228.

Barthes, R. (1957). *Mythologies*. Paris : Seuil.

Bleger, J. (1967). *Symbiosis and ambiguity: A Psychoanalytic Study*. London: New Library of Psychoanalysis.

Bollorino, F. and Rubini, A. (1999). *Ascesa e caduta del terzo stato digitale*. Milan: Apogeo.

Comolli, J. L. (2004). *Voir et pouvoir. L'innocence perdue: cinéma, télévision, fiction, documentaire*. Paris: Verdier.

Cutter, F. (1999). Virtual psychotherapy. *PsychNews International*, 1(3): 96.

Dupuy, N. (2014). www.lecinemaestpolitique.fr/her-un-film-qui-ne-parle-que-de-lui/

Foucault M. (1966). The utopian body. In: Caroline A. Jones (ed.), *Sensorium: Embodied Experience, Technology, and Contemporary Art*. Cambridge, MA: MIT Press.

Freud, S. (1923). *The Ego and the Id*. S.E., 19. London: Hogarth Press.

Freud, S. (1930). *Civilization and Its Discontents*. S.E., 21. London: Hogarth Press.

Galimberti, U. (2000). *Psiche e techne. L'uomo nell'età della tecnica*. Milan: Feltrinelli.

Grazia, A. (1999). *La ricerca in campo informatico e la nuova scienza della mente*. www.psychiatryonline.it/sites/default/files/Risorse/grazia2.pdf. In: F. Bollorino (ed.), *Psichiatria on line*. Milan: Apogeo.

Jullier, L. (1999). Quoted in De Vincenti, G., Moderno e postmoderno: dagli indici stilistici alle pratiche di regia. At: www.fucinemute.it

King, G. (1999). Killingly funny: Mixing modalities in New Hollywood's comedy-with-violence. In: S. J. Schneider (ed.), *New Hollywood Violence*. Mancester: Manchester University Press.

Kohut, H. (2011 [1978]). *The Search of the Self. Selected writings 1950–1978*. London: Karnac.

Kuhn, T. (1962). *The Structure of Scientific Revolutions*. Chicago: University of Chicago Press.

Lemma, A. (2014). The body and the analyst and the analytic setting: Reflections on the embodied setting and the symbiotic transference. *International Journal of Psychoanalysis*, 95: 225–244.

Lévy, P. (1995). *Qu'est-ce que le virtuel?* Paris: La Decouverte.

Lyotard, J. F. (1979). *The Postmodern Condition: A Report on Knowledge.* Minneapolis: University of Minnesota Press, 1984.

Morra, G. (1996). Il quarto uomo: post-modernità o crisi della modernità? Rome: Armando.

Rank, O. (1914). *The Double.* London: Karnac, 1989.

Scharff, J., (2012a). On Reply to "Skype and privacy." *International Journal of Psychoanalysis*, 93: 81–95.

Scharff, D. and Scharff, J. (2010). Telephone analysis. *International Journal of Psychoanalysis*, 91: 989–992.

Seta, A. (1999). Il corpo è necessario alla psicoterapia, www.psychiatryonline. it/sites/default/files/Risorse/seta.pdf. In: F. Bollorino (ed.), *Psichiatria on line.* Milan: Apogeo.

Sobchack, V. (1992). *The Address of the Eye: A Phenomenology of Film Experience.* Princeton, NJ: Princeton University Press.

Steiner J. (1993). *Psychic Retreats: Pathological Organizations in Psychotic, Neurotic and Borderline Patients.* London: Routledge.

Sterling, B. (1992). *The Hacker Crackdown: Law and Disorder on the Electronic Frontier.* New York: Bantam Books.

Studlar, G. (1993). *In the Realm of Pleasure.* New York: Columbia University Press.

Weizenbaum, J. (1976). *Computer Power and Human Reason: From Judgment to Calculation.* San Francisco: Miller Freeman.

Winnicott, D. (1971). *Playing and Reality.* London: Routledge.

INDEX

Abre los ojos (film) 146–8
"The Accident," (Lem) 139
A.I.: Artificial Intelligence (film) 143, 150
Aisenstein, M. 115
AI Therapy 14
Akhtar, Salman 14, 16
Allen, Woody 162
alter ego 141, 143; *see also* Ego
Amenabar, Alejandro 146
analysis *see* psychoanalysis
The Anatomy of Loving (Bergmann) 127
angels 141
animated games 145–6
Anzieu, D. 113
Apollo and Daphne 131
Aristotle 53
artificial intelligence 11, 16, 31, 47, 127, 134, 143–4, 185, 187; strong AI 12
artificial subjectivity 139
Asperger Syndrome 84
assemblage technique 148
Austen, Jane 128
autism 55–6, 142
Autómata (film) 143
Avatar (film) 141
avatars 146

Balint, Michael 134
Barthes, Roland 197–8
Baudrillard, Jean 145
Bauman, Z. 106
Being John Malkovich (film) 167
Benjamin, Walter 30
Ben-Ze'ev, A. 140
Bergmann, M. 127
The Best Offer (film) 105; ending 101; and love over the phone 90–1; plot 91–8
Bettelheim, Bruno 28
Beyond the Pleasure Principle (Freud) 145
Bicentennial Man (film) 143, 150
biology, computational 13
Black Mirror (miniseries) 69–70; "Be Right Back" episode 69–75
Blade Runner (film) 39, 134, 143
Blind Loves (film) 2
blindness 2
body language 192, 197
body-mind question 71
Bollas, C. 94, 169, 172
Bollorino, F. 181, 182
Bolter, J.D. 154

208   INDEX

borderline personality organization 137n2
boundaries, denial of 25–6
Bradbury, Ray 160
Brooks, Rodney 13
Buñuel, Luis 149

Cameron, James 141
cell phones 35–6, 91, 93, 94, 159, 160, 182
chat forum sex 118
chat rooms 8, 41
cinema: about 198–203; post-modern 201; virtual intimacy in 140–1; and the virtual other 143–5
clinical relationships 3, 90
cognitive behavioral therapy (CBT) programs 14
Coleman, B. 119
communication: in analysis 4–6, 15, 89, 192; body 197; digital 91; global 90; personal 168; remote 89, 99–100, 105, 106; semantic 151, 174; sensorial 100–1; technologies of 101, 104; tools for 3, 5, 90, 99–100; unconscious 15; verbal/non-verbal 192; virtual 3, 70, 82, 113
communication media 3
computational biology 13
computers: use by analysts 35–6; development of 12–13; in psychoanalytic space 5
Consequences of Love, The (film) 91
corporeality, denial of 24–5, 29
Correspondence, The (film) 90, 101–5; plot 101–5
countertransference 4, 107n5, 107n6, 191, 197, 203n6; elaboration of 22
couples 99–100; analytic 4, 5, 142, 198; conjugal 91; idealized 48; narcissistic 99; parent 43, 45; in therapy 99
creative acts 80
cyber-pornography 115
cybersex 118
cyberspace 4, 10, 111, 116, 117, 119, 183, 195; see also Internet
cyborg love 153; see also robot love movies

Dali, Salvador 149
Dante (Alighieri) 155

Da Ponte, Lorenzo 126
deafness 2
death: denial of 24–5, 29; and digital communication 91; experience of 101–5
defense mechanisms 56
Deleuze, Gilles 119
Dennett, D. C. 12
depression 25, 46, 77, 82, 83, 97, 172
Depression (software) 191
depressive breakdown 85
Der blaue Engel (film) 107n4
desire(s) 42, 57, 186, 187–8, 200, 202; appearance of 56–7; disintermediation of 110; flattening of 114–15; human 123–4, 199, 201; incestuous 24; for intimacy 151; law of 55, 57; for love 80, 87; for an object (object of) 54, 99, 110, 197; and reality 126; sexual 42, 53, 59, 66, 112; unfulfilled 176, 188; work of 110, 114–16
desire principle 55
Dick, Philip K. 141, 151
digital immigrants 7, 114, 172–3
digital natives 5, 172–3
dissociation 98, 99, 137n2
distance therapies 3–4; see also Skype analysis; telephone analysis
Divine Comedy (Dante) 155
double inscription 175
dreams 3, 8, 47, 49, 63, 78, 132, 143, 146–51, 183, 189, 197; of an adult 177–8; of a child 175–6
dream screen 143
dystopias 143

echoes and echoing 2, 78, 86, 133
Ego 24, 29, 40, 45, 53, 128, 130, 132, 137n1, 177, 179, 182–3, 190, 191, 195; alter 141, 143; foetal 168; super- 106
egoism 137n1
Eliza (software) 13–14, 191
Ellis, Havelock 132
empathic failures 21
empathy 152, 161, 186, 192, 193, 194
Enlightenment 141, 149
erotization 23
eXistenZ (film) 145, 150
Ex Machina (film) 139, 150, 151–2

Fahrenheit 451 (Bradbury) 160
Fahrenheit 451 (film) 160, 161
fantasy 139; in "The Accident"
    139; in *Black Mirror* 70; in *The*
    Correspondence 104; of the dead
    mother 171–2, 178; of the "double"
    36; harmfulness of 178; in *Her*
    9, 23, 25, 27, 41, 47, 78, 90, 159,
    161, 163, 174, 177, 178; and
    pornography 61–2; of the return
    to the womb 171; sexual 115, 116,
    161; unconscious 182; virtual
    reality as 119; in *Where the Wild*
    Things Are 176
Fassbinder, Rainer Werner 162
Fear of Flying (Jong) 106
feminism 106
Ferro, Antonino 36
film-concert 201
Fleischmann, Monika 118
Foucault, Michel 109
Frankenstein (Shelley) 141, 143–4
Frankenstein's Bride (film) 144
free association 5, 6, 9, 15, 20, 197
Freud, Sigmund 3–4, 90, 127, 132,
    137n1, 145, 149, 170–1, 175, 179,
    190; *The Freud/Jung Letters* 23; on
    hysteria 194; "Splitting of the Ego
    in the Process of Defense" 53;
    "The Uncanny" 46
Freudian hypothesis 170–1

Garland, Alex 139, 151
Gibson, William 145, 183
Giddens, A. 109
Gilead, Amihud 71
Gill, Merton 14, 16
Groundhog Day (film) 148
Grusin, R. 154

HAL (computer) 134
Haneke, Michael 148
Harris-Williams, Meg 72
Helgadottir, Fjola 14
Her (film) 7–9, 37–8, 90, 150–1, 159,
    160, 182–4, 199–200, 203; as adult
    dream 177; analytic techniques
    used by the OS 19–22; and the
    challenges of embodied nature
    119; character names 168;
    compared to *S1m0ne* 199–201;

differences between computer
    therapist and human analyst 22–7;
    ending 117, 134–6, 200; and the
    experience of love 127–8; and the
    first experience of satisfaction
    170; on the future of desire 123–5;
    illustrating computerized analytic
    therapy 15–16; on intimacy, sex,
    and the Internet 110–14; Isabella
    as sex surrogate 18, 24–5, 43–4,
    48, 112–13, 163–4, 187; love in
    the virtual world 167–9; and the
    man-machine relationship 38–40;
    and the operating system 173;
    plot 40–6, 184–90; role of the OS
    18–19; Samantha as Siren 161–5;
    and Samantha's emotions 44–5;
    Samantha's love for Theodore
    18, 23, 24, 27, 43, 48, 87, 117, 190;
    setting 77–8, 168; and Skype
    analysis 174–5; sound track to 161;
    story of Theodore 16–18; summary
    46–9; Theodore's "creative Act"
    80, 82–8; Theodore's love for
    Samantha 21, 23, 25, 27, 39, 40, 43,
    46–7, 87, 111, 151, 163, 184, 186,
    187, 188, 190; Theodore's recovery
    of humanity 133; Theodore's
    relationship with Samantha 78–9
Herzog, Werner 151
Hitchcock, Alfred 107n2
holodeck simulations 145
hook-up apps 118
Human Genome Project 13
human-machine interface 39, 110–11
Humans (TV series) 13, 31n4
hyper-realism 84
hypocrisy, technological 140
hysteria 194–5

idealization 23, 48; of disembodiment
    113; love and 128, 129, 130, 136,
    174
Inception (film) 145, 149–50, 150
information revolution 181–2
information systems 181
Internet: destructive power of 193,
    194; hysterics of 195; undesirable
    psychic implications 113–14; and
    virtual intimacy 140
Internet regression 192

210 INDEX

Internet use 37–8, 154–5, 181; case studies (Chiara) 81–2, 87; case studies (Daniele) 84, 87; case studies (Sara) 82–3, 87; and essential knowing 72–3; and intimacy 109–10; and love relationships 90; and pornography 114–16; and the possible self 72; psychic implications of 113–14; for psychoanalysis 5–7, 12
interpretation 21–2
Interstellar (film) 143
intimacy 2, 5, 13, 17, 28, 29, 42, 44, 45, 109, 110, 151, 169; pornography as block to 51–9; psychic 193; *see also* virtual intimacy
intimate partners, virtual 7–10; *see also* love relationships; virtual intimacy
intimate relationships 1; conducted online 10; and physical contact 2–3
intrapsychic space 93
Invisible Boyfriends 110

Janin, C. 112
Jobs, Steve 181
Jong, Erika 106
Jonze, Spike 7, 15, 77, 79, 90, 123, 133, 150, 167, 169, 172–4, 178–9
Jullier, Laurent 201

Kahn, M. R. 45
Kernberg, O. 129, 137n2
knowing, essential 72–3
Kristeva, Julia 126
Kubrick, Stanley 134, 139, 141, 144, 182
Kuhn, T. 182

Lang, Fritz 141
L'Année Dernière à Marienbad [*Last Year in Marienbad*](film) 129
"law of desire" 55, 57
The Legend of 1900 (film) 105
Lehotsky, Juraj 2
Lem, Stanislaw 139, 141, 144
Lemma, Alessandra 193
Le Nozze di Figaro (opera) 126
Le Rêve du Radjah (film) 149
Le Voyage dans la Lune (Méliès) (film) 141
Levy, David L. 13, 153
Lewin, Bertram 143
libido 55, 78, 137n1, 170, 176; withdrawal of 178

Liebestod 136
Life on the Screen (Turkle) 12
Liquid Love (Bauman) 106
Lo and Behold: Reveries of the Connected World (documentary) 151
loneliness 17, 40, 41, 92, 106, 125, 135, 159, 160, 163, 164, 169, 173, 174, 177, 178
loss 130–1, 202; acceptance of 87; avoidance of 90; experience of 45, 74, 90, 98–9, 106; love and 150; of the love object 21, 27, 44, 91, 99, 131, 133, 136, 170; mourning for 27, 80, 105, 177; of neutrality 23–4; processing of 98, 103, 106; traumatic 92, 93, 105, 132; vulnerability to 30
love 2, 24, 400; as cure 23–4, 174; and death 101–5; defined 126; as delusion 9; destruction of 3; digital 159; and essential knowing 73; excessive 136; experience of 127–8; human 48, 125, 141; ideal 46, 48; and idealization 128, 129, 130, 136, 174; as illusion 43, 46, 174; impossible 127, 130, 131; need for 129–30, 132, 136, 137n1; oedipal 86, 96; over the phone 91; passionate (romantic) 129, 132, 133, 136; passive 134; primary 79, 134, 155; and psychoanalysis 126–7; psychological elements of 128; with robots 13, 139, 140, 141, 142–3, 152, 153, 155; sensory experience of 98–100, 129; sex and 118; sublime 87; transference 174; transformative power of 91–2, 97; true 125, 127; and union with the beloved 128, 129, 133; virtual 16–17, 23, 46–7, 90, 101–5, 141, 142, 144, 150, 153, 167–70; in Western culture 15; *see also* love relationships
Love and Sex with Robots: The Evoluton of Human-Robot Relationshps (Levy) 13, 153
love object 83, 88, 129, 130, 136, 150, 152, 172, 176; external 131; internal 131; loss of 21, 27, 44, 91, 99, 131, 133, 136, 170; primary 105, 107n2, 179
love relationships: on the Internet 90; and the quest for true love 125–6;

sensory experience of 98–101;
transference 27; *see also* intimate
relationships; virtual relationships
lovesickness 126, 130, 132
Lyotard, J. F. 182

machine-ism 36, 49n1
Magic Flute (opera) 141
mainframes 181
Making Mr. Right (film) 143
Mandrioni, H.D. 173
man-machine relationship 38–40
masturbation 17, 23, 60, 61, 64, 124, 128
The Matrix (film) 145
The Matrix of the Mind (Ogden) 70–1
McDougall, J. 25
Méliès, George 141, 149
Meltzer, Donald 72
Memento (film) 146, 148–9
memory, loss of 148–9
Mendes, Sam 99
Metropolis (film) 141, 143
mimesis 141, 186
mirroring 2, 129–30, 144
mise-in-scène 145, 148
mixed reality 118
mobile dating apps 118
mobile phones 35–6, 91, 93, 94, 159,
160, 182
Moon (film) 143
mother-infant dyad 127
mourning 27, 83, 131; working through
30–1, 71, 73–4, 80

narcissism 15, 86, 90, 131, 137nn1–2,
145, 147, 152, 155, 159, 179, 182;
of Oldman (*The Best Offer*) 92;
pathological 142; of Samantha
(*Her*), 27; of Theodore (*Her*) 80,
83, 86
narcissistic couple 99–100
narcissistic defence 85
narcissistic Ego structures 128
narcissistic fragility 189
narcissistic infatuation 141
narcissistic level 23
narcissistic mirror 194, 195, 200
narcissistic objects 81; maternal 41, 172,
178, 186; self- 186
narcissistic projection 187
narcissistic regulation 142, 143, 148, 155
narcissistic relationships 47–8, 86, 90, 105

narcissistic security 99
narcissistic slip 82, 84
narcissistic turn 82
narcissistic wounds 2, 130, 133, 179
Narcissus 152–3, 154
The Net (film) 145
neutrality 23–4
Niccol, Andrew 198
No Country for Old Men (film) 148
Nolan, Christopher 143, 148, 150
nostalgia 38, 46, 47
Nuovo Cinema Paradiso (film) 105

object constancy 30
object relations 29, 86, 87, 145, 147, 173;
primary 134; total 137n2
objects: autistic 55–6; subjective 170
oedipal anxiety 143
oedipal conflicts 137n2
Oedipal fantasies 5, 23, 45
oedipal flights 148
Oedipal level 23, 47–8, 96, 104
Oedipal love 86
Oedipal object 107n2
oedipal scene of exclusion 187
Ogden, Thomas 70–1, 73–4
omnipotence 24, 25, 140, 160, 185; of
childhood 29, 30; defensive 61;
illusion of 183; narcissistic 145;
technical 145; wish for 31
online dating 118
On the Lyricism of the Mind (Amir) 71–2
Other 146, 193, 194, 196, 203; artificial
7, 143; devoted 149; disintegrated
147; loving 152; as mirror of self
83; robots as 13; subjectivity of
155; virtual 143–8, 153

paranoid-schizoid position 70–1
passion 43, 48, 55, 66, 98, 100, 125, 126,
128, 129, 130, 132, 133, 136
persecutionism 48
Person, Ethel 128, 130
perversion 44–5
pharmacology 13
phone sex 118
Picard, Rosalind 13
Poland, Warren 14, 15, 16
pornography: access to 115–16; bizarre
64–5; case studies (Avi) 60–2; case
studies (Gil) 62–5; case studies
(Joel) 59–60; cyber- 115; defined

212   INDEX

52–3, 65–6; "disciplining" scenes 61–2; effects of accessing 51–2; excessive use of 51–2; extreme 59; and fantasy 61–2; habituation to 58; and Internet use 114–16; limited sensory perception of 55–7; saturated perfection and the shock of sight 57–9; as substitute for normal relations 60
post-modernism 12, 182, 201, 202
projective identification 44, 98, 128, 130, 131, 136
psychic determinism 14
psychoanalysis: analytic techniques used by the OS (in *Her*) 19–22; computerized 12, 15–16, 22, 25–26, 29; by e-mail 6; environment for 35–6; film 142–3, 155; goals of 15, 22–3, 28; increasing popularity of 11; and love 126–7; main elements of 14–15; mass reproduction of 26, 30; at the movies 141–3; remote 89–90, 190–8; by video-phone 5, 6; virtual 3–7, 27–31
psychoanalytic relationships 3, 90
psychopharmacology 13
psychotherapy, online 191
The Purple Rose of Cairo (film) 162
Pygmalion 141, 143

Real Humans (theater production) 13
reality: denial of 24, 28; vs. the symbolic 20; in the therapeutic relationship 26; transference 20; *see also* mixed reality; virtual reality
reality principle 29, 65–6
relationships: intimate 1–3, 10; narcissistic 47–8, 86, 90, 105; psychoanalytical 3, 90; symmetrical vs. asymmetrical 21; virtual 78, 105–6
Resnais, Alain 129
Revolutionary Road (film) 99
RoboCop (film) 143
robot love movies 142, 143, 150, 153
robots: as the Beloved Cyborg 140, 142–3, 155; love with 13, 139, 140, 141, 142–3, 152, 153, 155; as "other" 13
role-play games 191

Rose, G. J. 2
Rubini, A. 181, 182
"rule of abstinence" 24

S1m0ne (film) 198–9; compared to *Her* 199–201
sado-masochism 62
Sandler, Joseph 131
saturated perfection 57–9, 65–6
Savege Scharff, J. 3
Saving Possibilities (Gilead) 71
Schopenhauer, Arthur 149
Scott, Ridley 143
Searle, John 12
Seidelman, Susan 143
self-construction 100
self-knowledge 15
self-regulation 148
semantics 151, 174
sensory disabilities 1–2
separatedness, denial of 24–5, 28
setting: in analysis 191, 193–4, 196; embodied 193
sexuality 40, 52, 95, 106, 109, 112, 113, 114, 143
sexualization 61
sexual revolution 106
Shafii, M. 20
Shelley, Mary 141
Shrink (software) 191
Simulakrons 162
simulation 12, 13, 29, 141, 145, 147, 162, 195
Siren song 53, 93, 94, 153, 165
Skype analysis 3–7, 11, 36, 174–5, 191, 192, 194, 196
Smith, Dinitia 6
snuff movie 59
software, therapeutic 191
Solaris (film) 141, 144, 145, 147, 155
solitude 175
Star Trek (TV series) 145
Stein, Alexander 41
Sterling, B. 195
Strachey, James 23
ST-TAS (TV series) 145
Studlar, Gaylin 202
subliminal perception 148
superego 106
symbolic, vs. real 20

"talking cure" 2
Taobao 110
Tarkovsky, Andrei 141, 144
technology: and the de-objectification of the body 112–13; effect on human behaviour 117–18
technophilia 153
teleanalysis 3–4
telephone analysis 3–4, 11, 36, 94–5, 196
therapeutic dyad 5
therapeutic relationship 94–5, 191; identification with human analyst 31; mass reproduction of 26–7, 30; symmetry and asymmetry in 21; virtual 26
therapy *see* psychoanalysis; psychotherapy
Thomas Aquinas (saint) 141
Three Essays on the Theory of Sexuality (Freud) 127
Tornatore, Giuseppe 90
Total Recall (film) 145
transference 4, 6, 61, 90, 104, 186, 191, 194, 196, 197, 203n6; erotic 48; and love 174; neutrality toward 23; symbiotic 193, 197; development of 20; oedipal fantasies 23
transference-countertransference engagement 14
transference fantasy 23
transference neurosis 14
transparency 123–4, 125, 135
Truffaut, François 160
Turing, Alan 31n1
Turkle, S. 12–13, 154
Tustin, Francis 55
Twombly, Cy 164
2001: A Space Odyssey (film) 39, 134, 139, 141, 144, 182

Uncanny 46
Un chien andalou (film) 149
unconscious: of the cinema audience 142, 201; desire in 114; fantasies of 6, 90, 99, 112, 128, 182, 191, 197; mind at work 114, 119, 133; multiple 78; in psychoanalysis 14, 15, 28–9, 65; repressed 94; unrepressed 100; voice of 197–8
utopias 140, 141

Vanilla Sky (film) 145, 146, 147
Vaucanson, Jacques de 96–7, 107n3
Verheuven, Paul 143
Vertigo (film) 107n2
Virilio, P. 116–17
virtual intimacy 139–40, 142, 148, 152, 153, 155; in cinema 140–1, 143; Internet-based 140
virtualisation 106
virtuality, as memory loss 148
virtual personality 69–70
virtual reality 25, 46–7, 69, 113, 118, 128, 147, 189, 191, 194, 200; and the fourth wall 145–6; vs. reality of the virtual 119
virtual relationships 78, 105–6
Virtual Sexuality (film) 143
voice 197–8; of the mother 2, 42; of the OS (disembodied) 19–20, 41–2, 111–12, 171, 197; in psychoanalysis 4; of the Siren 53, 93, 94, 153, 165
voyeurism 65
vulnerability 30–31, 98, 117, 147

Wall E (film) 143
Wallerstein, Robert 14–15, 16
Watts, Allan 18
web syndrome 82
Weiner, Oswald 145
Weizenbaum, Joseph 13–14
Welt am Draht (*World on a Wire*; film) 145, 162
West World (TV series) 13
Where the Wild Things Are (film) 176, 178
Williams, Robbie 58
Winnicott, D. W. 2, 178
work of desire *see* desire
World as Will and Representation (Schopenhauer) 149

Žižek, Slavoj 58